T0260213

Other related books from O'Reilly

iOS Swift Game Development Cookbook

iOS 15 Programming Fundamentals with Swift

Learning Swift

Practical Artificial Intelligence with Swift

Swift Pocket Reference

Native Mobile Development

Other books in O'Reilly's *Head First* series

Head First Android Development

Head First C#

Head First Design Patterns

Head First Git

Head First Go

Head First iPhone and iPad Development

Head First Java

Head First JavaScript Programming

Head First Learn to Code

Head First Object-Oriented Analysis and Design

Head First Programming

Head First Python

Head First Software Development

Head First Web Design

Head First **Swift**

Wouldn't it be dreamy to quickly learn Swift? I could build apps, websites, command-line tools...anything!

Paris Buttfield-Addison

Jonathon Manning

Beijing · Boston · Farnham · Sebastopol · Tokyo

Head First Swift

by Paris Buttfield-Addison and Jonathon Manning

Copyright © 2022 Secret Lab. All rights reserved.

Published by O'Reilly Media, Inc., 1005 Gravenstein Highway North, Sebastopol, CA 95472.

O'Reilly Media books may be purchased for educational, business, or sales promotional use. Online editions are also available for most titles (*http://oreilly.com*). For more information, contact our corporate/institutional sales department: (800) 998-9938 or *corporate@oreilly.com*.

Series Creators:	Kathy Sierra, Bert Bates
Acquisitions Editor:	Suzanne McQuade
Development Editor:	Michele Cronin
Cover Designer:	Karen Montgomery
Brain Image on Spine:	Eric Freeman
Production Editor:	Christopher Faucher
Proofreader:	Rachel Head
Indexer:	Potomac Indexing, LLC
Page Viewers:	Mars Buttfield-Addison, Argos and Apollo (dogs).

Printing History:

November 2021: First Edition.

The O'Reilly logo is a registered trademark of O'Reilly Media, Inc. The *Head First* series designations, *Head First Swift*, and related trade dress are trademarks of O'Reilly Media, Inc. Head First Swift is an independent publication and has not been authorized, sponsored, or otherwise approved by Apple Inc.

Many of the designations used by manufacturers and sellers to distinguish their products are claimed as trademarks. Where those designations appear in this book, and O'Reilly Media, Inc., was aware of a trademark claim, the designations have been printed in caps or initial caps.

Apple, the Apple logo, iOS, iPadOS, macOS, Mac, Xcode, Swift Playgrounds, SwiftUI, watchOS, tvOS, iPad, iPhone, iPod, and iPod touch are trademarks of Apple Inc., registered in the U.S. and other countries. Swift and the Swift logo are trademarks of Apple Inc.

Head First Swift is an independent publication and has not been authorized, sponsored, or otherwise approved by Apple Inc.

While every precaution has been taken in the preparation of this book, the publisher and the authors assume no responsibility for errors or omissions, or for damages resulting from the use of the information contained herein.

No parrots, robots, or chefs were harmed in the making of this book.

ISBN: 978-1-491-92285-9

[LSI]

[2021-11-17]

Thanks to the Swift open source team, the folks at Apple, and all of the folks from the /dev/world conference and wider Swift community.

And thanks to Swift, for being complex enough (and interesting enough!) to warrant this book.

Oh, and thanks to our families. Paris particularly thanks his Mum, and his wife, and Jon thanks his Mum, Dad, and wildly extended family for all of their support.

Authors of Head First Swift

Paris Buttfield-Addison

Jon Manning

Paris Buttfield-Addison and **Jon Manning** are the cofounders of Hobart, Tasmania, Australia–based video game development studio Secret Lab.

Both Paris and Jon have PhDs in computer science, and between them they've written around 30 technical books over the years. They worked together at the influential "Web 2.0"–era startup Meebo, and are part of the team behind one of the longest-running Apple-related developer conferences, AUC /dev/world.

Paris and Jon have worked on thousands of apps and games at Secret Lab. They're best known for the adventure game Night in the Woods, which won an Independent Game Festival award and a BAFTA, as well as their popular open source project Yarn Spinner at *https://yarnspinner.dev*, which powers thousands of narrative video games.

Paris and Jon both live and work in Hobart and enjoy photography, cooking, and giving far too many conference talks. Find Paris on Twitter *@parisba* and online at *https://paris.id.au*, Jon on Twitter *@desplesda* and online *at https://desplesda.net*, and Secret Lab on Twitter at *@thesecretlab* and online at *https://secretlab.games* .

Secret Lab

Table of Contents (the summary)

Table of Contents (the real thing)

Intro

Your brain on Swift. Here you are trying to learn something, while here your brain is doing you a favor by making sure the learning doesn't stick. Your brain's thinking, "Better leave room for more important things, like which wild animals to avoid and whether naked snowboarding is a bad idea." So how do you trick your brain into thinking that your life depends on knowing Swift?

introducing swift

Apps, Systems, and Beyond!

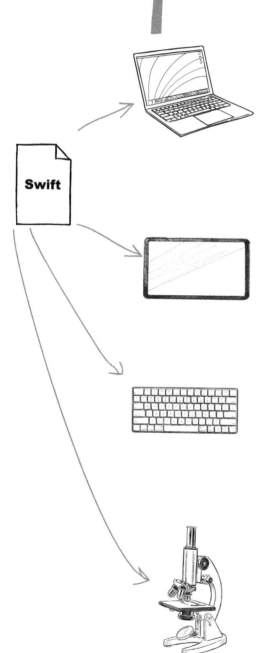

1

Swift is a programming language you can rely on. It's a programming language you can take home to meet your family. Safe, reliable, speedy, friendly, easy to talk to. And while Swift is **best known for being the programming language of choice for Apple's platforms**, such as iOS, macOS, watchOS, and tvOS, the open source Swift project also runs on Linux and Windows, and is gaining ground as a **systems programming language**, as well as on the server. You can build everything from mobile apps, to games, to web apps, to frameworks and beyond. Let's get started!

swift by name
Swift by Nature

2

You already know the gist of Swift. But it's time to dive into the building blocks in more detail. You've seen enough Swift to be dangerous, and it's time to put it into practice. You'll use Playgrounds to write some code, using **statements**, **expressions**, **variables**, and **constants**—the fundamental building blocks of Swift. In this chapter, you'll build the foundation for your future Swift programming career. You'll get to grips with **Swift's type system**, and learn the basics of **using strings to represent text**. Let's get going...and you can see for yourself how swiftly you can write Swift code.

Telling your variables
from your constants
from your spaceships...

collecting and controlling
Going Loopy for Data

3

You already know about expressions, operators, variables, constants, and types in Swift. It's time to consolidate and build on that knowledge and explore some more advanced Swift data structures and operators: **collections** and **control flow**. In this chapter, we're going to talk about putting **collections of data** into variables and constants, and how to **structure data**, **manipulate data**, and **operate on data using control flow statements**. We'll be looking at other ways to collect and structure data later in the book, but for now let's get started with **arrays**, **sets**, and **dictionaries**.

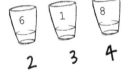

functions and enums
Reusing Code on Demand

4

Functions in Swift allow you to package up a specific behavior or unit of work into a single block of code that you can call from other parts of your program. Functions can be **standalone**, or they can be defined as part of a **class**, a **structure**, or an **enumeration**, where they are usually referred to as **methods**. Functions let you break down complex tasks into smaller, more manageable, and more testable units. They're a core part of the way you structure a program with Swift.

closures

Fancy, Flexible Functions

5

Functions are useful, but sometimes you need more flexibility. Swift allows you to **use a function as a type**, just like an integer or string. This means **you can create a function and assign it to a variable**. Once it's assigned to a variable, you can call the function using the variable, or pass the function to other functions as a parameter. When you create and use a function in this manner, it's called a **closure**. Closures are useful because they can **capture references** to constants and variables from the context in which they are defined. This is called **closing over a value**, hence the name.

We'll get some closure on the matter of closures...

structures, properties, and methods
Custom Types and Beyond

6

Working with data often involves defining your own kinds of data. **Structures**—often shortened to their Swift language keyword, **structs**—allow you to create your own **custom data types** (just like String and Int are data types) by **combining other types**. Using structs to represent the data that your Swift code is working with allows you to step back and consider how the data that flows through your code fits together. **Structs can hold variables and constants** (which are called **properties** when they're inside a struct) **and functions** (which are called **methods**). Let's add some structure to your world, and dive into structs.

7

classes, actors, and inheritance

Inheritance is Always a Thing

Structs showed us how useful it can be to build custom types. But Swift has a number of other tricks up its sleeve, including **classes**. Classes are **similar** to structs: they let you make **new data types that have properties and methods** within them. However, in addition to being **reference types**—instances of a specific class share a single copy of their data (unlike structs, which are value types and get copied)—**classes support inheritance**. Inheritance allows one class to build upon the features of another.

protocols and extensions

A Swift Lesson in Protocol

8

You know all about classes and inheritance, but Swift has a few more tricks for structuring programs, and they're a lot Swiftier. Meet protocols and extensions. **Protocols in Swift let you define a blueprint specifying methods and properties** that are required for some purpose, or some piece of functionality. **A protocol is adopted** by a class, structure, or enumeration, and the actual implementation happens there. Types that provide the functionality needed, and adopt a protocol, are referred to as **conforming** to that protocol. **Extensions** simply let you **add new functionality to existing types**.

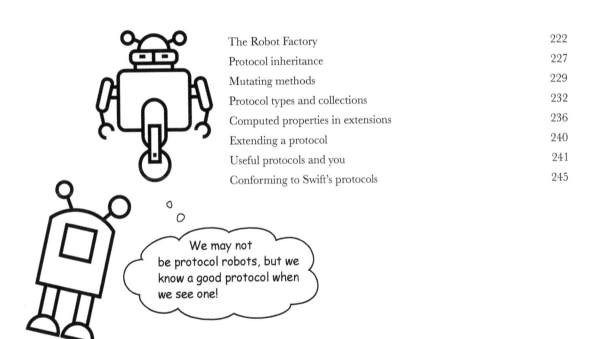

We may not be protocol robots, but we know a good protocol when we see one!

optionals, unwrapping, generics, and more

Nothing Optional About It

9

Dealing with data that doesn't exist can be challenging. Thankfully, Swift has a solution. Meet **optionals**. In Swift, an optional allows you to work with a value, or with **the absence of a value**. They're one of the many ways that Swift is designed to be a safe language. You've occasionally seen optionals in your code so far, and now we're going to explore them in more depth. **Optionals make Swift safe** because they keep you from accidentally writing code that would break if it's missing data, or if something can sometimes return a value that isn't actually a value.

getting started with swiftUI

User Interfaces...Swiftly

10

It's time to use your toolbox full of Swift techniques, features, and components: you're going to start building user interfaces. A Swift UI, if you will. We're going to bring everything together in this chapter to create our first true user interface. We'll build a whole experience using **SwiftUI, the user interface framework for Apple's platforms**. We'll still be using Playgrounds, at least initially, but everything we're doing here will lay the groundwork for an actual iOS application. Get ready: this chapter is full of code and a lot of new concepts.

There'll be time for beverages, but only after you learn SwiftUI...

11

putting swiftUI into practice

Circles, Timers, Buttons—Oh, My!

SwiftUI lets you do more than work with Buttons and Lists. You can also use shapes, animations, and more! In this chapter, we're going to look at some of the **more advanced ways you can construct a SwiftUI UI**, and connect it to a data source that isn't just user-generated content like todo items. SwiftUI lets you **build responsive UIs** that handle **events** coming from all sorts of places. We'll be working with Xcode, Apple's IDE, and we'll be focusing on iOS apps, but everything you'll learn is applicable to SwiftUI on iPadOS, macOS, watchOS, and tvOS as well. It's time to explore the depths of SwiftUI!

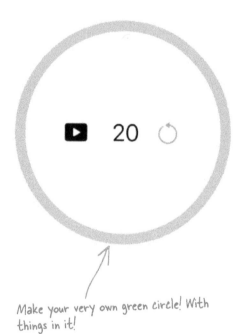

Make your very own green circle! With things in it!

apps, web, and beyond
Putting It All Together

12

You've done lots of Swift. You've used Playgrounds and Xcode.
We knew you'd have to **say goodbye** eventually, but the time has finally arrived. It's hard to part, but we know you've got what it takes. In this chapter, our final chapter together (at least in this book), we're going to do a **final pass through many of the concepts** you've learned, and build a handful of things together. We'll make sure your Swift is shipshape, and give you some **pointers on what to do next**. Some homework, if you will. It'll be fun, and we'll part on a high note.

how to use this book

Intro

> I can't believe they put *that* in a Swift book.

Who is this book for?

If you can answer "yes" to all of these:

1 Do you have access to a macOS or iPadOS device capable of running the latest public version of those operating systems?

2 Do you want to learn the principles of programming using the Swift programming language, so you can go further into the world of Swift?

3 Do you want to make apps one day, for iPhones or any other device in Apple's ecosystem, or learn a vibrant open source language for web apps?

This book is for you.

Who should probably back away from this book?

If you can answer "yes" to any of these:

1 You're already a powerful macOS, iOS, or Swift developer who wants a reference book.

2 You don't want to be a programmer, and have no desire to learn to code.

3 You dislike pizza, or food, or drinks, or bad jokes.

This book is not for you.

[Note from marketing: this book is for anyone with a credit card.]

We know what you're thinking

"How can *this* be a serious Swift book?"

"What's with all the graphics?"

"Can I actually *learn* it this way?"

We know what your *brain* is thinking

Your brain craves novelty. It's always searching, scanning, *waiting* for something unusual. It was built that way, and it helps you stay alive.

So what does your brain do with all the routine, ordinary, normal things you encounter? Everything it *can* to stop them from interfering with the brain's *real* job—recording things that *matter*. It doesn't bother saving the boring things; they never make it past the "this is obviously not important" filter.

How does your brain *know* what's important? Suppose you're out for a day hike and a tiger jumps in front of you. What happens inside your head and body?

Neurons fire. Emotions crank up. *Chemicals surge.*

And that's how your brain knows...

This must be important! Don't forget it!

But imagine you're at home, or in a library. It's a safe, warm, tiger-free zone. You're studying. Getting ready for an exam. Or trying to learn some tough technical topic your boss thinks will take a week, 10 days at the most.

Just one problem. Your brain's trying to do you a big favor. It's trying to make sure that this *obviously* non-important content doesn't clutter up scarce resources. Resources that are better spent storing the really *big* things. Like tigers. Like the danger of fire. Like how you should never have posted those "party" photos on your Facebook page. And there's no simple way to tell your brain, "Hey brain, thank you very much, but no matter how dull this book is, and how little I'm registering on the emotional Richter scale right now, I really *do* want you to keep this stuff around."

Your brain thinks THIS is important.

Your brain thinks THIS isn't worth saving.

Great. Only 400 more dull, dry, boring pages.

We think of a "Head First" reader as a <u>learner</u>.

So what does it take to *learn* something? First you have to *get* it, then make sure you don't *forget* it. It's not about pushing facts into your head. Based on the latest research in cognitive science, neurobiology, and educational psychology, *learning* takes a lot more than text on a page. We know what turns your brain on.

Some of the Head First learning principles:

Make it visual. Images are far more memorable than words alone, and make learning much more effective (up to 89% improvement in recall and transfer studies). They also make things more understandable. **Put the words within or near the graphics** they relate to, rather than on the bottom or on another page, and learners will be up to *twice* as likely to be able to solve problems related to the content.

Use a conversational and personalized style. In recent studies, students performed up to 40% better on post-learning tests if the content spoke directly to the reader, using a first-person, conversational style rather than taking a formal tone. Tell stories instead of lecturing. Use casual language. Don't take yourself too seriously. Which would *you* pay more attention to: a stimulating dinner party companion, or a lecture?

Get the learner to think more deeply. Unless you actively flex your neurons, nothing much happens in your head. A reader has to be motivated, engaged, curious, and inspired to solve problems, draw conclusions, and generate new knowledge. And for that, you need challenges, exercises, and thought-provoking questions, and activities that involve both sides of the brain and multiple senses.

Get—and keep—the reader's attention. We've all had the "I really want to learn this but I can't stay awake past page one" experience. Your brain pays attention to things that are out of the ordinary, interesting, strange, eye-catching, unexpected. Learning a new, tough, technical topic doesn't have to be boring. Your brain will learn much more quickly if it's not.

Touch their emotions. We now know that your ability to remember something is largely dependent on its emotional content. You remember what you care about. You remember when you *feel* something. No, we're not talking heart-wrenching stories about a boy and his dog. We're talking emotions like surprise, curiosity, fun, "what the...?" and the feeling of "I rule!" that comes when you solve a puzzle, learn something everybody else thinks is hard, or realize you know something that "I'm more technical than thou" Bob from engineering *doesn't*.

Metacognition: thinking about thinking

If you really want to learn, and you want to learn more quickly and more deeply, pay attention to how you pay attention. Think about how you think. Learn how you learn.

Most of us did not take courses on metacognition or learning theory when we were growing up. We were *expected* to learn, but rarely *taught* to learn.

But we assume that if you're holding this book, you really want to learn how to program with Swift. And you probably don't want to spend a lot of time on it. If you want to use what you read in this book, you need to *remember* what you read. And for that, you've got to *understand* it. To get the most from this book, or *any* book or learning experience, take responsibility for your brain. Your brain on *this* content.

The trick is to get your brain to see the new material you're learning as Really Important. Crucial to your well-being. As important as a tiger. Otherwise, you're in for a constant battle, with your brain doing its best to keep the new content from sticking.

So just how *DO* you get your brain to treat Swift like it was a hungry tiger?

There's the slow, tedious way, or the faster, more effective way. The slow way is about sheer repetition. You obviously know that you *are* able to learn and remember even the dullest of topics if you keep pounding the same thing into your brain. With enough repetition, your brain says, "This doesn't *feel* important, but they keep looking at the same thing *over* and *over* and *over*, so I suppose it must be."

The faster way is to do ***anything that increases brain activity,*** especially different *types* of brain activity. The things on the previous page are a big part of the solution, and they're all things that have been proven to help your brain work in your favor. For example, studies show that putting words *within* the pictures they describe (as opposed to somewhere else on the page, like a caption or in the body text) causes your brain to try to make sense of how the words and picture relate, and this causes more neurons to fire. More neurons firing = more chances for your brain to *get* that this is something worth paying attention to, and possibly recording.

A conversational style helps because people tend to pay more attention when they perceive that they're in a conversation, since they're expected to follow along and hold up their end. The amazing thing is, your brain doesn't necessarily *care* that the "conversation" is between you and a book! On the other hand, if the writing style is formal and dry, your brain perceives it the same way you experience being lectured to while sitting in a roomful of passive attendees. No need to stay awake.

But pictures and conversational style are just the beginning…

I wonder how I can trick my brain into remembering this stuff…

Here's what WE did

We used *visuals*, because your brain is tuned for visuals, not text. As far as your brain's concerned, a visual really *is* worth a thousand words. And when text and visuals work together, we embedded the text *in* the visuals because your brain works more effectively when the text is *within* the thing the text refers to, as opposed to in a caption or buried in a paragraph somewhere.

We used *redundancy*, saying the same thing in *different* ways and with different media types, and *multiple senses*, to increase the chance that the content gets coded into more than one area of your brain.

We used concepts and visuals in *unexpected* ways because your brain is tuned for novelty, and we used visuals and ideas with at least *some emotional* content, because your brain is tuned to pay attention to the biochemistry of emotions. That which causes you to *feel* something is more likely to be remembered, even if that feeling is nothing more than a little *humor*, *surprise*, or *interest*.

We used a personalized, *conversational style*, because your brain is tuned to pay more attention when it believes you're in a conversation than if it thinks you're passively listening to a presentation. Your brain does this even when you're *reading*.

We included more than 80 *activities*, because your brain is tuned to learn and remember more when you *do* things than when you *read* about things. And we made the exercises challenging yet doable, because that's what most people prefer.

We used *multiple learning styles*, because *you* might prefer step-by-step procedures, while someone else wants to understand the big picture first, and someone else just wants to see an example. But regardless of your own learning preference, *everyone* benefits from seeing the same content represented in multiple ways.

We include content for *both sides of your brain*, because the more of your brain you engage, the more likely you are to learn and remember, and the longer you can stay focused. Since working one side of the brain often means giving the other side a chance to rest, you can be more productive at learning for a longer period of time.

And we included *stories* and exercises that present *more than one point of view,* because your brain is tuned to learn more deeply when it's forced to make evaluations and judgments.

We included *challenges*, with exercises, and we asked *questions* that don't always have a straight answer, because your brain is tuned to learn and remember when it has to *work* at something. Think about it—you can't get your *body* in shape just by *watching* people at the gym. But we did our best to make sure that when you're working hard, it's on the *right* things. That *you're not spending one extra dendrite* processing a hard-to-understand example, or parsing difficult, jargon-laden, or overly terse text.

We used *people*. In stories, examples, visuals, etc., because, well, because *you're* a person. And your brain pays more attention to *people* than it does to *things*.

Here's what YOU can do to bend your brain into submission

So, we did our part. The rest is up to you. These tips are a starting point; listen to your brain and figure out what works for you and what doesn't. Try new things.

Cut this out and stick it on your refrigerator.

- -

① Slow down. The more you understand, the less you have to memorize.

Don't just *read*. Stop and think. When the book asks you a question, don't just skip to the answer. Imagine that someone really *is* asking the question. The more deeply you force your brain to think, the better chance you have of learning and remembering.

② Do the exercises. Write your own notes.

We put them in, but if we did them for you, that would be like having someone else do your workouts for you. And don't just *look* at the exercises. **Use a pencil.** There's plenty of evidence that physical activity *while* learning can increase the learning.

③ Read the "There are no Dumb Questions."

That means all of them. They're not optional sidebars, *they're part of the core content!* Don't skip them.

④ Make this the last thing you read before bed. Or at least the last challenging thing.

Part of the learning (especially the transfer to long-term memory) happens *after* you put the book down. Your brain needs time on its own, to do more processing. If you put in something new during that processing time, some of what you just learned will be lost.

⑤ Talk about it. Out loud.

Speaking activates a different part of the brain. If you're trying to understand something, or increase your chance of remembering it later, say it out loud. Better still, try to explain it out loud to someone else. You'll learn more quickly, and you might uncover ideas you hadn't known were there when you were reading about it.

⑥ Drink water. Lots of it.

Your brain works best in a nice bath of fluid. Dehydration (which can happen before you ever feel thirsty) decreases cognitive function.

⑦ Listen to your brain.

Pay attention to whether your brain is getting overloaded. If you find yourself starting to skim the surface or forget what you just read, it's time for a break. Once you go past a certain point, you won't learn faster by trying to shove more in, and you might even hurt the process.

⑧ Feel something.

Your brain needs to know that this *matters*. Get involved with the stories. Make up your own captions for the photos. Groaning over a bad joke is *still* better than feeling nothing at all.

⑨ Write a lot of code!

There's only one way to learn to program: **writing a lot of code**. And that's what you're going to do throughout this book. Coding is a skill, and the only way to get good at it is to practice. We're going to give you a lot of practice: every chapter has exercises that pose a problem for you to solve. Don't just skip over them—a lot of the learning happens when you solve the exercises. We included a solution to each exercise—don't be afraid to **peek at the solution** if you get stuck! (It's easy to get snagged on something small.) But try to solve the problem before you look at the solution. And definitely get it working before you move on to the next part of the book.

Read me

This is a learning experience, not a reference book. We deliberately stripped out everything that might get in the way of learning whatever it is we're working on at that point in the book. And the first time through, you need to begin at the beginning, because the book makes assumptions about what you've already seen and learned.

We begin by teaching the concepts of Swift, bit by bit, and only bring it together once the foundations are in place.

You might want to write apps, but you can't write apps for iPhones unless you know how variables and constants (and a whole lot more) work. So, we start with the basics before we get to the whole lot more. You'll thank us later.

We don't exhaustively cover everything.

There's a lot of Swift to learn, and there are a lot of other good books out there (some of them even by us!) that cover Swift for readers with varying levels of expertise. There's no point in this book discussing every facet of Swift. We cover the bits you need to know to get started and feel confident.

We pick the best bits to learn.

There are a lot of ways you can make a UI with Swift, from AppKit to UIKit to SwiftUI. We chose to teach a bit of SwiftUI in this book, and not cover the others. But because you'll read about all the building blocks in this book, if you want to go and learn AppKit later, you'll find it much easier.

The activities are NOT optional.

The exercises and activities are not add-ons; they're part of the core content of the book. Some of them are to help with memory, some are for understanding, and some will help you apply what you've learned. ***Don't skip the exercises.*** The crossword puzzles are the only thing you don't *have* to do, but they're good for giving your brain a chance to think about the words and terms you've been learning in a different context.

The redundancy is intentional and important.

One distinct difference in a Head First book is that we want you to *really* get it. And we want you to finish the book remembering what you've learned. Most reference books don't have retention and recall as a goal, but this book is about *learning*, so you'll see some of the same concepts come up more than once.

The examples are as lean as possible.

Our readers tell us that it's frustrating to wade through 200 lines of an example looking for the 2 lines they need to understand. Most examples in this book are shown within the smallest possible context, so that the part you're trying to learn is clear and simple. Don't expect all of the examples to be robust, or even complete—they are written specifically for learning, and aren't always fully functional.

We've placed a lot of the code on the web, so you can copy and paste it into Playgrounds and Xcode as you go. You'll find the code at *https://secretlab.com.au/books/head-first-swift*.

The Brain Power exercises don't have answers.

For some of them, there is no right answer, and for others, part of the learning experience is for you to decide if and when your answers are right. In some of the Brain Power exercises, you will find hints to point you in the right direction.

The technical review team

Tim Nugent

Nik Saers

Ishmael Shabazz

Technical Reviewers:

Huge thanks to the folks that helped us get the technology perfect for this book. They all spent a lot of time checking it over, and making sure it was good, and telling us off for doing something silly. We didn't always take your comments literally, but they always drove us to make a better book.

Extra special thanks to **Tim Nugent**, **Nik Saers**, and **Ishmael Shabazz**.

O'Reilly Online Learning

O'REILLY®

For more than 40 years, O'Reilly Media has provided technology and business training, knowledge, and insight to help companies succeed.

Our unique network of experts and innovators share their knowledge and expertise through books, articles, and our online learning platform. O'Reilly's online learning platform gives you on-demand access to live training courses, in-depth learning paths, interactive coding environments, and a vast collection of text and video from O'Reilly and 200+ other publishers. For more information, visit http://oreilly.com.

Acknowledgments

Our editor:

We literally couldn't have written this book without **Michele Cronin**'s support, and we'd write something worthy of her and put it here if it were possible to do such a thing. We've written a lot of books over the years, and this one was probably the hardest, and had the longest process. We went through several editors before we found Michele (and they were all amazing), but when we found Michele this book started forming properly. She's been supportive, and funny, and we've had some fantastic chats during our many, many meetings. We're excited to be working with you on other things. Again: couldn't have done this without you.

Michele Cronin

The O'Reilly team:

Massive and sincere thanks to **Christopher Faucher**, the production editor on this book, without whom this book would not have cleanly come together. We're really sorry we're so terrible at InDesign.

Likewise, thanks to **Kristen Brown** for making sure everything was polished and **Rachel Head** for your fantastic copyedit (as usual) and support.

Thanks also to **Zan McQuade**, for not only being incredibly interesting and fun at all our meetings, but putting up with us complaining about InDesign, Apple, and everything in between.

Rachel Roumeliotis

Similarly, huge thanks to our friend and (one of our) original O'Reilly editors: **Rachel Roumeliotis**. We miss seeing you at conferences every few months, and we hope that starts happening again when this whole *gestures broadly* thing is over.

Thanks also to one of our original long-standing editors, **Brian MacDonald**, as well as the person who got us into writing books, **Neal Goldstein**.

We're also really sorry for always using Australian English, mate.

Thanks to everyone at O'Reilly Media, broadly. They are literally the best. There is no team like them, and every new person at O'Reilly that we get to work with has been a pleasure to work with, the best at their job, and just an all-round fascinating person. They're amazing.

1 introducing swift

Apps, Systems, and Beyond!

There are a lot of places you can go with Swift. But it's always safe, quick, and easy to read!

Swift is a programming language you can rely on.

It's a programming language you can take home to meet your family. Safe, reliable, speedy, friendly, easy to talk to. And, while Swift is **best known for being the programming language of choice for Apple's platforms**, such as iOS, macOS, watchOS, and tvOS, the open source Swift project also runs on Linux and Windows, and is gaining ground as a **systems programming language**, as well as on the server. You can build everything from mobile apps, to games, to web apps, to frameworks and beyond. Let's get started!

Swift is a language for everything

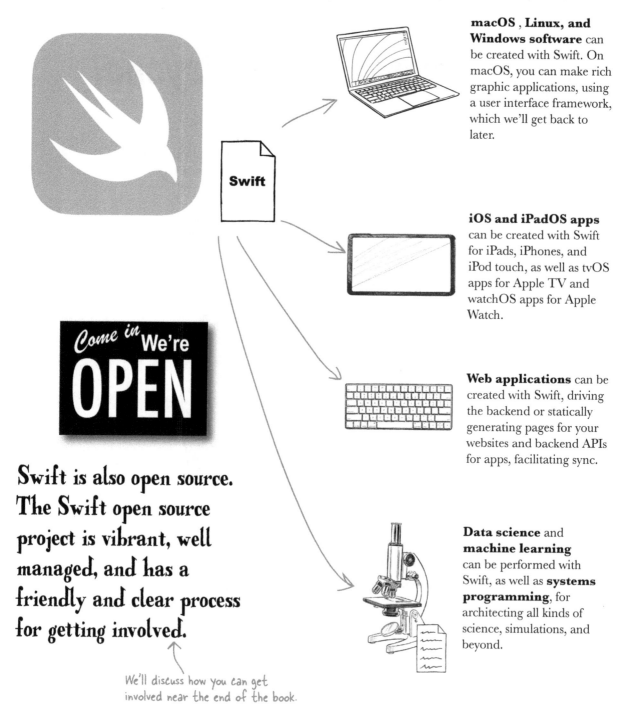

macOS , Linux, and Windows software can be created with Swift. On macOS, you can make rich graphic applications, using a user interface framework, which we'll get back to later.

iOS and iPadOS apps can be created with Swift for iPads, iPhones, and iPod touch, as well as tvOS apps for Apple TV and watchOS apps for Apple Watch.

Web applications can be created with Swift, driving the backend or statically generating pages for your websites and backend APIs for apps, facilitating sync.

Data science and **machine learning** can be performed with Swift, as well as **systems programming**, for architecting all kinds of science, simulations, and beyond.

Swift is also open source. The Swift open source project is vibrant, well managed, and has a friendly and clear process for getting involved.

We'll discuss how you can get involved near the end of the book.

No matter what you want to make, you can do it with Swift.

Swift has evolved fast.

From humble beginnings with Swift 1, all the way through to today, and into the future, Swift is a constantly evolving language, with new additions every year.

Each *major* Swift update has added new **language features**, as well as deprecating certain **syntax** elements. Since its announcement and release in 2014, Swift has been one of the fastest growing and most popular languages in programming language history.

There are a lot of different ways this is counted, and some counts are more meaningful than others. Swift has ranked highly across all the different lists, though!

Swift has regularly been ranked in the **top 10 programming languages** for the past few years, and the number of users and projects using the language continues to grow.

Swift skills are also in high demand, so don't forget to add it your résumé when you're finished with this book!

Swift originally started as a language solely for Apple's platforms—iOS, macOS, tvOS, watchOS—but has grown and expanded its possibilities since it was open sourced in 2015. It's great for systems programming, science, the web, and beyond.

No matter what you want to make, Swift is a great choice of programming language.

We won't be covering absolutely every facet of Swift in this book, but you'll know everything you need to move swiftly everywhere!

Bullet Points

- **Language features** are things like structs, protocols, and SwiftUI views.

- **Syntax** refers to the specific positioning and use of things like ! and ?, and brackets and the like.

The swift evolution of Swift

2014

Swift 1

Swift was introduced, to great surprise and fanfare, at Apple's big developer conference (WWDC) in June 2014. At this point, Swift was a proprietary language, only useful for developing for Apple's platforms, and it was closed source.

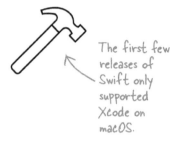

The first few releases of Swift only supported Xcode on macOS.

Swift was open sourced in December 2015, at version 2.2. Since then, Swift's development has taken place in the open at https://github.com/apple/swift.

2015

Swift 2

Swift 2 arrived on the scene at WWDC 2015, changing a lot of the syntax based on community feedback and evolving the features of the language. Swift continued to grow in popularity and community acceptance.

2016

Swift 3

Swift 3, released in September 2016, brought a raft of syntax changes, again based on community feedback. Swift 3 heralded a new era of stability for Swift, with the promise that the syntax would change less in the future.

Swift Playgrounds was released for the iPad at the same time Swift 3 was released.

Hammer by Iconic from the Noun Project

Swift into the future

Swift 4

Swift 4 came out in September 2017, bringing new features but maintaining slightly more stability between versions than previously. The Swift open source project continued to gain ground, and the language's popularity continued to skyrocket.

SwiftUI, the Swift-powered user interface framework, was launched in mid-2019.

A Bright Future

Swift has a bright future. Swift 6 is on the horizon; it will maintain the syntax and features of Swift 5, and add brand new exciting things. And Swift 5 has just gained new features, like Actors, which we'll touch on later in this book.

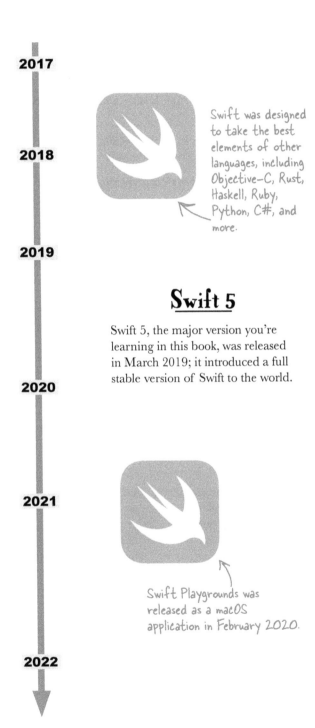

2017

2018

2019

2020

2021

2022

Swift was designed to take the best elements of other languages, including Objective-C, Rust, Haskell, Ruby, Python, C#, and more.

Swift 5

Swift 5, the major version you're learning in this book, was released in March 2019; it introduced a full stable version of Swift to the world.

Swift Playgrounds was released as a macOS application in February 2020.

How you're going to write Swift

Yes, you!

Every programming language needs a tool for you to program in and use to run the code you're writing. Basically, you can't do much with Swift without running some Swift code.

So, how's that done? For most of this book, we'll be using an app developed by Apple called **Playgrounds**!

Playgrounds are just like (collections of) big old-fashioned text files, but it also turns out you can run each and every line written through the Swift compiler and see the result.

Much of the Swift you'll be writing via this book will involve Playgrounds.

But not all of it. We'll explain more, a bit later.

Working with Swift in Playgrounds involves three stages:

Writing

1

You write your Swift code in a Playground, which is a **programming editor** just like you might use when working with a variety of other languages. You can put all your Swift code in one file, or you can split it up across *multiple files*. It's your choice.

We'll talk about how you can do this a bit later.

Running

2

You can then run your Swift code, either *all at once* or *line by line*, within the Playground. You can see errors, as well as the *output* of your code, inline next to each line, as well as in the console below the code editing area.

Using a Playground is the fastest way to switch between running and tweaking, so you can get a good understanding of what's going on.

Tweaking

3

The Playground has such a rapid write/run cycle that it's easy to make tweaks, improve your code, and evolve it into the form you need to accomplish your programming goals. Swift's speed of development is one of its primary selling points. Use it wisely!

> But I want to learn Swift to write **apps**, so I can share my ideas in the App Store! What's the point of Playgrounds when I could just write an **app in Xcode** right now?!

It's easier, and better, to learn Swift in a Playground.

Working in a Playground means you don't have to worry about all the *boilerplate* code that comes with building an app, as well as compiling your code into an app, testing it on an iOS device simulator, testing it on a physical iOS device, and troubleshooting the code for the slight differences between all the various pieces of iOS and iPadOS hardware.

A Playground lets you *focus on the Swift code*, and not worry about any of the other things that come with building an app (or writing a website backend, or doing data science, or any of the other things you might want to do with Swift). That's why we start in Playgrounds.

It removes all the distractions.

It's not lesser in any way: it's real, actual Swift code, and it lets you work up to building **apps** and more using Swift. You can also use Playgrounds to write apps.

We'll get to this later.

If you're here because you want to write iOS apps (that's awesome, by the way!), then please stick with us through the Playgrounds. It really is the best way to learn.

Xcode vs. Playgrounds

It's really tempting to jump straight to Xcode when you start learning Swift, particularly if you're already a programmer.

If you want to learn Swift instead of learning Swift plus the idiosyncracies of the (very powerful, very complex) Xcode environment, then start with Playgrounds. It lets you focus on the Swift.

The path you'll be taking

You need to be comfortable programming with Swift before you write apps with Swift.

Playgrounds

Playgrounds are our starting point. They're available for macOS and for iPadOS, and they let you code real Swift, using the Swift compiler. You can and quickly view the output, test new ideas, and separate your work into logical pages within a single Playground. We cannot emphasize this enough: everything you do in a Playground is real Swift.

iOS, macOS, tvOS, and watchOS apps

Once your Swift skills are big and strong, you'll take them out of the Playground and into Xcode. In Xcode, you'll use Swift to make apps for all of Apple's platforms.

Along the way, you'll learn SwiftUI, Apple's Swift-powered user interface framework. We'll start using it in Playgrounds, and move to Xcode a little later.

Websites

To cap things off, we'll briefly show you how to take Swift into the web with Vapor and Publish, frameworks for building websites and backends using Swift.

Data Science

It might be tempting to jump straight into Xcode.

Feel free to install Xcode, but we won't need it right now. We'll get back to it later on in the book.

Getting Playgrounds

Downloading and installing Playgrounds on macOS

1 Open the App Store app on your computer, find the **search field**, and enter "playgrounds" in it. Press Return on your keyboard.

2 Wait for the App Store to load the search results page, and then click on the **Swift Playgrounds** entry in the list (the icon is an orange bird).

3 Click the **install button** and wait for Playgrounds to download and install on your computer.

Searching is the easiest way to find it.

Look for the orange Swift bird logo.

The install button will be right here.

> I am very mobile. I use my iPad for everything, as much as I can. I noticed that iPadOS has a version of Playgrounds in its App Store. Can I use that, instead of on my Mac?

Yes, everything we do in macOS Playgrounds in this book can be done in iPadOS Playgrounds.

You can do everything we do in this book that needs Playgrounds on macOS or iPadOS, or mix and match between both. Searching the App Store for Playgrounds on iPadOS will get you to the iPadOS version of Playgrounds, and helpfully iCloud will sync your code between macOS and iPadOS, so technically you can use both!

If I've got Swift Playgrounds installed, where do I find it and open it?

Look for Playgrounds in your Applications folder.

To launch Swift Playgrounds, browse to your Applications folder and double-click on the Swift Playgrounds icon.

If you prefer to use Launchpad or Spotlight to launch your other apps, you can do that with Swift Playgrounds too. On iPadOS, look for the Playgrounds icon, or launch it via Spotlight there.

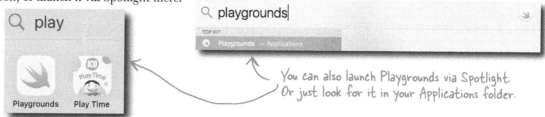

You can also launch Playgrounds via Spotlight. Or just look for it in your Applications folder.

⸻ Bullet Points ⸻

- Writing Swift requires a tool, or multiple different tools, that let you write Swift code, run Swift code, and tweak Swift code (before running it again, tweaking it again, and so on).

- One such tool is Apple's Playgrounds app, which is available for iPadOS and macOS. It's minimal, and keeps the focus on using the Swift programming language instead of needing to learn both the tool and the language.

- Apple's Xcode is another (more complicated) tool. Xcode is a fully integrated development environment,

- similar to Visual Studio and others. It's a very big, very complicated tool that serves many purposes.

- Xcode is necessary if you want to write more complex apps for Apple's platforms, like iOS. We'll be using Xcode later in the book.

- Playgrounds is the best tool for learning Swift. It can even let you write apps!

- Everything in this book that's designed for Playgrounds will work on iPadOS or macOS, or both. Your choice.

Creating a Playground

Once you've launched Swift Playgrounds, you can create a blank Playground to work with, or open an existing Playground that you've previously created.

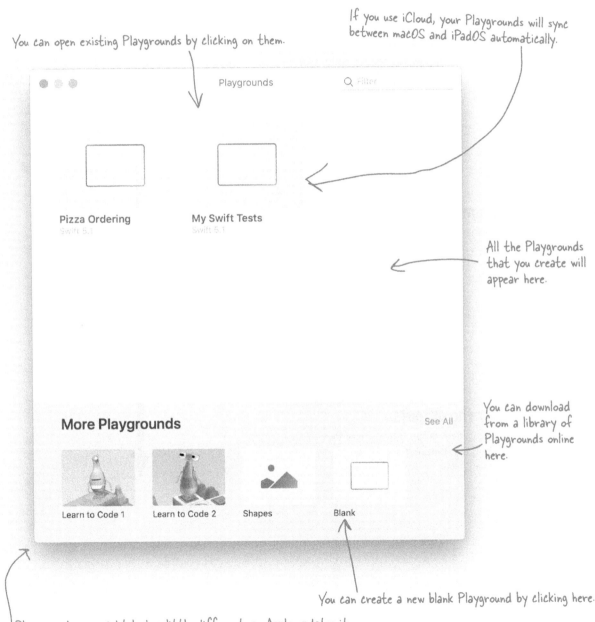

If you use iCloud, your Playgrounds will sync between macOS and iPadOS automatically.

You can open existing Playgrounds by clicking on them.

All the Playgrounds that you create will appear here.

You can download from a library of Playgrounds online here.

You can create a new blank Playground by clicking here.

Your Playgrounds app might look a little different, as Apple updates it often. Don't panic! All the same elements will be present.

Using a Playground to code Swift

❶ Create a Playground

Create a Playground in the Playgrounds app.

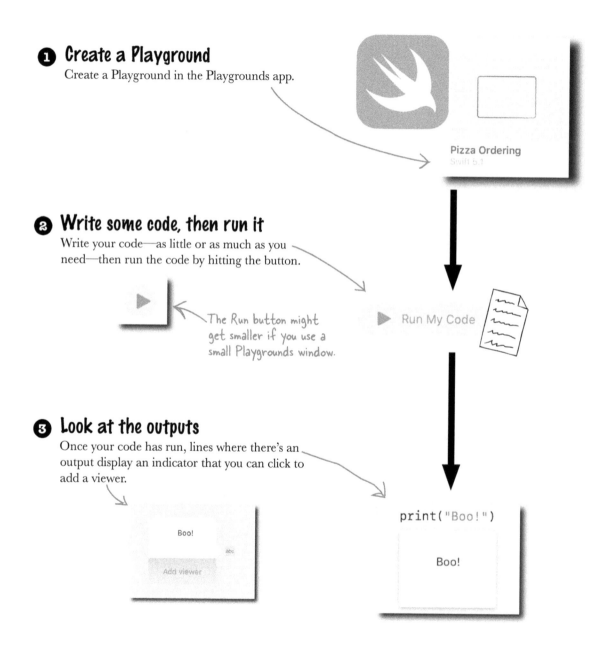

Pizza Ordering
Swift 5.1

❷ Write some code, then run it

Write your code—as little or as much as you need—then run the code by hitting the button.

▶ Run My Code

The Run button might get smaller if you use a small Playgrounds window.

❸ Look at the outputs

Once your code has run, lines where there's an output display an indicator that you can click to add a viewer.

Boo!

Abc

Add viewer

```
print("Boo!")
```

Boo!

A Playground will highlight your code in pleasant colors that make it easier for you to read.

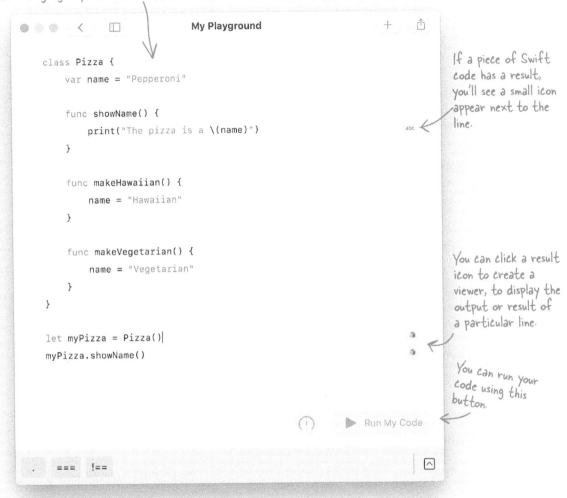

If a piece of Swift code has a result, you'll see a small icon appear next to the line.

```
class Pizza {
    var name = "Pepperoni"

    func showName() {
        print("The pizza is a \(name)")
    }

    func makeHawaiian() {
        name = "Hawaiian"
    }

    func makeVegetarian() {
        name = "Vegetarian"
    }
}

let myPizza = Pizza()
myPizza.showName()
```

You can click a result icon to create a viewer, to display the output or result of a particular line.

You can run your code using this button.

Test Drive

Go ahead and type the contents of the Playground into a brand new Swift Playground of your own.

Run it.

What does it display? Use the result icons to add viewers where there are results to view.

Basic building blocks

Our journey through Swift will take a while, but we can get you up to speed on the basics pretty fast. We're going to whiz through the basics of Swift to give you a taster of many areas of the language. After this, we'll come back and take a chapter-by-chapter approach to unpack each and every feature of Swift.

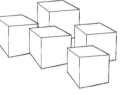

There are certain basic building blocks that make up almost every programming language on the planet (and probably any programming languages that might exist off the planet, too; programming is pretty universal).

Those basic building blocks consist of things like **operators**, **variables and constants**, **types**, **collections**, **control flow**, **functions**, **protocols**, **enumerations**, **structures**, and **classes**.

Who Does What?

We haven't told you what each basic building block does yet, but you might be able to guess. Match each building block to what it does. The solution is on page 27 (and we've done one, to start you off).

Operators	Named pieces of repeatable code
Variables and constants	Symbols or phrases used to check, change, or combine values
Types	A way to store data by name
Collections	Blueprints for functionality that can be adopted
Control flow	Certain kinds of data you can store or represent
Functions	Store groups of values
Enumerations	A way to group related values and functionality
Structures	A way to group related values and functionality that can also inherit those things from another one
Protocols	Ways to perform tasks multiple times, or under certain conditions
Classes	A way to group related values

Answers on page 27.

Relax

We don't expect you to be reading Swift code like an expert, memorizing Swift's history and evolution, and spouting off facts about Swift like you invented it.

However, you spent your hard-earned pennies on this book, so we're not going to let you get away without jamming many tender morsels of Swift knowledge into your mind. You might not understand everything yet, but in time (swiftly, you might say) you will recognize how the building blocks fit together.

Remember the code from a few pages ago? We're going to go through it to get an idea of what it might do.

We're creating a class named Pizza. This lets us group the facets of a Pizza together. Later, we can create an instance of a Pizza, and do something with those facets.

```swift
class Pizza {
    var name = "Pepperoni"

    func showName() {
        print("The pizza is a \(name)")
    }

    func makeHawaiian() {
        name = "Hawaiian"
    }

    func makeVegetarian() {
        name = "Vegetarian"
    }
}

var myPizza = Pizza()
myPizza.showName()
```

This creates a variable called name and assigns it the value "Pepperoni".

This creates a function called showName that prints the name (which is the contents of the name variable).

print tells Swift to display something to the user. More on that soon.

This creates a function called makeHawaiian that assigns the string "Hawaiian" to the name variable.

And this does the same, but for "Vegetarian".

Everything before this was part of the Pizza class.

This creates a variable called myPizza, which contains an instance of our Pizza class.

This calls the showName function of the instance of the Pizza class that we created (myPizza).

Excuse me...but I've used other programming languages, and in many of those everything has to be wrapped in, like, a main method or something? What's the deal with Swift?

At least, you don't need to write it. Code just gets run in Playgrounds.

You don't need a main method, or anything else (like semicolons).

In Swift, you can just start your code however you like. In the case of the Playgrounds we're working with at the moment, execution starts at the top of the file and proceeds from top to bottom.

Some of the building blocks that we'll be learning about, like classes, won't be executed in a way that lets you see them working immediately, because they rely on having an instance of them created elsewhere in the code. In general, though, you don't need a main method, or any specific starting point.

When we move on from Playgrounds to building apps using Swift, we'll look at the various potential starting points an app can have. For now, though, push it from your mind.

You also don't need semicolons at the end of your lines, and whitespace has absolutely no effect on anything.

If you're coming from other languages, you might be used to ending lines with a semicolon (;) or whitespace having some substantive meaning to your code's logic. None of these things matter, or apply, in Swift.

You can use semicolons to end statements if you miss them that badly from other languages, but we don't recommend it. It's not Swifty, and it won't reinforce that you're programming in Swift.

Sharpen your pencil

You've only just started learning Swift, but you're a clever egg and can probably make a pretty good guess about what's going on in some Swift code. Take a look at each line of code in the Swift program below, and see if you can figure out what it does. Write your answers on the blank lines. There's one that's already completed to get you started! If you want to check your answers, or if you get stuck, you can find a completed version on page 19.

```swift
class Message {
    var message = "Message is: 'Hello from Swift!'"    Declares a variable named message and assigns it a string value.
    var timesDisplayed = 0

    func display() {
        print(message)
        timesDisplayed += 1
    }

    func setMessage(to newMessage: String) {
        message = "Message is: '\(newMessage)'"
        timesDisplayed = 0
    }

    func reset() {
        timesDisplayed = 0
    }
}

let msg = Message()
msg.display()
msg.timesDisplayed
msg.display()
msg.timesDisplayed
msg.setMessage(to: "Swift is the future!")
msg.display()
msg.timesDisplayed
```

➤ Answers on page 19.

I've heard that Swift is a modern programming language. What does that mean? How can a programming language be modern?

What's <u>safe</u> in this context? It sounds good, but what does it really mean?

Swift is the culmination of decades of programming language development and research.

It's modern because it has incorporated the learnings of other programming languages, and refined the user experience—the user being the programmer—to the point where it's easier to read the code and easier to maintain the code. There's **less to type**, compared with many languages, and Swift's language features make the code **cleaner** and **less likely to have errors**. Swift is a *safe* language.

Swift also supports features that other languages often do not, such as **international languages, emoji, Unicode**, and **UTF-8 text encoding**. And you don't need to pay much attention to memory management. It's kind of magic.

Swift is safe because it automatically does many things that other languages require code for, or make it challenging to do at all.

There are a lot of reasons why Swift is often described as safe. For example, variables are always initialized before use, and arrays are automatically checked for overflow, and the memory your program uses is automatically managed.

Swift also heavily leans on the use of *value types*, which are types that are copied instead of referenced—so you know your value won't be modified anywhere else when you're in the midst of using it for something.

Swift's objects can never be nil, which helps you prevent runtime crashes in your programs. You can still use nil though, as and when you need it, via **optionals**.

nil is the absence of a value. You might have seen it in other languages, or seen null. A big source of crashes in programming, no matter the language, is trying to access a value that isn't there: those values are often nil.

Sharpen your pencil
Solution

From page 17.

Don't worry about whether you understand any of this yet! Everything here is explained in great detail in the book, mostly within the first 40 pages. If Swift resembles a language you've used in the past, some of this will be simple. If not, don't worry about it. We'll get there...a

Creates a class (everything within the squiggly brackets) named Message.

```swift
class Message {
    var message = "Message is: 'Hello from Swift!'"
    var timesDisplayed = 0

    func display() {
        print(message)
        timesDisplayed += 1
    }

    func setMessage(to newMessage: String) {
        message = "Message is: '\(newMessage)'"
        timesDisplayed = 0
    }

    func reset() {
        timesDisplayed = 0
    }
}

let msg = Message()
msg.display()
msg.timesDisplayed
msg.display()
msg.timesDisplayed
msg.setMessage(to: "Swift is the future!")
msg.display()
msg.timesDisplayed
```

Declares a variable named message, and assigns a string value to it.

Declares a variable named timesDisplayed, and assigns an integer to it.

Declares a function named display. Inside the function the message variable is printed, and the timesDisplayed variable is incremented by 1.

Declares a function named setMessage, which takes a String parameter named newMessage. Inside the function the message variable is updated to contain the string passed in as newMessage, and the timesDisplayed variable is set to 0.

Declares a function named reset. Inside the function the timesDisplayed variable is set to 0.

This is the end of our Message class declaration.

Creates an instance of our Message class, and stores it in a constant named msg.

These four lines call the display function of our instance of the Message class (msg), access the timesDisplayed variable, call the display function again, and access the timesDisplayed variable again, respectively.

Calls the setMessage function of our instance of the Message class (msg), passing a String in as the parameter.

Calls the display function of our instance of the Message class (msg).

This expression accesses the timesDisplayed variable of our instance of the Message class (msg).

A Swift example

All this Swift is hard work. A pizza is required! It just so happens that the local pizza place has heard you're learning Swift and wants to put your new skills to work.

We need some new pizza names. Can you code something up to generate some names for me? I'm not very creative.

Just some ideas so far...

Pizza name ideas
Swiss Hawaiian
Cheesey Meat
Bacon and Avocado
Apple and Gruyere
Tomato and (more) Tomato

Here's what you need to build

You're going to make a quick little Swift Playground that takes the list of all the possible pizza ingredients the chef has available, and generates a random pizza with four of those ingredients. Got it?

There are <u>three</u> things you'll need to do to make this happen:

❶ Get the list of ingredients

You'll need a list of ingredients. The chef can help with that, but you'll need to store it somehow. An array of strings is probably the most sensible solution.

❷ Randomly choose an ingredient

You'll also need a way to pick a random ingredient from that list, four times over (because our pizza needs four ingredients).

If we use an array to store our ingredients list, then we can use the `randomElement` function on our array to get back a random ingredient.

❸ Display the randomly generated pizza

Finally, you'll need to display the randomly generated pizza in the form of "ingredient 1, ingredient 2, ingredient 3, and ingredient 4."

The print function

Ready Bake Code

You might have noticed that sometimes our code contains a line that looks like this:

```
print("Some text to get printed!")
```

This is Swift's built-in **print function**. It tells Swift to display the given items as text.

Sometimes you'll see it used like this, too:

```
print("The pizza is a \(name)")
```

Used like this, print will substitute the value of the variable wrapped in **\ (** and **)** into what's printed. Handy, right? We'll cover this more later in the book, when we talk about **string interpolation**.

❶ Building a list of ingredients

The first step is to store the list of ingredients that the chef provided in a useful data structure.

We're going to use one of the collection types that Swift provides: specifically, we're going to make an **array** of strings. Each string stored in the array will be one of the ingredients.

We'll create our array of ingredients like this:

```swift
let ingredients = [
    "Pepperoni", "Mozzarella",
    "Bacon", "Sausage",
    "Basil", "Garlic", "Onion", "Oregano",
    "Mushroom", "Tomato",
    "Red Pepper",
    "Ham", "Chicken",
    "Red Onion",
    "Black Olives",
    "Bell Pepper",
    "Pineapple",
    "Canadian Bacon", "Salami",
    "Jalapeño",
    "Spinach",
    "Italian Sausage", "Provolone",
    "Pesto", "Sun-Dried Tomato",
    "Feta",
    "Meatballs",
    "Prosciutto",
    "Cherry Tomato",
    "Pulled Pork", "Chorizo",
    "Anchovy", "Capers"
]
```

The start of the list is defined with a [.

This is item 0.

There are 33 things in this array of strings (which is storing ingredients). This means you can access items 0 to 32, because the first thing in a Swift array is item 0. We'll be using arrays more in the next chapter.

The grouping of some items together has no special meaning, it's simply for code presentation.

The end of the list is defined with a].

This is item 32.

Exercise

Create a new Swift Playground, and code your list of ingredients.

Use the print function to to print some of the ingredients. You can access an individual ingredient using this syntax: `ingredients[7]`. Which ingredient will that access?

⟶ Answer on page 27.

❷ Picking four random ingredients

The second step is to pick a random ingredient four times over (from the list that we just put into an array).

Swift's `Array` collection type has a handy function, `randomElement` returns a randomly selected element from the array it is called on.

To get a random element from the `ingredients` array, we can do this:

```
ingredients.randomElement()!
```

We need to put the `!` at the end, because this function returns an **optional**. We'll talk more about this later, but the summary is: there might be a value there (if there are things in the array), and there might not (because an array can be empty, yet still perfectly valid).

So, to be safe, Swift has the concept of optionals, which may, or may not, contain a value. The `!` forces the possibility of an optional to be ignored, and if there's a value it will just give us the value. ***You really should never do this once you've learned how it works.*** More on that much later in the book.

If there was any possibility of this array changing (there's not, because it's been declared as a constant—which cannot ever change—using the `let` keyword) then this would be unsafe programming (because we'd be calling `randomElement()` and disregarding the possibility of an optional when, if it wasn't a constant, the array would have the possibility of being empty).

`randomElement` is a convenience property that we can use on our array (and other Swift collection types). There are other properties and conveniences on arrays, including `first` and `last`, which return the first and last array element, respectively, and `append`, which adds something new to the end of the array.

Exercise

Open your Swift Playground that contains the list of ingredients.

Use the print function again, and print a selection of random ingredients using `ingredients.randomElement()!`.

Try printing the last element of the array, by using the `last` property. What is it?

Append a new ingredient to the end of the array using the syntax `ingredients.append("Banana")`, then print the last element of the array again to check that your new ingredient is where you expected it to be.

⟶ Answer on page 27.

❸ Displaying our random pizza

Finally, we need to use our array of ingredients and the `randomElement` function to generate and display our random pizza.

Because we want four random ingredients, we need to call this four times, and we may as well do it inside a call to the print function, like this:

```
print("\(ingredients.randomElement()!), \(ingredients.randomElement()!),
\(ingredients.randomElement()!), and \(ingredients.randomElement()!)")
```

> I'm only just starting to learn, but it looks like I could get the same random ingredient more than once?

Yes, you might get the same random ingredient more than once.

Each call to `randomElement()` has no knowledge of how you're using its returned element, or that you're calling it multiple times. So yes, it is possible you might generate a pizza that's nothing but Pineapple.

```
Red Pepper, Ham, Onion, and Pulled Pork
Pineapple, Mozzarella, Bacon, and Capers
Salami, Tomato, Prosciutto, and Meatballs
Pineapple, Pineapple, Pineapple, and Anchovy
```

Brain Power

Comment out everything but the list ingredients array in your Swift Playground.

Implement the code that's needed to print a four-ingredient randomly generated pizza, as above.

Test it out. Does it work OK?

The chef seems to think that it might be annoying to get the same ingredient more than once.

Can you figure out how to code it so that that never happens? Give it a go.

Congrats on your first steps with Swift!

You've done **a lot** in this chapter. You've been dropped in at the deep end, and been asked to decipher some actual, real Swift code as you became familiar with programming Swift in a Playground.

You've also built a little tool to help a pizza chef generate random names for their pizzas. Very useful!

In the next chapter, we're going to write some longer-form Swift code. Some real, serious, actual code that does something useful (kind of). You'll be learning about all the Swift building blocks: **operators**, **variables and constants**, **types**, **collections**, **control flow**, **functions**, **enumerations**, **structures**, and **classes**.

Before you get there, though, we have the answers to a few questions you might have, a crossword puzzle, and a tiny bit more sassy commentary. And don't forget to get a nice cup of coffee, or some sleep.

The chef is going to have a lot more ideas for things you can code in Swift if you keep this up. You might be looking at a new career as Chief Swift Engineer at a pizza shop at this rate.

there are no
Dumb Questions

Q: Where are the semicolons? I thought programming was meant to be full of semicolons!

A: While lots of other programming languages require you to end lines with semicolons (;), Swift doesn't require it. If it makes you feel more comfortable, you can do it anyway. It's still valid, it's just not necessary!

Q: How do I run my code on an iPhone or iPad? I bought this book so I could learn to make iOS apps and get filthy rich.

A: We'll explain everything you need to know to use your Swift knowledge to make iOS apps much, much later in the book. We make no promises about getting rich, but we do promise that you'll know how to build iOS apps by the end.

Q: I'm used to Python. Does whitespace mean anything in Swift?

A: No, whitespace is not meaningful in Swift the same way it is in Python. Don't worry about it!

Q: I really just want to make iPhone apps. Do I have to do all this stuff with the Playgrounds? I want to jump straight to apps!

A: As we said, you really need to work through Swift code by itself before you start working with apps. It'll be a much, much better experience for you, as a programmer, if you start with the fundamentals of Swift before you get into creating apps.

Swiftcross

Put your brain to the test with some Swift terminology. Check back throughout the chapter if you get stuck!

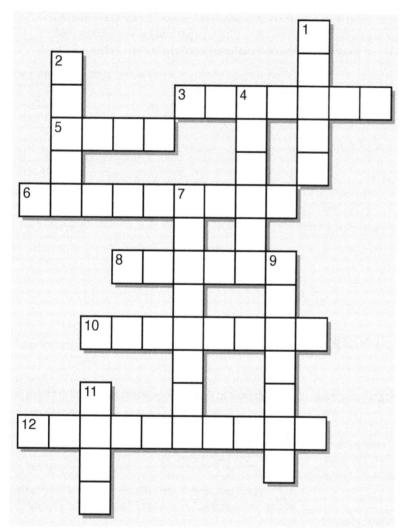

Across

3) The first stage of working with Swift in a Playground.

5) Swift is an _____ source project, which means its source code is available, and development is done in public.

6) Other programming languages use these to signify the end of a line. Swift does not.

8) A feature of Swift Playgrounds that allows you to look at the result or output of a line of code.

10) The third stage of working with Swift in a Playground.

12) A Swift _____ is an environment for running code and exploring Swift.

Down

1) This function is used to output text from Swift.

2) Apple's big, powerful Swift integrated development environment (IDE).

4) The popular phone, made by Apple, that you can write Swift apps for.

7) Check, change, or combine a value with one of these.

9) The second stage of working with Swift in a Playground.

11) A _____ method is the starting point for many programs in other languages, but isn't needed in Swift.

⎯⎯⎯⎯⎯► Answers on page 28.

Exercise Solution

From page 22.

Arrays start at 0. This means accessing index 7 of an array will actually access the 8th item of the array.

`ingredients[7]` will access `"Oregano"`.

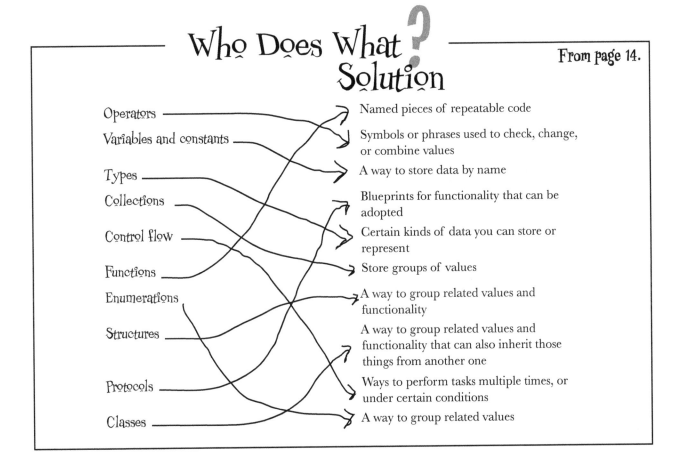

Who Does What?
Solution

From page 14.

Operators —————————————————————→ Named pieces of repeatable code

Variables and constants —————————→ Symbols or phrases used to check, change, or combine values

Types —————————————————————→ A way to store data by name

Collections ————————————————→ Blueprints for functionality that can be adopted

Control flow ————————————————→ Certain kinds of data you can store or represent

Functions ————————————————→ Store groups of values

Enumerations ————————————————→ A way to group related values and functionality

Structures ————————————————→ A way to group related values and functionality that can also inherit those things from another one

Protocols ————————————————→ Ways to perform tasks multiple times, or under certain conditions

Classes ————————————————→ A way to group related values

Exercise Solution

From page 23.

The last element in the `ingredients` array is "Capers".

After you've appended a new ingredient (`"Banana"`) to the array, the new last ingredient will be "Banana", because `append` adds things to the end of the array.

Swiftcross Solution

From page 26.

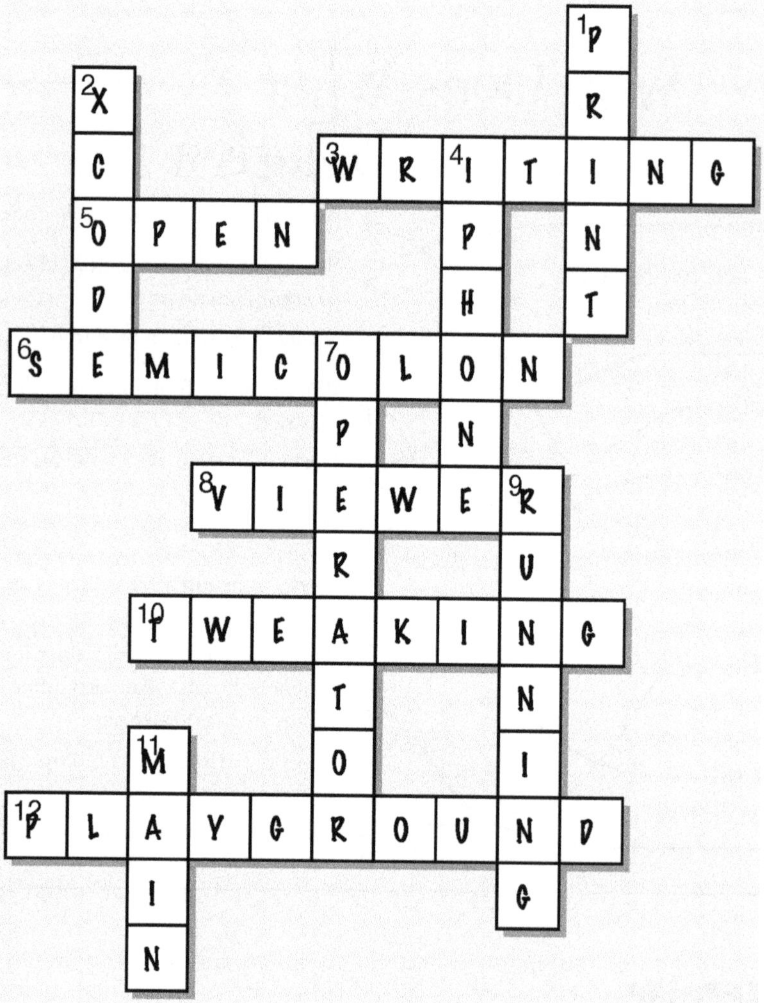
1 PRINT
2 XCODE
3 WRITING
4 IPHONE
5 OPEN
6 SEMICOLON
7 OPERATOR
8 VIEWER
9 RUNNING
10 TWEAKING
11 MAIN
12 PLAYGROUND

2 swift by name

Swift by Nature

Just follow my lead and we'll have you swiftly doing Swift without even needing to use the blackboard.

$2 + 7 = 9$

You already know the gist of Swift. But it's time to dive into the building blocks in more detail. You've seen enough Swift to be dangerous, and it's time to put it into practice. You'll use Playgrounds to write some code, using **statements**, **expressions**, **variables**, and **constants**—the fundamental building blocks of Swift. In this chapter, you'll build the foundation for your future Swift programming career. You'll get to grips with **Swift's type system**, and learn the basics of **using strings to represent text**. Let's get going...and you can see for yourself how swiftly you can write Swift code.

The puns will now stop.

Building from the blocks

Every program you write in Swift is *composed* of different elements. Through the chapters of this book, you'll be learning what those elements are, and how to combine them to get Swift to do what you want it to do.

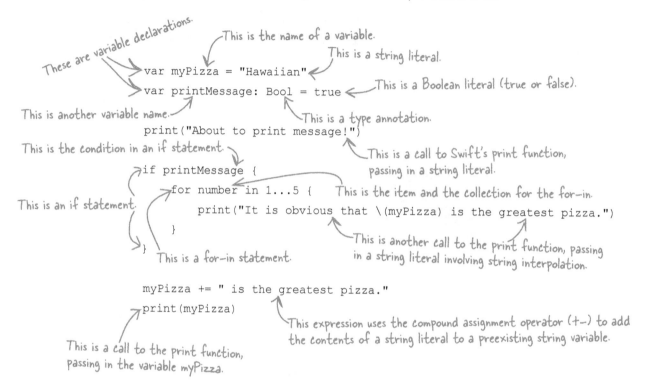

These are variable declarations.

This is the name of a variable.

This is a string literal.

```
var myPizza = "Hawaiian"
var printMessage: Bool = true
```

This is a Boolean literal (true or false).

This is another variable name.

This is a type annotation.

```
print("About to print message!")
```

This is the condition in an if statement.

This is a call to Swift's print function, passing in a string literal.

```
if printMessage {
    for number in 1...5 {
```

This is an if statement.

This is the item and the collection for the for-in.

```
        print("It is obvious that \(myPizza) is the greatest pizza.")
    }
}
```

This is a for-in statement.

This is another call to the print function, passing in a string literal involving string interpolation.

```
myPizza += " is the greatest pizza."
print(myPizza)
```

This is a call to the print function, passing in the variable myPizza.

This expression uses the compound assignment operator (+=) to add the contents of a string literal to a preexisting string variable.

Bullet Points

- There are numerous elements that make up a Swift program. These are the building blocks.

- The most fundamental building blocks are expressions, statements, and declarations.

- A statement defines an action for your Swift program to take.

- An expression returns a result, which is a value of some sort.

- A declaration introduces a new name into your Swift program, for example for a variable.

- Variables let you store named data of a certain type.

- Types define what kind of data is stored in something.

- Literals represent literal values (e.g., 5, true, or "Hello").

Basic operators

The first building block we're going to look at is the **operator**. An operator is a phrase or a symbol that is used to change, check, or combine values that you're working with in your program.

Operators can be used to do mathematics, perform logical operations, assign values, and more. Swift has all the operators that are common building blocks of most programming languages, plus a whole bunch that are reasonably unique to Swift...or at least used uniquely in Swift. You'll learn more about operators as you read more of this book.

Operators can be *unary*, *binary*, or *ternary*: ← ─── This is just a fancy way of saying single target (unary), two target (binary), and three target (ternary).

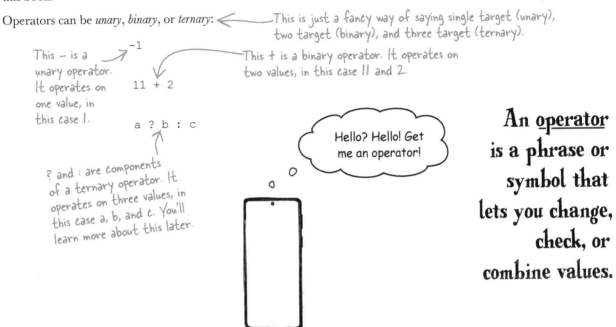

This – is a unary operator. It operates on one value, in this case 1.

This + is a binary operator. It operates on two values, in this case 11 and 2.

$$-1$$
$$11 + 2$$
$$a ? b : c$$

? and : are components of a ternary operator. It operates on three values, in this case a, b, and c. You'll learn more about this later.

Hello? Hello! Get me an operator!

An <u>operator</u> is a phrase or symbol that lets you change, check, or combine values.

Relax

It's easy to feel intimidated if you don't understand or know all of the potential operators and the symbols for them.

As you increase your knowledge of and experience with Swift, many of the operators will become second nature (and many will already be second nature, like the math operators). But many won't.

It's totally normal for a programmer to need to look up operators, keywords, and syntax, even if they've been programming in that language for years or decades. There's nothing wrong with having to check your memory by looking things up.

Operating swiftly with mathematics

When you're programming, you're often doing math. Swift isn't going to let you down when it comes to doing math. All the classics are there, including operators for ***adding, subtracting, dividing, multiplying,*** and ***modulo***.

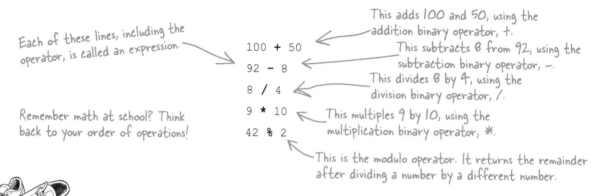

Each of these lines, including the operator, is called an expression.

This adds 100 and 50, using the addition binary operator, +.

```
100 + 50
92 - 8
8 / 4
9 * 10
42 % 2
```

This subtracts 8 from 92, using the subtraction binary operator, -.

This divides 8 by 4, using the division binary operator, /.

Remember math at school? Think back to your order of operations!

This multiples 9 by 10, using the multiplication binary operator, *.

This is the modulo operator. It returns the remainder after dividing a number by a different number.

Exercise

Create a new Playground and do some math! You can combine operators, just like you learned in high school.

Try multiplying something by 42, and then dividing it by 3 and subtracting 4.

Try 4 + 5 * 5.

Check if a number is even by using the modulo operator (if there's no remainder from dividing something by 2, then it's an even number). What do you think the result will be?

⟶ Answers on page 37.

Express yourself

A combination of values and operators that produces a value is called an expression.

```
917 - 17 + 4
```

This is an expression, because it's a combination of values (917, 17, and 4) and operators (- and +) that produces a value (904).

Actually, any code that returns a value is called an expression. Even if the value that's produced is the same as the expression, it's still an expression.

Expressing yourself

If you input these **expressions** into a Playground and run it, you can see what their value is (what they *evaluate* to):

100 **+** 50

92 **−** 8

8 **/** 4

9 ***** 10

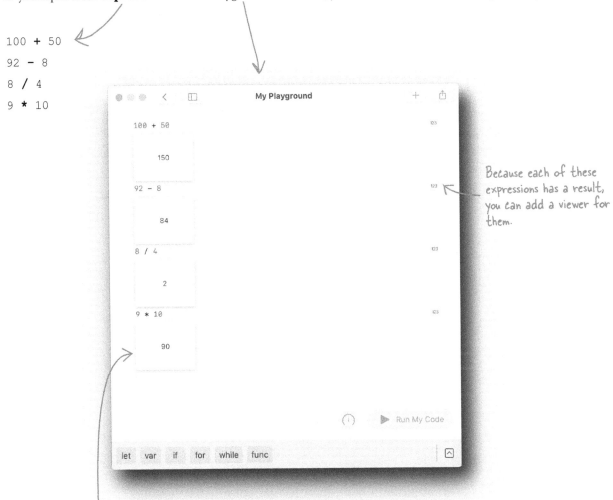

Because each of these expressions has a result, you can add a viewer for them.

The results viewers that you add will appear below each expression that you add them for.

You can't mix and match whitespace styles...

...you have to pick one style and stick with it. So your expressions and operators can either be like 8 / 4 *or be like* 8 / 4, *but they can't be like* 8 /4 *or be like* 8/ 4.

Bullet Points

- Swift programs are built from statements.

- A simple statement is built from expressions and declarations.

- An expression is code that evaluates to a result.

- A statement does not return a result.

- A declaration is when a new variable, constant, function, structure, class, or enumeration is introduced.

- Operators are phrases or symbols used to change, check, or combine values in Swift.

- Some of the most common operators let you perform mathematical operations.

- Other operators let you assign things, compare things, or check the result of things.

Who Does What?

Solidify your knowledge of the basic operators you can use in Swift expressions, and match each expression on the left to its result on the right.

7 + 3	2
9 - 1	10
10 / 5	20
5 * 4	8
9 % 3	0
-11	-11

⟶ Answers on page 37.

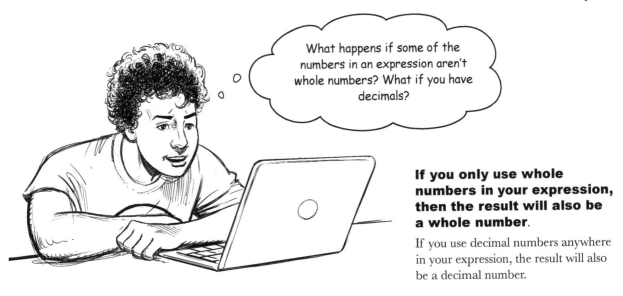

What happens if some of the numbers in an expression aren't whole numbers? What if you have decimals?

If you only use whole numbers in your expression, then the result will also be a whole number.

If you use decimal numbers anywhere in your expression, the result will also be a decimal number.

Say you want to divide 10 by 6. You'd expect the result to be something resembling 1.666666666666667 if you did this:

```
10 / 6
```

But you'd end up with a result of 1, because the result can only be a whole number and it's been rounded down to the closest one.

Whereas, if you ask Swift to use decimal numbers, like this:

```
10.0 / 6.0
```

you'll end up with the more precise answer of 1.666666666666667, because Swift is working exclusively with decimal numbers.

Swift also has another math operator: **modulo**. You can use it to figure out how many multiples of a number will fit inside another number.

For example, if you wanted to know how many times 2 would fit inside 9, you'd do this:

```
9 % 2
```

The answer to this is 1. You can fit 4 units of 2 inside 9, before the remainder that's left isn't enough to make another 2—only 1 remains.

In Swift, whole numbers are more properly known as "integers" and decimal numbers as "doubles" or "floats." Integers, doubles, and floats are known as types.

Other types you might have heard of include strings and Booleans.

Names and types: peas in a pod

Like with pets and seasonal beverages, it's much easier to work with data that has a name. **Constants** and **variables** are used to store some data, and refer to it by name. You assign data to them using the **assignment operator**, =.

A **variable** is a piece of named data whose *value can be changed*, while a **constant** is one whose *value can never be changed*. Here are a few examples:

The keyword <u>let</u> defines a constant, and the keyword <u>var</u> defines a variable.

This = is another operator. It's called the assignment operator.

```
let favNumber = 8.7
```
This statement declares a constant named favNumber and assigns the double value 8.7 to it.

```
var coffeesConsumed = 17
coffeesConsumed = 25
```
This one declares a variable named coffeesConsumed and assigns the integer value 17 to it.

A variable can be updated later. Because it's variable. Get it?

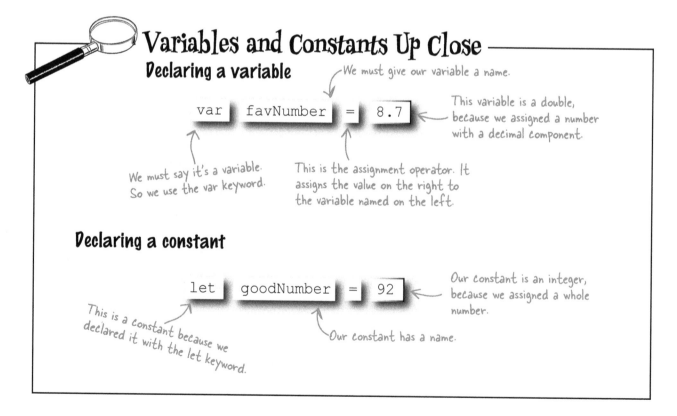

Variables and Constants Up Close

Declaring a variable

We must give our variable a name.

```
var   favNumber   =   8.7
```

This variable is a double, because we assigned a number with a decimal component.

We must say it's a variable. So we use the var keyword.

This is the assignment operator. It assigns the value on the right to the variable named on the left.

Declaring a constant

```
let   goodNumber   =   92
```

Our constant is an integer, because we assigned a whole number.

This is a constant because we declared it with the let keyword.

Our constant has a name.

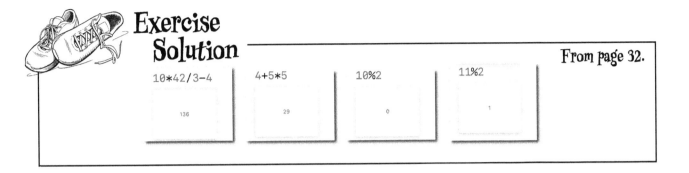

Exercise Solution

From page 32.

10*42/3-4	4+5*5	10%2	11%2
136	29	0	1

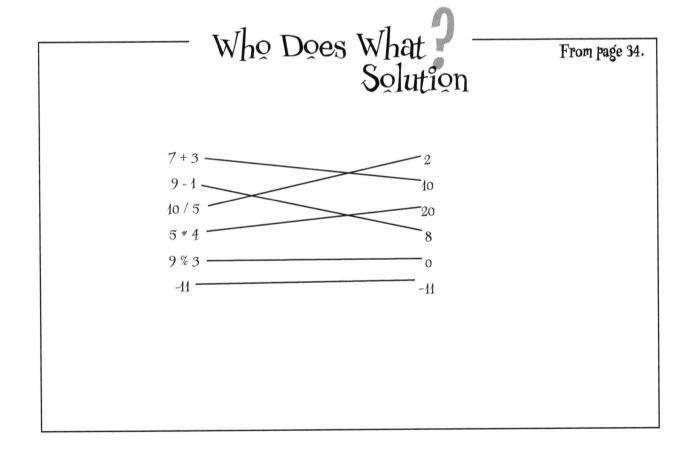

Who Does What? Solution

From page 34.

```
7 + 3 ────────┐  ┌──── 2
9 - 1 ──────┐ │  │ ┌── 10
10 / 5 ─────┘ │  │ └── 20
5 * 4 ────────┘  └──── 8
9 % 3 ─────────────── 0
-11 ───────────────── -11
```

I'm very used to being in control when I code. Are you sure I can't change a constant once I've set it?

That's so inflexible. I'm a variable. I can have my value updated again, and again, and again.

8.7

favNumber

17

coffeesConsumed

A variable can have its value changed, but its type can never change.

I'm a constant in the world. Once I'm set, I never change my value.

Not even if you're the boss!

You <u>cannot change</u> <u>a constant</u> once it's set. Ever.

You can change the value of a **variable** as many times as you need to, but once you've assigned a value to a **constant** you can't change the value. Let's take a closer look at the ways you can declare variables and constants:

```
let myNumber = 10
```
This defines a constant named myNumber, and assigns the value 10 to it. Swift figures out that this constant is a whole number, an integer, because we assigned the value as one.

```
let myDouble = 10.5
```
This expression creates a constant called myDouble, storing the decimal number 10.5 in it (a double).

```
var number = 55
```
This expression declares a variable called number, which we assign the integer 55 to, making the variable an integer.

```
number = 9.7
```
Because number is an integer, we can't assign a double to it (even though it's a variable). This will error.

```
number = 10
```
We can update number to a new integer, though. Because it's a variable.

```
let myConstant = 5
```
This creates a constant named myConstant and assigns the integer 5 to it, making it a constant integer.

```
myConstant = 7
```
Once it has a value, it can't be changed. So we can't then do this. This will error.

Sharpen your pencil

Create a new Swift Playground, and write some Swift code that does the following:

☐   Create a variable named pizzaSlicesRemaining and set it to 8.

☐   Create a constant named totalSlices and set it to 8.

☐   Divide totalSlices by pizzaSlicesRemaining.

☐   Update the value of pizzaSlicesRemaining to 4.

☐   Divide totalSlices by pizzaSlicesRemaining again.

⟶ Answers on page 43.

Exercise

Create a new Playground and declare an Integer variable, assign some data (an integer, naturally) to it, and then, on the next line, attempt to assign a string to it, and see what happens.

What error does Swift give you?

⟶ Answer on page 43.

Relax

This is a lot to take in.

There are a lot of elements to consider, even at this early point in your Swift journey. You'll build on your knowledge, and you'll feel more comfortable as we continue.

Not all data is numbers

You already know how to create and name both **constants** and **variables** when you need to store something in numerical form, whether or not a decimal point is involved! ***Not all values are numbers, though.*** It's time to introduce one of the biggest stars of the Swift world: the <u>**type system**</u>.

These are all <u>types</u>

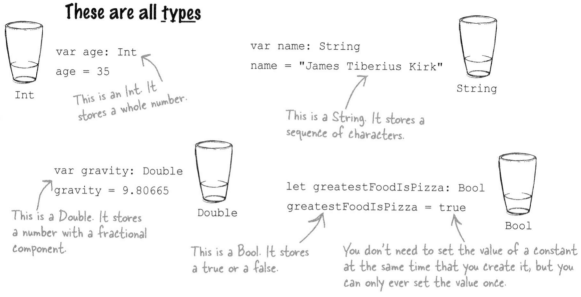

```
var age: Int
age = 35
```

Int

This is an Int. It stores a whole number.

```
var name: String
name = "James Tiberius Kirk"
```

String

This is a String. It stores a sequence of characters.

```
var gravity: Double
gravity = 9.80665
```

This is a Double. It stores a number with a fractional component.

Double

```
let greatestFoodIsPizza: Bool
greatestFoodIsPizza = true
```

Bool

This is a Bool. It stores a true or a false.

You don't need to set the value of a constant at the same time that you create it, but you can only ever set the value once.

Sometimes you want a number, sometimes you want a string, and sometimes you want something else entirely. Swift has a **type system**, which lets you tell Swift what kind of data to expect using a **type annotation** or **type inference**.

You've already seen some types (integers, doubles, floats, and strings), and we've been setting the types of our variables and constants using ***type inference***, where we let Swift figure out what type of data something is when the value is assigned.

There are a bunch more types to learn about, though, and we'll cover all of them in this book. It's important to understand them, because once a variable has its type set there's no changing it, and you can't assign it data that's of the wrong type.

"Hawaiian Pizza"

I'm just not your type...sorry. There are plenty of other variables out there for you.

Int

Type inference means that Swift figures out what the data is, and assigns the type for you. You can also use type annotation to specify the type.

Swift Safety
Today's Lesson

Mutability

While it might be conceptually obvious that variables are designed to have their values change and constants are not, it pays to look at this in practice. Create a Swift Playground and declare the following variable, representing the name of a pizza shop:

```
var pizzaShopName = "Big Mike's Pizzeria"
```

Now suppose the pizza shop gets acquired, and the new owner (who, naturally, is no longer Big Mike) wants to change the name to "Swift Pizza." Because the pizzaShopName is a variable, you can add something like this to your Playground and there'll be absolutely no problem:

```
pizzaShopName = "Swift Pizza"
```

However, if you change the first line in your Playground to this:

```
let pizzaShopName = "Big Mike's Pizzeria"
```

You'll see that the second line, where you try to change the name, now has an error (as does the first line, suggesting you change it to a variable to make it mutable).

This is one of the simplest safety features of Swift:

If something isn't meant to change, Swift will tell you about it.

A red indicator will appear on each line with an error, or with code related to an error.

When there are issues with your code, you'll see a red indicator.

This is the line with the error, in this case. The first line also has an indicator because changing it will fix the error.

You can click it to see a full list of all the errors in your Playground.

Clicking either of the Fix buttons, in this case, will change the constant to a variable in the first line.

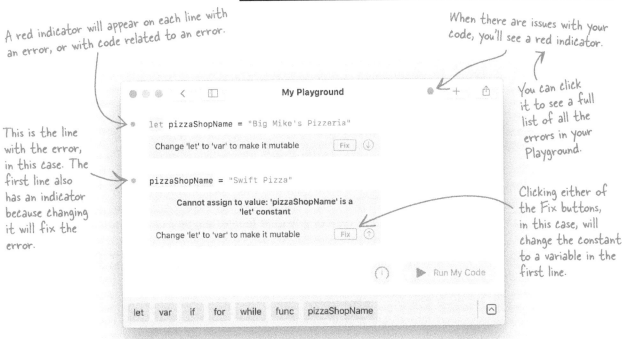

Stringing things along with types

When you're programming, as we said, you're often doing math. But you're also often working with text. Programming languages represent text using a type called a String. As you saw on the previous page, you can create a String like this:

```
var greeting = "Hi folks, I'm a String! I'm very excited to be here."
```

Or like this:

```
var message: String = "I'm also a String. I'm also excited to be here."
```

When you include a predefined value that happens to be a string in your code like we just did, it's called a **string literal**. A string literal is, quite literally, a sequence of characters surrounded by double quotation " " marks.

If you want to create an empty variable that stores a string, you can do that too, like this:

```
var positiveMessage = ""
```

← In this case, positiveMessage is a String because the data "" is a String (however short), and type inference makes the variable a String.

Or like this:

```
var negativeMessage: String
```

← negativeMessage is a String because a String type annotation is provided.

You can then assign values to your strings:

```
positiveMessage = "Live long and prosper"

negativeMessage = "You bring dishonor to your house."
```

Types are, by design, inflexible.

You cannot do this:

```
var pizzaTopping
        pizzaTopping = "Oregano"
```

This is because when we declared the variable `pizzaTopping` *we didn't supply any data for Swift to perform type inference with, and we also didn't supply a type annotation explicitly telling Swift what type it would be.*

So, while it's normally perfectly fine to declare a variable and then assign some data to it (or change the data) at a later point—that's the entire point of a variable—in this case, because we declared the `pizzaTopping` *variable without a type and without any data to infer a type from, it's not safe, so it can't be done.*

If we want to declare a variable in advance without supplying some data, we must supply a type annotation, like this:

```
        var pizzaTopping: String
```

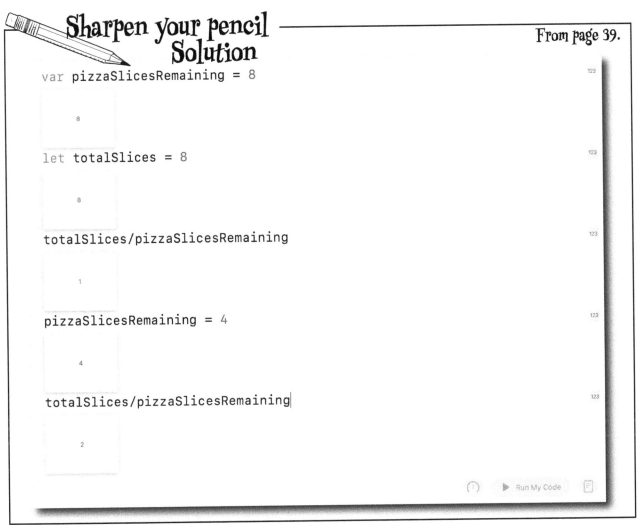

Sharpen your pencil
Solution

From page 39.

```
var pizzaSlicesRemaining = 8
```
8

```
let totalSlices = 8
```
8

```
totalSlices/pizzaSlicesRemaining
```
1

```
pizzaSlicesRemaining = 4
```
4

```
totalSlices/pizzaSlicesRemaining
```
2

Run My Code

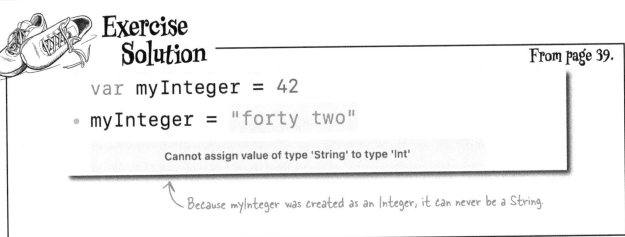

Exercise
Solution

From page 39.

```
var myInteger = 42
• myInteger = "forty two"
```

Cannot assign value of type 'String' to type 'Int'

Because myInteger was created as an Integer, it can never be a String.

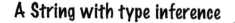

Anatomy of a Type

A String with type inference

The variable is named pizzaShopName.

```
var   pizzaShopName   =   "Swift Pizza"
```

It's a variable, so the stored value can change.

This is the assignment operator. It assigns the value on the right to the variable named on the left.

This is the value, a string of characters.

pizzaShopName

Swift knows that my type is String because it looked at the type of data that was assigned (a string of characters).

**When you let Swift determine the type based on the data you assign it's referred to as type inference.
When you specify a type, it's referred to as type annotation.**

A String with type annotation

This is a type annotation, telling Swift our variable is a String.

```
var   pizzaName:   String   =   "Swift Pizza"
```

We add a colon after our variable name and before the type annotation.

Swift knows that my type is String because a type annotation was provided declaring me to be a String.

pizzaName

Bullet Points

- **String** stores strings of characters. There could be any number of characters in a string, including zero.

- **Int** stores whole round numbers, with no decimal point. They can be negative, though.

- **Double** stores numbers that have a decimal point. They can also be negative.

- **Bool** stores `true` or `false`. Nothing else.

If a variable or constant is declared with a type annotation but no data, the data can be assigned later. The data <u>must match</u> the type annotation.

> I understand type annotations and type inference. But I don't see how it works with a constant. Can you declare a constant and then give it a value at a later date? How does the type system play into that?

Constants and variables need a type annotation, or a value that is assigned at declaration. Or both.

When you declare a variable or constant, you can **either supply a type annotation or immediately assign a value**.

If you assign a value, that's all you need to do; the type system will use type inference, and you're done.

If you don't want to assign a value at declaration, that's fine, but you must supply a type annotation so that Swift knows what type of data to expect when some data is assigned.

For example, this is OK because we assigned some data to this constant at the time of declaration:

```
let bestPizzaInTheWorld = "Hawaiian"
```

This is a constant (we used the <u>let</u> keyword to declare it), so once we assign the string literal "Hawaiian" to it, it will be of type String (thanks to <u>type inference</u>).

But if we do not assign any data at the time the constant or variable is declared, there will be an error:

```
let bestPizzaInTheWorld
bestPizzaInTheWorld = "Hawaiian"
```

We must supply a type annotation if we want to do this, like this:

```
let bestPizzaInTheWorld: String
bestPizzaInTheWorld = "Hawaiian"
```

Because we provide a <u>type annotation</u>, this declaration is OK.

We eventually put a string into this constant, as per its type annotation. Because it's a constant, once it has some data assigned it can't be changed again.

Who am I?

A bunch of Swift **types**, in full costume, are playing a party game, "Who am I?" Each one will give you a clue, and you have to guess what their name is based on what they say about themselves.

Assume they always tell the truth about themselves. Draw an arrow from each clue to the name of one attendee. We've already guessed one of them for you.

If you find this challenging, it's totally OK to sneak a peek at the answers at the end of this chapter!

Tonight's attendees:

I exclusively focus on whether things are true or false. I don't care about anything else.

String

I just love characters and prefer to focus on one character at a time.

Bool

I am interested in working with as many characters as I can, all at once.

Int

I love whole numbers. Positive and negative. I just don't do fractions.

Double

I'm in love with fractional components. I'm a big fan of numbers that have them. That's all I like, really.

Character

—————————▶ Answers on page 54.

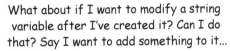

What about if I want to modify a string variable after I've created it? Can I do that? Say I want to add something to it...

Modifying a string after you've created it is easy. It (mostly) just works like it does for numbers.

You can add something to a string. Let's say you were storing a nice motivational speech:

```
var speech = "Our mission is to seek out new
                      life and new civilizations."
```

And then, later on, you wanted to add some more:

```
speech +=
      " To boldly go where no one has gone before!"
```

This += is an operator. It's called the compound assignment operator. It means "take speech, and store speech plus the following thing in speech."

The speech variable will now contain:

```
"Our mission is to seek out new life and new
civilizations. To boldly go where no one has gone
before!"
```

You can only use the += operator to add to a string. You cannot use -= to remove from a string.

Exercise

Create a new Swift Playground, and code the following:

- Create a String variable named favoriteQuote.
- Assign a snippet of your favorite quote to the variable.
- Add the string "by" and then the author of the quote to the favoriteQuote variable.
- Print the favoriteQuote variable.

→ Answers on page 52.

String interpolation

You'd be forgiven for thinking string interpolation was something from science fiction, but it's not, and it's very useful. **String interpolation** lets you construct a string from a mix of values—constants, variables, string literals, and expressions—by including their values inside a new string literal.

Let's say you had a number that represented the speed of your hypothetical spaceship, measured in warp factors (just like on a certain popular science fiction television show):

```
var warpSpeed = 9.9
```

And you also had the name of the hypothetical spaceship, stored as a string constant:

```
let shipName = "USS Enterprise"
```

And your ship was en route to some far-off planet, and you had that stored as a variable:

```
var destination = "Ceti Alpha V"
```

You could use string interpolation to construct a brand new string, incorporating all this useful information:

```
var status = "Ship \(shipName) en route to \(destination),
traveling at a speed of warp factor \(warpSpeed)."
```

Ship `shipName`

en route to

`destination`

traveling at a speed of warp factor

`warpSpeed` .

If you then printed this new status string variable, the result would be:

```
Ship USS Enterprise en route to Ceti Alpha V, traveling
at a speed of warp factor 9.9.
```

The placeholder is replaced with the actual value of the constant, variable, string literal, or expression that is being named.

You might have noticed us using string interpolation when calling Swift's print function, to display the values of variables and constants as part of the printed output.

Exercise

Create a new Swift Playground, and add the following code:

```
var name = "Head First Reader"
var timeLearning = "3 days"
var goal = "make an app for my kids"
var platform = "iPad"
```

Use string interpolation to print a string that says "Hello, I'm Head First Reader, and I've been learning Swift for 3 days. My goal is to make an app for my kids. I'm particularly interested in the iPad platform." Use the variables and string interpolation to customize the printed string with your own details. ⟶ Answers on page 52.

What's this you keep saying about "literals"? Isn't everything in programming a literal? Literally everything...ha ha ha...

Literals values are any value that appear directly in your code.

For example, if you define a variable named `peopleComingToEatPizza` and you assign the value 8 to it (because that's how many people you have coming over to eat pizza), then the value that appears directly in your source code, which is 8, is an integer literal:

```
var peopleComingToEatPizza = 8
```

If you define a variable to represent the percentage of your delicious pizza pie that's remaining and assign the value 3.14159 to it, then you've assigned a floating-point literal to your variable:

```
var pieRemaining = 3.14159
```

And if you describe a pizza using words and store that description in a variable, you've created a String variable thanks to type inference because you assigned a string literal:

```
var pizzaDescription =

    "A delicious mix of

            pineapple and ham."
```

good questions

there are no
Dumb Questions

Q: I thought Swift had something called "protocols." When are we learning about those? What about classes?

A: Swift does have something called "protocols," and we promise that we'll get to them shortly. We'll also get to classes very soon. Swift has more than one way to structure a program, and both classes and protocols offer useful paths forward.

Q: Why would I ever use a constant when I could just make everything a variable in case it needs to change?

A: Swift places a much greater emphasis on using constants than other programming languages do. It can help, a lot, with making your program safer and more stable if you only use variables for values that you expect to change. Additionally, if you tell the Swift compiler that your values with be constants, the compiler can make your programs faster by performing certain optimizations for you.

Q: Why can't I change the type of a value after I've assigned it? Other languages can do this.

A: Swift is a strongly typed language. It puts a lot of emphasis on the way the type system works, and encourages you to learn it. You cannot change the type of a variable after you've created it. You can create a new variable and cast the type to something new if you need to.

Q: So are variables and constants also types?

A: No, variables and constants are named locations to store data. The data in a variable or constant has a type, so the variable or constant has a type, but it in itself is not a type.

Q: What if I need to store some data that Swift doesn't have a type for?

A: Great question. We'll be looking at ways you can create your own types later on in the book.

Bullet Points

- Operators are phrases or symbols that are used to change, check, or combine values that you're working with in your program.
- Variables and constants let you store data and refer to it by name.
- Variables and constants have a type (like Int or String). Swift will assign a type for you based on what you store in the variable or constant at creation, or you can explicitly specify a type.
- Variables can have their value, but not their type, changed at any time.
- Constants can never change value or type.
- Swift programs are comprised of expressions, statements, and declarations.

Swiftcross

It's time to test your brain. Gently.

This is just a normal crossword, but all the solutions are concepts we covered in this chapter. How much did you learn?

Across

3) A value that appears directly in your code.

4) The kind of data that is stored.

5) I'm true or false.

8) When a string is placed within another string.

10) Mutable stored, named data.

11) Type _____ is when Swift figures out the type of something based on what the data looks like.

13) A type that stores words, characters, or sentences.

14) The type for a number with a decimal place.

Down

1) A type _____ is used to mark a type on a variable.

2) A line of code that introduces a new named piece of data to a program.

6) A phrase or symbol that is used to change, check, or combine values.

7) A type for a whole number.

9) A statement that results in a value.

12) A named piece of data where you cannot modify the data after it's created.

→ Answers on page 54.

Exercise Solution

From page 47.

```
var favoriteQuote: String
favoriteQuote = "I love it when a plan comes together!"          abc
favoriteQuote += " by John 'Hannibal' Smith"                     abc
print(favoriteQuote)                                             abc
```

```
I love it when a plan comes together! by John 'Hannibal' Smith
```

Exercise Solution

From page 48.

```
var name = "Head First Reader"
var timeLearning = "3 days"
var goal = "make an app for my kids"
var platform = "iPad"
print("Hello, I'm \(name), and I've been learning Swift for
  \(timeLearning). My goal is to \(goal). I'm particularly
  interested in the \(platform) platform.")
```

```
Hello, I'm Head First Reader, and I've been learning Swift for 3
days. My goal is to make an app for my kids. I'm particularly
interested in the iPad platform.
```

Swiftcross
Solution

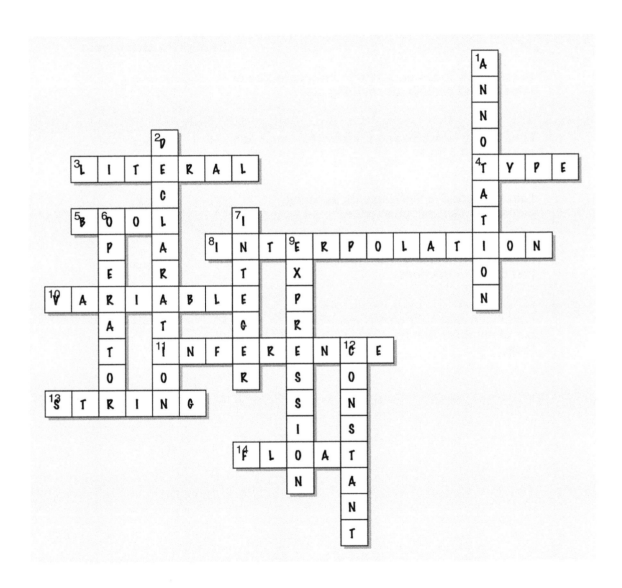

Who am I? Solution

From page 46.

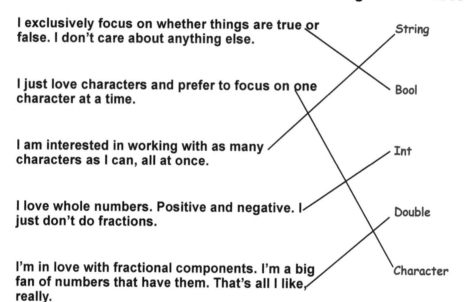

Tonight's attendees:

I exclusively focus on whether things are true or false. I don't care about anything else.

String

I just love characters and prefer to focus on one character at a time.

Bool

I am interested in working with as many characters as I can, all at once.

Int

I love whole numbers. Positive and negative. I just don't do fractions.

Double

I'm in love with fractional components. I'm a big fan of numbers that have them. That's all I like, really.

Character

3 collecting and controlling

Going Loopy for Data

I love to collect things. I want to learn how to collect and count things. What were we doing, again?

You already know about expressions, operators, variables, constants, and types in Swift. It's time to consolidate and build on that knowledge and explore some more advanced Swift data structures and operators: **collections** and **control flow**. In this chapter, we're going to talk about putting **collections of data** into variables and constants, and how to **structure data**, **manipulate data**, and **operate on data using control flow statements**. We'll be looking at other ways to collect and structure data later in the book, but for now let's get started with **arrays**, **sets**, and **dictionaries**.

Sorting pizzas

Meet the *Swift Pizzeria*, the fastest pizza place in town.

Get it? Hilarious.

The Chef, who is pretty grumpy at the best of times, wants to sort the restaurant's pizzas alphabetically using Swift (after all, it's in the name).

They're facing some issues, though. Can you help the chef **sort** their pizzas?

> I want to alphabetize my pizzas. Why is this so difficult? I've stored each pizza name as a string variable...

```swift
var pizzaHawaiian = "Hawaiian"
var pizzaCheese = "Cheese"
var pizzaMargherita = "Margherita"
var pizzaMeatlovers = "Meatlovers"
var pizzaVegetarian = "Vegetarian"
var pizzaProsciutto = "Prosciutto"
var pizzaVegan = "Vegan"
```

Swift has a range of special types that can store collections of things. Unsurprisingly, these are called <u>collection types</u>.

The name says it all, really!

There are three main collection types you can use to store collections in Swift: **arrays**, **sets**, and **dictionaries**. They all have differences, and knowing when to use each is a fundamental Swift programming skill.

The quickest way to store a list of pizzas in a collection and then sort them alphabetically is an array—but we'll come back to that. To decide how best to help the chef, you need to understand each of the collection types and what they can do.

Swift collection types

The Swift types you've used so far allow you to store individual pieces of data, of different types (for the most part). For example, String lets you store strings, Int lets you store integers, Bool lets you store Boolean values, and so on.

Swift's **collection types** allow you to store **multiple pieces** of data.

Bet you didn't see that coming.

A collection type makes storing collections of things much easier.

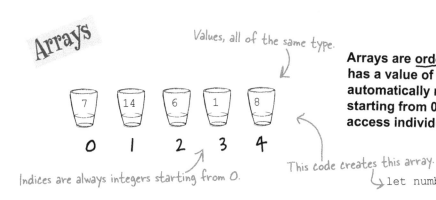

Arrays

Values, all of the same type.

7 14 6 1 8

0 1 2 3 4

Indices are always integers starting from 0.

This code creates this array.

```
let numbers = [7, 14, 6,1, 8]
```

Arrays are <u>ordered</u>, and every element has a value of the <u>same type</u> and is automatically numbered with an <u>index</u>, starting from 0. This means you can access individual values using the indices.

Sets

Values, all of the same type.

1 7 9 13 3

Only one element of each value.

Sets are <u>unordered</u>, and every element has a value of the <u>same type</u>. There are <u>no index values</u> for sets, so you need to access them using features of the set, or by iterating through the whole set.
Each value can only be stored in a set <u>once</u>.

Both of these pieces of code create this set.

```
var numbers = Set([1, 7, 9, 13, 3])
var numbers: Set = [1, 7, 9, 13, 3]
```

Dictionaries

Values, all of the same type.

1 7 9 13 3

"Tom" "Bob" "Tim" "Mars" "Tony"

Keys, all of the same type. Each key maps to a value.

Dictionaries are <u>unordered c</u>ollections of <u>keys and values.</u> Every key is the same type, and every value is the same type. A value can be accessed using its key, just like with indices in arrays. The keys can be different types than the values.

This code creates this dictionary.

```
var  scores = ["Tom": 5, "Bob": 10, "Tim": 9, "Mars": 14, "Tony": 3]
```

Collecting values in an <u>array</u>

The first ***collection type*** we're going to look at is an **array**. An array is a collection of things, of the *same type*, that has a specific order. You can create an array simply, like this array of strings representing potential names for a cat:

The values stored in the array are placed between square brackets.

```
let catNames = ["Lucy", "Tom", "Billy", "Bruce", "Lady", "Doug", "Susan"]
```

This array is a constant.

Swift's <u>type inference</u> system will figure out that this is an array of strings, because they're all strings!

An array is an ordered collection of values of the <u>same type</u>.

Or you could create an array like this variable array of integers, where a type annotation is provided:

```
var numbers: [Int] = [7, 14, 6, 1, 8]
```

The <u>type annotation</u> is wrapped in square brackets here to designate it as an <u>array</u> of that type.

Arrays number the values they hold with indices, starting from 0. The indices the array we just created look like this:

You can access the individual components of an array using the index.

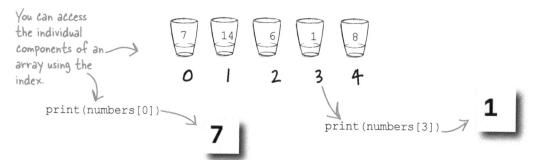

```
print(numbers[0])
```

7

```
print(numbers[3])
```

1

We can add things to variable arrays in a variety of ways, including appending:

```
numbers.append(42)
```

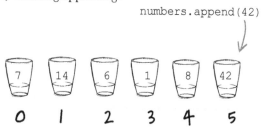

We can also remove elements:

```
numbers.remove(at: 3)
```

And inserting:

```
numbers.insert(11, at: 2)
```

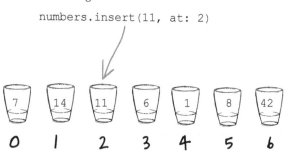

And change the value of specific elements:

```
numbers[2] = 307
```

Sharpen your pencil

Consider the following array, containing a collection of our favorite pizzas:

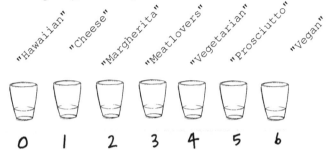

"Hawaiian" "Cheese" "Margherita" "Meatlovers" "Vegetarian" "Prosciutto" "Vegan"

0   1   2   3   4   5   6

Create a new Playground and write some code to do the following:

☐ Create this array, as a variable, storing the pizza names in it.

☐ Print the element of the array that contains `"Vegetarian"`.

☐ Append the pizza `"Pepperoni"` to the array, without changing the rest of the array.

☐ Insert a new pizza, `"Ham, Pineapple, and Pesto"`, at index 2, shuffling everything after along by one index.

☐ Remove the `"Cheese"` pizza from the array entirely, leaving the rest intact.

☐ Swap the `"Prosciutto"` pizza for a `"Pumpkin and Feta"` pizza, without changing the rest of the array.

☐ Print out the whole array.

Once you've completed all of these steps, your array should look something like this. ↓

```
["Hawaiian", "Ham, Pineapple, and Pesto", "Margherita", "Meatlovers", "Vegetarian", "Pumpkin and Feta", "Vegan", "Pepperoni"]
```

→ Answers on page 62.

How big is that array, exactly? Is it empty?

You knew exactly how big the arrays we've worked with so far were (because you created them), but what if you need to work with an array that you don't know the length of in advance?

Imagine you've been asked to do something with an array named `ingredients` that contains the ingredients you need for a specific pizza. It's been created somewhere else, so you don't know how many elements are in it.

Let's take a peek behind the curtain. Here's the array being created:

```
var ingredients =
        ["Oregano", "Ham", "Tomato", "Olives", "Cheese"]
```
This is a simple array of strings.

Every collection type in Swift has a count property available that lets you get the number of elements in the collection, like this:

```
print("There are \(ingredients.count)
            ingredients in this pizza.")
```
There are 5 ingredients in this pizza.

You can also do other useful things, like check if the array is empty:

```
print(ingredients.isEmpty)
```
false

And there are some convenience methods that let you get the minimum and maximum elements of an array:

```
print(ingredients.max())
print(ingredients.min())
```

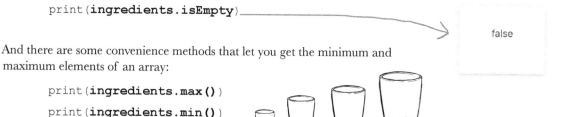

Bullet Points

- Arrays collect elements of the same type. If you create an array of integers, it can only ever store integers.

- Array elements are indexed from 0, and arrays can store as many elements of the same type as you want.

- If you remove an element from an array, the array is reordered. There are no empty gaps.

- Arrays can have specific elements removed, by index number.

- Elements can be appended at the end.

- And elements can be inserted between two other elements (with a reordering taking place).

- There are many useful properties (like count) and convenience methods (like max and min) available on arrays.

- Arrays in Swift might look a lot like lists from other languages. They basically are that. But they're also arrays.

Collecting values in a set

The second collection type that we're going to use is the **set**. Sets are similar to arrays and must also contain just one type, but **sets are unordered, and <u>there can only be one of each distinct value in a set</u>**.

You can create a set like this:

```
var evenNumbers = Set([2, 4, 6, 8])
```

Or like this:

```
var oddNumbers: Set = [1,3,5,7]
```

There are other ways to create sets, and we'll cover them later in the book.

> **Sets are useful when you need to make sure each item only appears once.**

You can insert items into sets, just like with an array:

```
oddNumbers.insert(3)
```
← This will not fail, or throw any sort of error, but won't do anything. This is because 3 is already in this set, and sets only allow one of each value. This is a feature, not a bug.

```
oddNumbers.insert(9)
```
↖ This insert will result in the addition of 9 to the set.

And likewise, you can easily remove elements (even if they don't exist in the set, you can still ask for them to be removed):

```
oddNumbers.remove(3)
```
← This results in the removal of 3 from the set, if it was in the set to begin with. It won't error if it wasn't.

Sharpen your pencil

Consider the following questions about sets, and see if you can figure out the answer. You run them in a Playground to find out, or take a peek at the answers on the next page.

```
var pizzas = Set(["Hawaiian", "Vegan", "Meatlovers", "Hawaiian"])
print(pizzas)
```
What will be printed? _____

```
let favPizzas = ["Hawaiian", "Meatlovers"]
```
What's in this set? _____

```
let customerOrder = Set("Hawaiian", "Vegan", "Vegetarian", "Supreme")
```
What's in this set? _____

Sharpen your pencil **Solution**

From page 59.

```
var favoritePizzas = ["Hawaiian", "Cheese", "Margherita",
 "Meatlovers", "Vegetarian", "Prosciutto", "Vegan"]
print(favoritePizzas[4])
favoritePizzas.append("Pepperoni")
favoritePizzas.insert("Ham, Pineapple, and Pesto", at: 2)
favoritePizzas.remove(at: 1)
favoritePizzas[5] = "Pumpkin and Feta"
print(favoritePizzas)
```

```
Vegetarian
 ["Hawaiian", "Ham, Pineapple, and Pesto", "Margherita", "Meatlovers",
  "Vegetarian", "Pumpkin and Feta", "Vegan", "Pepperoni"]
```

Sharpen your pencil **Solution**

Sets can only contain one instance of each thing, so "Hawaiian" is only in there once.

```
var pizzas = Set(["Hawaiian", "Vegan", "Meatlovers", "Hawaiian"])
print(pizzas)
```

What will be printed? `["Meatlovers", "Hawaiian", "Vegan"]`

```
let favPizzas = ["Hawaiian", "Meatlovers"]
```

What's in this set? `["Hawaiian", "Meatlovers"]`

Also it's an Array, not a Set. Surprise!

```
let customerOrder = Set("Hawaiian", "Vegan", "Vegetarian", "Supreme")
```

What's in this set? Nothing, because the syntax is incorrect. The list of items needs to be wrapped in [ ].

Collecting values in a dictionary

The final collection type we're going to use right now is a **dictionary**. As you might be able to intuit from the name, a dictionary collects things by mapping one thing to another...just like a real-world dictionary maps a word to a definition. Like sets, **dictionaries in Swift are unordered**.

The data items that dictionaries map are referred to as **keys** and **values**.

If you wanted to create a dictionary that represented some people who played a board game and the scores they got, you could do it like this:

These are the names of the people that played the board game.

```
var scores = ["Paris": 5, "Marina": 10, "Tim": 9, "Jon": 14]
```

In this case, Swift's type inference will infer that the keys are strings.

These are the game scores for each player.

And Swift's type inference will infer that the values are integers.

Or like this, where you tell the Swift compiler explicitly which types you'd like the keys and values to be:

```
var scores: [String: Int] = ["Paris": 5, "Marina": 10, "Tim": 9, "Jon": 14]
```

The type annotation for our dictionary says we want strings on the left (for the keys) and integers on the right (for the values).

We can also create an empty dictionary like this, but we have to specify the types in advance, because (obviously) the compiler can't figure that out without any values present:

```
var scores: [String: Int] = [:]
```

> So how do I get something out of a dictionary?
> Even better, how do I put something in?

Reading a value from a dictionary might look a little strange, compared to what we've done so far.

To read a value from a dictionary, you can simply use the key:

```
print(scores["Paris"]!)
```

The exclamation mark afterward is used to directly access the value of the key. This is called *force unwrapping* an optional. We'll come back to this syntax a little bit later, when we use optionals. But, once you've learned about force unwrapping, you should never actually do it.

You can also add new values or change existing ones in the dictionary, like this:

```
scores.updateValue(17, forKey: "Bob")
```

Or like this:

```
scores["Josh"] = 4
```

Exercise

It's time to put your newly developed Swift collection skills to work. We've got a couple of collections that need to have their elements accessed and modified. See if you can complete these exercises Don't worry if you need to check the answers.

Consider the following set, representing a set of forbidden pizzas that must never be ordered:

```
var forbiddenPizzas: Set =
        ["Lemon and Pumpkin",
                "Hawaiian with a Fried Egg", "Schnitzel and Granola"]
forbiddenPizzas.insert("Chicken and Boston Beans")
forbiddenPizzas.remove("Lemon and Pumpkin")
```

What does **forbiddenPizzas** contain now?

Consider the following dictionary, representing a bunch of dessert pizzas and the quantities that have been ordered:

```
var dessertPizzaOrders = ["Rocky Road": 2, "Nutella": 3, "Caramel Swirl": 1]
```

Print the quantity of Rocky Road, and the quantity of Caramel Swirl. Then add a new order for 17 Banana Split pizzas.

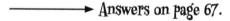

➜ Answers on page 67.

Bullet Points

- In addition to regular types, Swift also features collection types, which allow you to store a group of collected things.

- Arrays are a collection type that stores an ordered collection of the same type, accessibile with an integer index.

- Sets store an unordered (not sorted) collection of distinct elements of the same type. Every element is unique, and there can be no duplicates.

- Dictionaries store an unordered collection of paired keys and values. All keys are the same type, and all values are the same type. A value can be accessed by its key.

Is that it? That's not many collection types. Are there any others?

Yep, the three main collection types are the array, set, and dictionary.

But Swift has a few more tricks up its metaphorical sleeve. There is a generic collection type, which we'll get to much later, that allows you to create your own collection types, but there's also the humble **tuple**.

Tuples let you store multiple values in a single variable or constant, but without the overhead of being, for example, an array.

Tuples are perfect for when you need a very specific collection of values where each item has an exact position or name.

Tuples

A **tuple** can store as many values as you like, as long as their amount and type are defined up front. For example, you could use a tuple to represent coordinates, like x and y, and store them in one variable:

```
var point = (x: 10, y: 15)
print(point.x)
```

Both components of this tuple are integers, because of type inference.

This will print 10.

Tuples can have names for each component or have no names at all. You can update or modify tuples without using the names for the components, as long as the types of the values match:

```
point = (50, 10)
```

The x value will be updated to 50, and the y value will be updated to 10.

You can also always access the contents of tuples using integers, starting from 0:

```
print(point.0)
```

This will print 50.

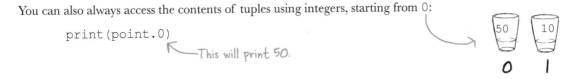

Everyone needs a good <u>alias</u>

When you're working with the various data types in Swift, one of the ways you can make your code easier to read is by using **type aliases**: giving a new name to an existing type.

Let's take a look at a quick example: a simple, one-way, Celsius to Fahrenheit temperature convertor, written without any type aliases.

Our Celsius value is stored in an integer variable called temp.

```
var temp: Int = 35
var result: Int
```

And we'll store our converted Fahrenheit result in an integer variable called result.

```
result = (temp*9/5)+32
print("\(temp) °C is \(result) °F")
```

The result is calculated by converting the Celsius value in temp into Fahrenheit and stored in the result variable.

And we print the whole thing out, showing the conversion.

While this is a very small, simple piece of code, it can be made even easier to follow using type aliases:

```
typealias Celsius = Int
typealias Fahrenheit = Int
```

We define type aliases for Int, named after each of the two temperature systems our code is dealing with.

```
var temp: Celsius = 35
var result: Fahrenheit
```

Our temperature values are now typed based on what they are.

```
result = (temp*9/5)+32
print("\(temp) °C is \(result) °F")
```

Type aliases don't change anything about the type. They just give you a new name to call the type.

Type aliases are a great way to make your code more readable. But be careful.

It's easy to get carried away and make it unmanageable to figure out what types your code is actually working with if you alias everything. Both Celsius and Fahrenheit are still just integers underneath. There's nothing stopping you from assigning a Celsius value to a Fahrenheit variable, because they're just integers.

Exercise Solution

From page 64.

```
var forbiddenPizzas: Set = ["Lemon and Pumpkin", "Hawaiian
 with a Fried Egg", "Schnitzel and Granola"]
forbiddenPizzas.insert("Chicken and Boston Beans")
forbiddenPizzas.remove("Lemon and Pumpkin")
print(forbiddenPizzas)

var dessertPizzaOrders = ["Rocky Road": 2, "Nutella": 3,
 "Caramel Swirl": 1]
print(dessertPizzaOrders["Rocky Road"]!)
print(dessertPizzaOrders["Caramel Swirl"]!)
dessertPizzaOrders["Banana Split"] = 17
```

```
["Chicken and Boston Beans", "Hawaiian with a Fried Egg",
 "Schnitzel and Granola"]

2
1
```

Control flow statements

When you're coding in Swift (and other programming languages, naturally), it's often useful to be able to **do something repeatedly** or **do something under certain conditions**. These two concepts, broadly, are often called *control flow*.

There are lots of tools in your control flow toolbox, and they all work a little differently and all have their place.

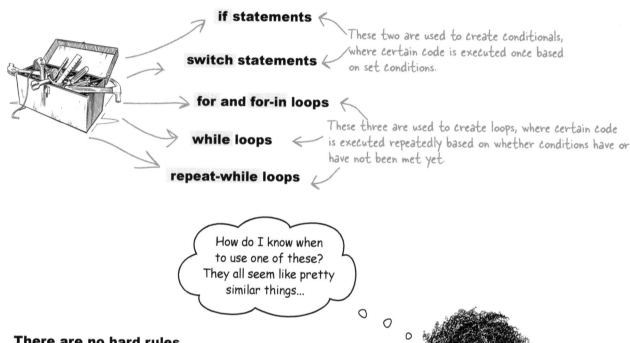

if statements

switch statements

These two are used to create conditionals, where certain code is executed once based on set conditions.

for and for-in loops

while loops

These three are used to create loops, where certain code is executed repeatedly based on whether conditions have or have not been met yet.

repeat-while loops

How do I know when to use one of these? They all seem like pretty similar things...

There are no hard rules.

You can use all of these control flow statements in a variety of situations. **There's no single rule that tells you when to use what, but it will usually be relatively obvious.**

`if` **statements** are best for executing some code only if a certain condition is true.

`switch` **statements** are useful in the same context, but if you have lots of possible different cases, depending on the conditions.

Loops—`for`, `for-in`, `while`, and `repeat-while`— allow you to repeatedly execute some code based on certain conditions.

You'll find uses for all of these control flow statements as you code more.

if statements

`if` statements allow you to do something under certain conditions. They allow you to execute some specific code if certain conditions are met. `if` statements, broadly, are part of a group of concepts known as **conditionals**.

If you have a Bool named `userLovesPizza` and you wanted to use it to determine whether you should give the user a pizza based on whether they love pizza or not, you could use an `if` statement.

```
var userLovesPizza: Bool = true

if(userLovesPizza) {
    print("Enjoy! 🍕 ")
}
```

This is only printed if the user loves pizza (the expression is true) →

Enjoy! 🍕

The conditional in an if statement must be a Boolean expression. This means it must evaluate to either true or false. If the expression is true, the code inside the if statement between the two { } is run.

The `if` statement can be combined with `else` and `else if` in order to provide more options:

```
if(userLovesPizza) {
    print("Enjoy! 🍕 ")
} else {
    print("Sorry!")
}
```

You'll see else if in action on the next page...

The else is run if the if is false!

Exercise

Consider the following Bool variables, each representing whether a certain kind of pizza has been ordered (and therefore should be delivered):

```
var hawaiianPizzaOrdered = true
var veganPizzaOrdered = true
var pepperoniPizzaOrdered = false
```

In a Swift Playground, construct some `if` statements to check if each of these pizzas needs to be delivered. If they need to be delivered, print a message for the delivery driver saying as much, and then set the Bool to `false` so that too many pizzas don't get delivered.

Once you've done that, consider converting this code to use a dictionary of pizza orders and using the `if` statement to check the count of each pizza type in the dictionary before printing the delivery message (which will now include a count).

→ Answers on page 72.

switch statements

You often have to think about a lot of possibilities when you're creating conditionals with `if` statements. Going back to the pizza shop ordering example, imagine how *unwieldy* things could get if we also wanted to send a special message with each type of pizza...let's see how we might do this.

We'll check if a string variable contains a certain type of pizza, and display a message based on that type. We'll need to use a new operator, the **equal to operator**, to check. The equal to operator is two equals signs together: `==`.

```
var pizzaOrdered = "Hawaiian"
```
The pizza that's been ordered is set.

This is the equal to operator. It's used for checking if the things on either side are the same. It returns true if they are.

```
if(pizzaOrdered == "Hawaiian") {
    print("Hawaiian is my favorite. Great choice!")
} else if(pizzaOrdered == "Four Cheese") {
    print("The only thing better than cheese is four cheeses.")
} else if(pizzaOrdered == "BBQ Chicken") {
    print("Chicken and BBQ sauce! What could be better?")
} else if(pizzaOrdered == "Margherita") {
    print("It's a classic for a reason!")

}
```

And then we use lots of if and else if statements to check which pizza was ordered, so we can display the right message.

✎ Sharpen your pencil

Take the following `if` statement, which is designed to print facts about some planets, and add the planets Neptune, Mars, and Earth:

```
var planet = "Jupiter"
if planet == "Jupiter" {
    print("Jupiter is named after the Roman king of the gods.")
} else {
    print("All the planets are pretty cool.")
}
```

→ Answers on page 75.

> I know elegant when I see it! This cake is elegant! And all those if statements are not elegant! Surely there's a better way?

A switch statement often serves you better if you need to execute different code depending on the value of a variable or constant.

Code with lots of `if` statements becomes unreadable, and very inelegant, fast. A `switch` statement lets you **switch** which bits of code get run, based on the values of variables or constants that you want to *switch* on.

A `switch` statement can have multiple clauses, and is not simply limited to testing for equality or comparing. We'll come back to this later.

Going back to our pizza shop, we can rewrite the potential giant series of `if` statements as a nice, clean `switch` statement:

```
var pizzaOrdered = "Hawaiian"
```
The pizza that's been ordered is set.

We switch on the pizzaOrdered variable

```
switch(pizzaOrdered) {
case "Hawaiian":
    print("Hawaiian is my favorite. Great choice!")
case "Four Cheese":
    print("The only thing better than cheese is four cheeses.")
case "BBQ Chicken":
    print("Chicken and BBQ sauce! What could be better?")
case "Margherita":
    print("It's a classic for a reason!")
default:
    break
}
```

And then, for each case...

we display the right message.

The default case is executed if none of the others are matched.

The break keyword causes a switch statement to end immediately, and the code immediately after the switch statement is executed.

Exercise
Solution

From page 69.

```swift
var hawaiianPizzaOrdered = true
var veganPizzaOrdered = true
var pepperoniPizzaOrdered = false


if(hawaiianPizzaOrdered) {
    print("Please deliver a Hawaiian pizza.")
    hawaiianPizzaOrdered = false
}
if (veganPizzaOrdered) {
    print("Please deliver a Vegan pizza.")
    veganPizzaOrdered = false
}
if (pepperoniPizzaOrdered) {
    print("Please deliver a Pepperoni pizza.")
    pepperoniPizzaOrdered = false
}


var pizzaOrder = ["Hawaiian": 2, "Vegan": 1, "Pepperoni": 9]


if (pizzaOrder["Hawaiian"]! > 0) {
    print("Please deliver \(pizzaOrder["Hawaiian"]!)x Hawaiian pizza.")
}
if (pizzaOrder["Pepperoni"]! > 0) {
    print("Please deliver \(pizzaOrder["Pepperoni"]!)x Pepperoni pizza.")
}
if (pizzaOrder["Vegan"]! > 0) {
    print("Please deliver \(pizzaOrder["Vegan"]!)x Vegan pizza.")
}
```

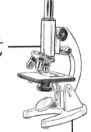

── Anatomy of a switch Statement ──

❶ Start with the switch keyword
Switch statements start with the `switch` keyword.

❷ Then the value you want to check
This value can be a variable or a constant. It's the thing the `switch` is checking for, in each case.

```
switch   value   {

case  a value  :

    // code to be executed

case  another value  :

    // code to be executed

default:

    // code to be executed

}
```

❸ Then the cases you want
Each case is compared against the value you want to check, but you can also use more complicated matching patterns, which we'll come back to later in the book. You can even check multiple values in one case.

❹ Provide code for each case
The code is executed if that case is matched.

❺ And finally, a default case and code
The default case gets executed if nothing else in the `switch` statement is matched. A default case is required if the switch is not exhaustive.

Exercise

Construct a `switch` statement to test whether a number is lucky. Provide some printouts of a variety of different lucky numbers, each for a different kind of luck. Print "I've told you everything I know about lucky numbers." if the number being switched on is not lucky in any way, or the code is done printing what it knows.

⟶ Answers on page 75.

Building a switch statement

So, if you (for some reason) wanted to check if a number was 9, 42, 47, or 317, you could use a `switch` statement.

Start with the <u>switch</u> keyword

❷ Then the value you want to check

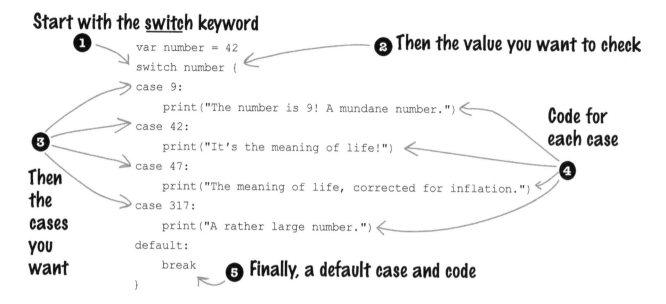

❸ Then the cases you want

Code for each case

❹

❺ Finally, a default case and code

```
var number = 42
switch number {
case 9:
    print("The number is 9! A mundane number.")
case 42:
    print("It's the meaning of life!")
case 47:
    print("The meaning of life, corrected for inflation.")
case 317:
    print("A rather large number.")
default:
    break
}
```

This only looks a tiny bit more elegant! What's the deal?

A switch statement is easier to maintain in the long term, and makes for more readable code.

We'll come back to `switch` statements later in book (when we look at enumerations).

But, in general, if you have more than a handful of things you're checking for in a large block of `if-else` statements, then you might want to consider a `switch` statement.

Sharpen your pencil
Solution

From page 70.

```
var planet = "Jupiter"
if(planet == "Jupiter") {
    print("Jupiter is named after the Roman king of the gods.")
} else if(planet == "Neptune") {
    print("Neptune is inhospitable to life as we know it.")
} else if(planet == "Mars") {
    print("Mars has a lot of Earth-made rovers on it.")
} else if(planet == "Earth") {
    print("Earth is infested with something called 'humans'.")
} else {
    print("All the planets are pretty cool.")
}
```

Exercise
Solution

From page 73.

```
var number = 6

switch(number) {
case 6:
    print("6 means easy and smooth, all the way!")
case 8:
    print("8 means sudden fortune!")
case 99:
    print("99 means eternal!")
default:
    print("I've told you everything I know about lucky numbers.")
}
```

Range operators

In addition to the mathematical operators you've already seen, and the assignment operator, Swift has several other useful operators, including a selection of range operators. **Range operators are shortcuts for expressing a range of values.**

These both represent the range 1, 2, 3, 4:

> **Range operators are particularly useful for loops and other control flow statements.**

```
1...4
```
← This is the closed range operator.

```
1..<5
```
← This is the half-open range operator.

The **closed range operator** defines a range that runs from the value on the left side of the operator to the value on the right side.

The **half-open range operator** defines a range that runs from the value on the left side of the operator to the value immediately before the value on the right side.

There's also a **one-sided range operator** that lets you consider a range that continues as far as it can in one direction. For example, the following constants define a range that starts at 5 and continues infinitely and a range that goes from an infinitely negative number to 100, respectively:

```
let myRange = 5...
```
← This is the one-sided range operator.

```
let myOtherRange = ...100
```

We can then check if the constant contains a certain value:

```
myRange.contains(1)
```
← This returns false, because 1 is not contained within 5 to infinity.

```
myRange.contains(70)
```
← This returns true, because 70 is.

```
myOtherRange.contains(50)
```
← This returns true, because 50 is contained within infinitely negative to 100.

```
myOtherRange.contains(-10)
```
← This returns true, because -10 is too.

Exercise

Create a new Swift Playground, and create range operators for the following ranges:

- 72 to 96

- −100 to 100

- 9 to infinity

- Negative infinity to 37,000

→ Answers on page 81.

More complex switch statements

Say you need to help a school write some code that prints out a text representation of a student's final grade. The school grades on a system of Fail (0 to 49 points), Pass (50 to 59), Credit (60 to 69), Distinction (70 to 79), and High Distinction (80 to 99). You could do this with a bunch of `if` statements, but it wouldn't look very nice.

Consider a `switch` statement instead:

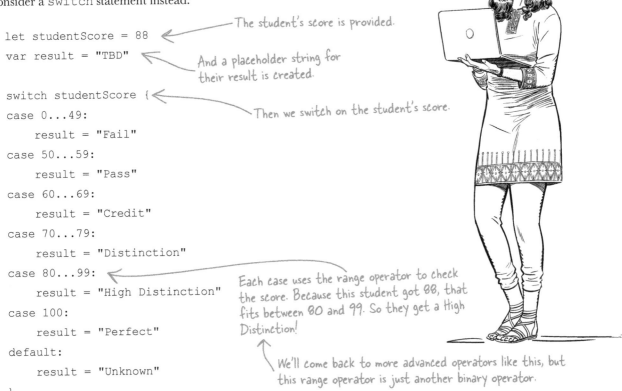

```
let studentScore = 88
```
← The student's score is provided.

```
var result = "TBD"
```
← And a placeholder string for their result is created.

```
switch studentScore {
case 0...49:
    result = "Fail"
case 50...59:
    result = "Pass"
case 60...69:
    result = "Credit"
case 70...79:
    result = "Distinction"
case 80...99:
    result = "High Distinction"
case 100:
    result = "Perfect"
default:
    result = "Unknown"
}
```

← Then we switch on the student's score.

Each case uses the range operator to check the score. Because this student got 88, that fits between 80 and 99. So they get a High Distinction!

We'll come back to more advanced operators like this, but this range operator is just another binary operator.

But the `switch` statement has more tricks up its its sleeve. We'll look at one final trick here, before we come back to switches later in the book.

Imagine you want to switch on a number, and check whether it's an odd number or an even number. You can do it like this:

Using the modulo operator you can check if a number is odd or even.

Don't worry if this syntax isn't familiar to you yet, we'll come back to it!

```
var num = 5
switch num {
case _ where num % 2 == 0:
    print("This number is an Even number!")
default:
    print("This number is an Odd number!")
}
```

Getting repetitive with loops

Swift has two major loop statements. You can use **for (and for-in) loops** for running some code a certain number of times or iterating through every item in a collection type, and **while (and repeat-while) loops** for running some code over and over again until something becomes true or false.

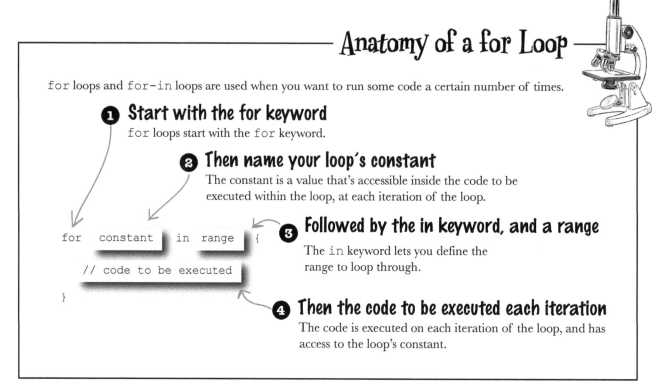

─ Anatomy of a for Loop ─

for loops and for-in loops are used when you want to run some code a certain number of times.

❶ Start with the for keyword
for loops start with the for keyword.

❷ Then name your loop's constant
The constant is a value that's accessible inside the code to be executed within the loop, at each iteration of the loop.

```
for   constant   in   range   {

    // code to be executed

}
```

❸ Followed by the in keyword, and a range
The in keyword lets you define the range to loop through.

❹ Then the code to be executed each iteration
The code is executed on each iteration of the loop, and has access to the loop's constant.

┌ Bullet Points ─

- for loops can run code repeatedly, usually based on some sort of numeric range.

- for-in loops can iterate over a sequence—most commonly items in a collection, but also ranges of numbers.

- while loops can run some code until a condition becomes true or false.

- You can put as many loops as you want inside other loops. Loops all the way down.

Building a for loop

Let's unpack this and write some code that displays the numbers from 1 to 10 using a `for` loop:

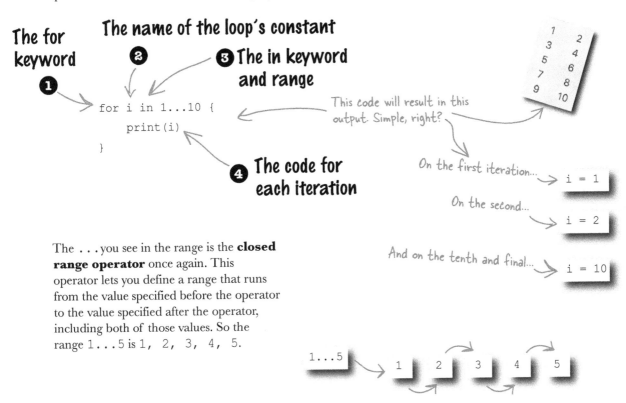

The for keyword ❶

The name of the loop's constant ❷

❸ The in keyword and range

```swift
for i in 1...10 {
    print(i)
}
```

This code will result in this output. Simple, right?

❹ The code for each iteration

On the first iteration... → i = 1

On the second... → i = 2

And on the tenth and final... → i = 10

The . . . you see in the range is the **closed range operator** once again. This operator lets you define a range that runs from the value specified before the operator to the value specified after the operator, including both of those values. So the range `1...5` is `1, 2, 3, 4, 5`.

`1...5` → 1 2 3 4 5

Exercise

Combine your knowledge of Swift's math operators with your knowledge of Swift's `for` loop syntax and write a `for` loop that prints the odd numbers between 1 and 20. Here are a few hints, but you might want to fire up a new Swift Playground for this:

- Think back to the modulo operator we mentioned earlier. It lets you get the remainder of a division operation.

- The closed range operator makes it easy to count from 1 to 20.

- Use the print function to print the odd numbers. You can perform the check for odd numbers in a variety of ways: consider an intermediate variable, or an `if` statement, or both. Or something else entirely!

——————————————→ **Answer on page 81.**

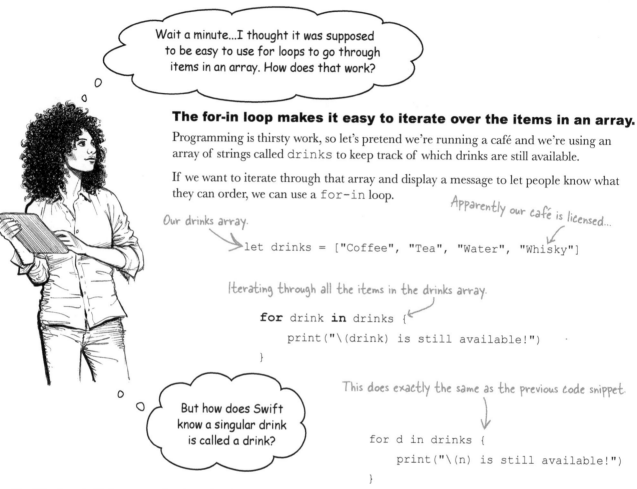

Wait a minute...I thought it was supposed to be easy to use for loops to go through items in an array. How does that work?

The for-in loop makes it easy to iterate over the items in an array.

Programming is thirsty work, so let's pretend we're running a café and we're using an array of strings called `drinks` to keep track of which drinks are still available.

If we want to iterate through that array and display a message to let people know what they can order, we can use a `for-in` loop.

Apparently our café is licensed...

Our drinks array.

```swift
let drinks = ["Coffee", "Tea", "Water", "Whisky"]
```

Iterating through all the items in the drinks array.

```swift
for drink in drinks {
    print("\(drink) is still available!")
}
```

This does exactly the same as the previous code snippet.

But how does Swift know a singular drink is called a drink?

```swift
for d in drinks {
    print("\(n) is still available!")
}
```

Swift doesn't know what a single drink is called.

We can use a word that makes it easier for a human to understand what's going on.

If the only purpose of your loop is to iterate through some sort of data structure, you might be able to use `forEach` instead:

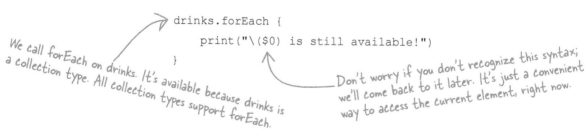

```swift
drinks.forEach {
    print("\($0) is still available!")
}
```

We call forEach on drinks. It's available because drinks is a collection type. All collection types support forEach.

Don't worry if you don't recognize this syntax; we'll come back to it later. It's just a convenient way to access the current element, right now.

Exercise Solution

From page 76.

- 72 to 96
- –100 to 100
- 9 to infinity
- Negative infinity to 37,000

```
72...96
-100...100
9...
...37000
```

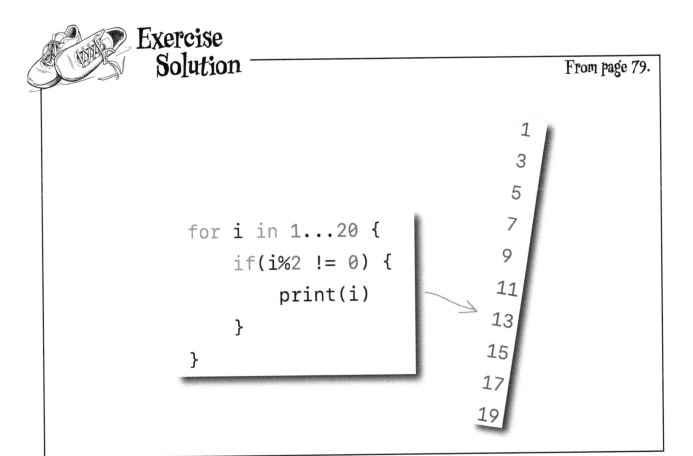

Exercise Solution

From page 79.

```
for i in 1...20 {
    if(i%2 != 0) {
        print(i)
    }
}
```

```
1
3
5
7
9
11
13
15
17
19
```

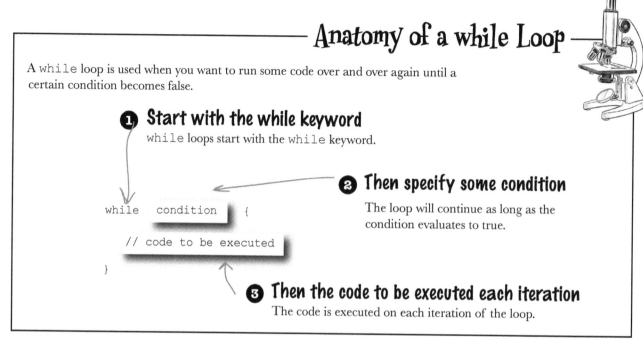

Anatomy of a while Loop

A while loop is used when you want to run some code over and over again until a certain condition becomes false.

1 Start with the while keyword
while loops start with the `while` keyword.

2 Then specify some condition
The loop will continue as long as the condition evaluates to true.

```
while    condition    {
    // code to be executed
}
```

3 Then the code to be executed each iteration
The code is executed on each iteration of the loop.

Building a while loop

Let's unpack this and write a while loop that, while a number is less than 100, multiplies the number by 2:

A while loop
is particularly
useful when
you're not sure
how many
iterations the
loop will go
through until it's
finished.

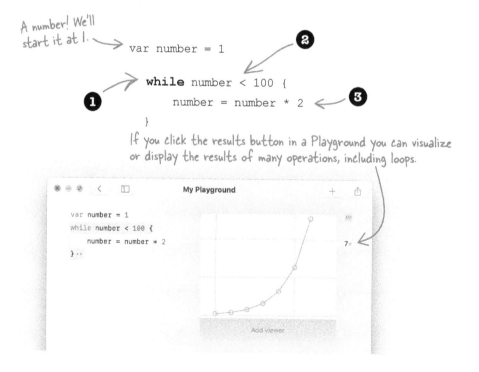

A number! We'll start it at 1.

```
var number = 1

while number < 100 {
    number = number * 2
}
```

If you click the results button in a Playground you can visualize or display the results of many operations, including loops.

Anatomy of a repeat-while loop

A `repeat-while` loop is just like a `while` loop, except that the condition is evaluated at the end of the loop, instead of at the beginning. It will always run at least once.

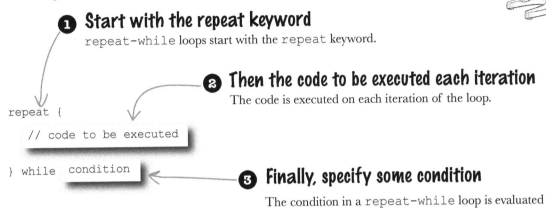

1 Start with the repeat keyword

`repeat-while` loops start with the `repeat` keyword.

2 Then the code to be executed each iteration

The code is executed on each iteration of the loop.

```
repeat {
    // code to be executed

} while  condition
```

3 Finally, specify some condition

The condition in a `repeat-while` loop is evaluated at the end of the loop, instead of the beginning.

Building a repeat-while loop

Let's rewrite our `while` loop using `repeat-while` instead:

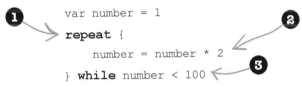

```
var number = 1
repeat {
    number = number * 2
} while number < 100
```

Exercise

Consider the following simple game. The game starts at level 1, and finishes at level 10. We've partially written a `repeat-while` loop to run the game. Fill in the two gaps.

```
var currentLevel = 1
var winningLevel = 10


repeat {
    print("We're at level \(currentLevel) of \(winningLevel)!")
    currentLevel = _____
} while (_____)
print("Game finished!"):
```

Answers on page 95.

Solving the pizza-sorting problem

> All this is great, but you still haven't solved my pizza sorting issue! How do we do it? I have some ideas, but you're the programmer...

```
var pizzaHawaiian = "Hawaiian"
var pizzaCheese = "Cheese"
var pizzaMargherita = "Margherita"
var pizzaMeatlovers = "Meatlovers"
var pizzaVegetarian = "Vegetarian"
var pizzaProsciutto = "Prosciutto"
var pizzaVegan = "Vegan"
```

Exercise

Consider the chef's list of pizzas, which they've stored as independently created String variables, and come up with:

☐   A better way to represent the list of pizzas, using one of the collection types that you've learned about.

☐   A way to operate on your new pizza collection to sort the pizzas into alphabetical order and print them.

———→ Answers on page 95.

there are no
Dumb Questions

Q: Can I make my own collection types?

A: We'll get to this in Chapter 9, as it requires some advanced Swift features. But the answer is yes: you can make your own collection types that are just as capable as the provided three (arrays, sets, and dictionaries).

Q: What do I do if I need to create a variable, but don't know what type to set it to in advance?

A: Great question! You might have noticed that in our code so far, sometimes we specify a type in the expression that creates a variable, and sometimes we

don't. Swift's type system is able to infer types, or use a provided type annotation to determine the type.

Q: In other languages I've looked at switch statements don't seem very powerful, and I've never used them. Swift seems to have considerably more powerful switch statements. What's the deal?

A: You're right. Swift's `switch` statement is considerably more capable than most other languages'. `switch` statements are super useful, and Swift has a really good implementation of them.

Q: How do you decide when to use a different control flow statement?

A: It's kind of a you'll know it when you see it situation unfortunately. The more you program, the more you'll feel comfortable choosing between them.

Q: Do I have to use the for-in syntax to iterate through items in an array?

A: No, you could just do it manually, like you might find in other older programming languages, but why would you bother?

Q: When using a for-in loop, do you have to name the iterating variable i?

A: No, you can call it whatever you'd like.

If you're interested in even more collection types, you can visit Apple's GitHub project for the Swift Collections project. It's not part of Swift, but it's maintained by Apple and the open source community to contribute a bunch more useful collection types!

https://github.com/apple/swift-collections

Brain Power

Write your own `for-in`, `while`, and `repeat-while` loops. Get creative, and see if you can make an infinite loop that can never be escaped from. What's the condition for your infinite loop? Think about ways to prevent infinite loops in your code.

building blocks

expressions

constants

Many features

operators

variables

types

Wow

Such Swift

Phew, that's a lot of Swift!

collections

arrays

Incredibly, you're only **three chapters** into your Swift journey, but you've already done so much! You've learned about the building blocks of Swift, and how to create a Swift Playground and build programs out of operators, expressions, variables, constants, types, collections, and control flow. Phew.

sets

dictionaries

The next few pages contain some exercises to test your understanding of the concepts we've covered here. We've also included some bullet points to recap key information and a crossword covering concepts from the past three chapters.

Repeating your Swift knowledge helps solidify what you've learned. Don't skip these pages! When you're done with the exercises, take a break and get some rest so you're refreshed to march onward.

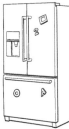

Code Magnets

A Swift program is all scrambled up on the fridge. Can you rearrange the code snippets to make a working program that produces the output on the next page? The code uses concepts we've looked at in detail, as well as a few that we haven't.

```swift
var fido = Dog(name: "Fido", color: .brown, age: 7)
```

```swift
enum DogColor {
    case red
    case brown
    case black
}
```

```swift
listDogsInPack()
```

```swift
var pack: [Dog] = [fido, bruce]
```

```swift
var moose = Dog(name: "Moose", color: .red, age: 11)
```

```swift
addDogToPack(dog: moose)
```

```swift
var bruce = Dog(name: "Bruce", color: .black, age: 4)
```

```swift
class Dog {
    var name: String
    var color: DogColor
    var age: Int

    init(name: String, color: DogColor, age: Int) {
        self.name = name
        self.color = color
        self.age = age
    }
}
```

```swift
func listDogsInPack() {
    print("The pack is:")
    print("--")
    for dog in pack {
        print(dog.name)
    }
    print("--")
}
```

```swift
listDogsInPack()
```

```swift
func addDogToPack(dog: Dog) {
    pack.append(dog)
    print("\(dog.name) (aged \(dog.age)) has joined the pack.")
}
```

⟶ Answers on page 92.

Code Magnets, cont.

Organize code magnets from the previous page here.

This is the output of the jumbled program. Can you get the code snippets into the right order? Every snippet is used.

```
The pack is:
--
Fido
Bruce
--
Moose (aged 11) has joined the pack.
The pack is:
--
Fido
Bruce
Moose
--
```

Pŏŏl Puzzle

Your **job** is to take lines of code from the pool and place them into the blank lines in the Playground. You may **not** use the same line more than once, and you won't need to use all the lines. Your **goal** is to make the code that will generate the output shown below, given the starting variables:

```
var todaysWeather = "Windy"
var temperature = 35
```

```
var message = "Today's Weather"



    message = "It's a lovely sunny day!"


    message = "Strap your hat on. It's windy!"


    message = "Pack your umbrella!"


    message = "Brr! There's snow in the air!"
default:
    message = "It's a day, you know?"
}
```

```
    message += " And it's not cold out there."


    message += " And it's chilly out there."
} else {
    message += " And it's not cold or hot!"
}
```

Strap your hat on. It's windy! And it's not really cold or hot!

Note: each thing from the pool can only be used once!

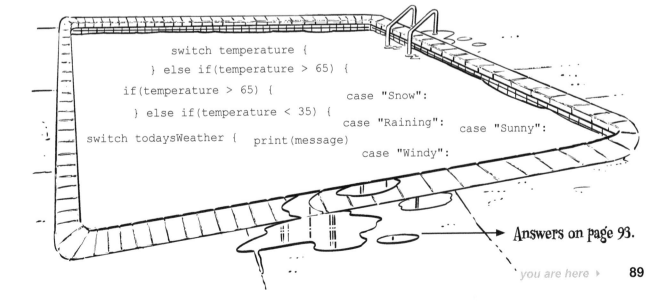

```
            switch temperature {
        } else if(temperature > 65) {
    if(temperature > 65) {                case "Snow":
        } else if(temperature < 35) {     case "Raining":    case "Sunny":
    switch todaysWeather {   print(message)
                                          case "Windy":
```

Answers on page 93.

BE the Swift Compiler

Each of the Swift code snippets on this page represents a complete Playground. Your job is to play Swift compiler, and determine whether each of these will run or not. If they will not compile, how would you fix them?

A

```
let dogsAge = 10
let dogsName = "Trevor"

print("My dog's name is \(dogsName) and
they are \(dogsAge) years old.")

dogsAge = dogsAge + 1
```

B

```
var number = 10

for i in 1...number {
    print(number*92.7)
}
```

C

```
var bestNumbers: Set = [7, 42, 109, 53, 12, 17]

bestNumbers.remove(7)
bestNumbers.remove(109)
bestNumbers.remove(242)

bestNumbers.insert(907)
bestNumbers.insert(1002)
bestNumbers.insert(42)
```

Answers on page 93.

Swiftcross

All the solutions to this crossword are from concepts we covered in this chapter.

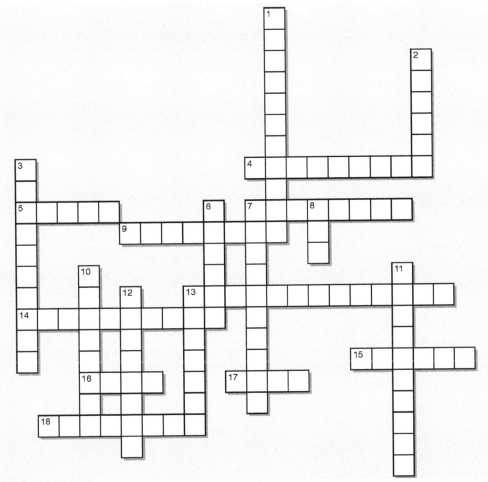

Across

4) Related functionality and values.
5) An ordered collection of values of the same type.
7) A named piece of data that can never change.
9) A named piece of repeatable code.
13) Mixing values with a string.
14) Checking what's inside an optional.
15) This statement helps you run different code depending on the value of a variable (among other things).
16) A type that can store positive or negative.
17) A way to execute some code over and over again.
18) Something to check, combine, or change a value.

Down

1) A group of related values.
2) A decimal number.
3) A place to code Swift without the clutter of an IDE.
6) A type that can store some words. Or a word.
7) A way to store groups of values.
8) An unordered collection of values of the same type.
10) A named piece of data that can change later.
11) A collection of values mapped to other values.
12) Representing a value, as well as the potential absence of a value.
13) A whole number.

———————→ Answers on page 94.

Code Magnets Solution

From page 87.

```swift
class Dog {
    var name: String
    var color: DogColor
    var age: Int

    init(name: String, color: DogColor, age: Int) {
        self.name = name
        self.color = color
        self.age = age
    }
}
enum DogColor {
    case red
    case brown
    case black
}
var fido = Dog(name: "Fido", color: .brown, age: 7)
var bruce = Dog(name: "Bruce", color: .black, age: 4)
var moose = Dog(name: "Moose", color: .red, age: 11)
var pack: [Dog] = [fido, bruce]

func addDogToPack(dog: Dog) {
    pack.append(dog)
    print("\(dog.name) (aged \(dog.age)) has joined the pack.")
}
func listDogsInPack() {
    print("The pack is:")
    print("--")
    for dog in pack {
        print(dog.name)
    }
    print("--")
}
listDogsInPack()
addDogToPack(dog: moose)
listDogsInPack()
```

Pool Puzzle Solution

From page 89.

```
var todaysWeather = "Windy"
var temperature = 35
var message = "Today's Weather"

switch todaysWeather {
case "Sunny":
    message = "It's a lovely sunny day!"
case "Windy":
    message = "Strap your hat on. It's windy!"
case "Raining":
    message = "Pack your umbrella!"
case "Snow":
    message = "Brr! There's snow in the air!"
default:
    message = "Its a day, you know?"
}
if(temperature > 65) {
    message += " And it's not cold out there."
} else if(temperature < 35) {
    message += " And it's chilly out there."
} else {
    message += " And it's not cold or hot!"
}
print(message)
```

BE the Swift Compiler Solution

From page 90.

A The code will error because we're trying to modify a constant (dogsAge). We need to change the dogsAge constant to a variable for this to work.

B The code will error when you try and multiply a double (92.7) by an integer (number). Additionally, we're not using the i that's counting up inside the loop at all.

C This works fine, exactly as it is.

Swiftcross Solution

From page 90.

```
                                            1E
                                            N
                                            U
                                            M                    2D
                                            E                    O
                                            R                    U
                                            A                    B
                          4S  T  R  U  C  T  U  R  E             L
3P                                          I
L                                                                
5A  R  R  A  Y              6S    7C  O  N  8S  T  A  N  T
Y                9F  U  N  C  T  I  O  N     E
G                           R         L      T
R            10V            I         L                    11D
O            A     12O     13I  N  T  E  R  P  O  L  A  T  I  O  N
14U  N  W  R  A  P  P  I  N  G              C
N            I     T        T                C
D            A     I        E      16B  15S  W  I  T  C  H
             16B  O  O  L   G      17L  O  O  P  O
                   O        E      N         N
             18O  P  E  R  A  T  O  R         A
                   L                         R
                                             Y
```

Exercise Solution

From page 83.

```
var currentLevel = 1
var winningLevel = 10

repeat {
    print("We're at level \(currentLevel) of \(winningLevel)!")
    currentLevel = currentLevel + 1
} while (currentLevel <= winningLevel)
print("Game finished!"):
```

```
We're at level 1 of 10!
We're at level 2 of 10!
We're at level 3 of 10!
We're at level 4 of 10!
We're at level 5 of 10!
We're at level 6 of 10!
We're at level 7 of 10!
We're at level 8 of 10!
We're at level 9 of 10!
We're at level 10 of 10!
Game finished!
```

Exercise Solution

From page 84.

```
var pizzas = ["Hawaiian", "Cheese", "Margherita", "Meatlovers", "Vegetarian",
"Prosciutto", "Vegan"]
pizzas = pizzas.sorted()
print(pizzas)
```

```
["Cheese", "Hawaiian", "Margherita",
"Meatlovers", "Prosciutto", "Vegan",
"Vegetarian"]
```

4 functions and enums

Reusing Code on Demand

> We've all got a function to perform. But naming your function, and making it clear what you give back, is always important...

Functions in Swift allow you to package up a specific behavior or unit of work into a single block of code that you can call from other parts of your program. Functions can be **standalone**, or they can be defined as part of a **class**, a **structure**, or an **enumeration**, where they are usually referred to as **methods.** Functions let you break down complex tasks into smaller, more manageable, and more testable units. They're a core part of the way you structure a program with Swift.

Wouldn't it be dreamy if we could create self-contained pieces of code that could be reused over and over again to perform specific tasks? And even more amazing if we could name them.

Functions in Swift let you <u>reuse code</u>

Like many programming languages, Swift has a feature known as ***functions***. Functions let you **package up some code, and reuse it if you need to run it more than once**.

We've been using functions a fair bit already: the `print` function, for example, is a built-in function that lets us print things for display. Swift has lots of other built-in functions, and you'll get a chance to use some of them in a moment.

What can functions do?

Including, but not limited to!

Functions can, in no particular order, do all sorts of things, including: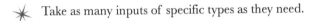

* Be defined as a block of code that just does something, and doesn't need any inputs or have any outputs.

* Take as many inputs of specific types as they need.

* Return as many outputs of specific types as they need.

* Have a variable number of inputs.

* Modify the original values of variables passed to them, separately to also returning values (or not).

> **Functions let you <u>package up code</u> that performs specific tasks, give it a name, and reuse it by calling it at will.**

If you're a seasoned programmer, you might conflate functions and methods.

We haven't covered classes yet in this book, but when we do we'll come back to methods. To cut a long story short, functions are called methods when they're associated with a particular type: you can create a function inside a class, structure, or enumeration, and that function (method) encapsulates some reusable code that relates to working with an instance of the type it's inside. If this means nothing to you yet, don't worry—you'll get there!

Built-in functions

Before we look at implementing some functions of our own, let's take a few moments to consider some of Swift's built-in functions. These are built directly into the language.

The first two we'll consider are **min** and **max**. You might be able to guess from their names that they will return their smallest and largest arguments (respectively) as their result.

Here's a really simple example of both that you can test in a Playground:

```
print (min(9, -3, 12, 7))
print (max("zoo", "barn", "cinema"))
```

Experiment with your own examples here—for example, what happens if you enter "Zoo" instead of "zoo"?

As you would expect, the first example will print out `"-3"`, since that is the smallest value in the argument list.

The second example might look odd at first, but it will print `"zoo"`. That's because, since the arguments are all strings, the comparison between the elements in the list is a string comparison, and "zoo" comes after "barn" and "cinema," so it's considered to be greater than them.

Brain Power

Your job is to play Swift compiler and figure out what each of these calls to Swift's built-in functions does. Do they all work? If they work, what's the result?

```
print(max(8, "Hello", -1))
```

```
print("Hello, world!")
```

```
print(min("Potato", "Tomato", "Cabbage"))
```

```
print(min(7*2,3+4,82-9,76))
```

```
print(max(8,9,10,11,104,-104))
```

What can we learn from built-in functions?

From just these two functions, we can glean some important information about functions in Swift:

- The functions are taking some input values (called *arguments* to the function) and returning a result.

- Some functions can support a variable number of arguments. **min** and **max**, for example, can take an arbitrary number of arguments as long as there are two or more, and they're all of the same type.

> We call this feature a variadic parameter—we'll cover it soon.

- Some functions support more than one type of argument. For example, both **min** and **max** can work with integers, floating-point values, and strings, as long as all arguments are of the same type. Under the hood, if Swift knows how to compare two instances of a type, then that type can be used with **min** and **max**.

> Understanding how this "generic" argument feature works will require you to have some more Swift under your belt first. We'll get you there, promise!

You may have remembered from the previous chapters, or at least deduced from the preceding examples, that **print** is also a built-in function.

It can take a variable number of arguments, and those arguments can be of any type. Swift already knows how to print simple types like numbers and strings, and complex types like arrays and dictionaries.

For user-defined types (like classes and structures), by default **print** will output the type name, but you can add a special property to a type that describes how it should be represented in string form. If such a description exists, **print** will output it instead of the type name.

Relax

Functions are fiddly.

There's a lot going on with returns, parameters, and the like. You don't need to make everything a function, and it's not always apparent when something should be a function until you've gone some way into implementing and building whatever it is you want to build.

Don't necessarily try to make everything a function from the first moment you begin coding in Swift. Trust your judgment as things emerge and you begin to recognize where discrete, individual units of reusable code would be useful, and don't try to plan too far in advance.

Sharpen your pencil

Take a look at the following code, and think about how it works. Does it look sensible? Once you've read it (you can create a Playground and run the code if you like), write up a little analysis of the code. We've started you off with some thoughts of our own on the next page, but have a think about it on your own before you check that out.

```
var pizzaOrdered = "Hawaiian"
var pizzaCount = 7

if (pizzaCount > 5) {
    print("Because more than 5 pizzas were ordered, a discount of 10% applies to the order.")
}

if (pizzaOrdered == "Prosciutto") {
    print("\(pizzaCount)x Prosciutto pizzas were ordered.")
}

if (pizzaOrdered == "Hawaiian") {
    print("\(pizzaCount)x Hawaiian pizzas were ordered.")
}

if (pizzaOrdered == "Vegan") {
    print("\(pizzaCount)x Vegan pizzas were ordered.")
}

if (pizzaOrdered == "BBQ Chicken") {
    print("\(pizzaCount)x BBQ Chicken pizzas were ordered.")
}

if (pizzaOrdered == "Meatlovers") {
    print("\(pizzaCount)x Meatlovers pizzas were ordered.")
}
```

Solution

The code on the previous page was fine in the same way leftover, cold pizza where most of the toppings have fallen off is fine. It worked, but it wasn't very sensible, in a few ways.

In fact, it's definitely not fine. Not fine at all.

The *fine* code is really only doing **two** key things:

```
var pizzaOrdered = "Hawaiian"
var pizzaCount = 7
```

We check if the pizzaCount variable is greater than 5 so we can print out a message notifying that the order qualifies for a discount if it is. **1**

```
if (pizzaCount > 5) {
    print("Because more than 5 pizzas were ordered, a discount of 10%
            applies to the order.")
}
```

```
if (pizzaOrdered == "Prosciutto") {
    print("\(pizzaCount)x Prosciutto pizzas were ordered.")
}
```

```
if (pizzaOrdered == "Hawaiian") {
    print("\(pizzaCount)x Hawaiian pizzas were ordered.")
}
```
`...<snip>`

For each possible pizza, we check, then we print a custom message about it. Each of these if statements is doing exactly the same thing. **2**

It's pretty tedious to write the same check over and over again for each pizza, not to mention that it's hard to add pizzas, and it's hard to change the logic if the requirements change (because you'd have to change it for each pizza), and it's easy to make mistakes. For example, you might forget to update what's printed (so you might have the logic check how many Hawaiian pizzas were ordered, then print a message about Vegan pizzas!).

The possible problems are numerous.

Brain Power

What can we do to fix this code? If you're already familiar with functions, think about the sensible possibilities for breaking this up into pieces. There are a few possible answers here, and all of them are more or less correct, depending on the overall goals for your code.

Improving the situation with a function

On the previous pages, we had some messy Swift code that basically did the same thing over and over again: it checked if enough pizzas were ordered to qualify for a special volume discount, and then it printed out the count and type of pizza that was ordered.

Let's write a `pizzaOrdered` function.

A function is defined with the `func` keyword, followed by the desired name of the function, any parameters the function has, and then the function's return type.

Our `pizzaOrdered` function will be able to take care of the ordering process from the previous page, but with less potentially error-prone code. It has a name, which we already know, plus two parameters: the name of the pizza as a string, and the count of the pizza as an integer. It doesn't have a return type (because it doesn't return anything, it just prints things).

Here's the definition for our new function:

It gets a function name, so we can call it to use it.

We define a function using the func keyword.

To work, our function needs to know two things: the type of pizza ordered, and a count of pizzas.

```
func pizzaOrdered(pizza: String, count: Int) {

}
```

The _body_ of the function goes here. The body is the code that gets run when the function is called.

The named, typed values that the function takes as input are called parameters.

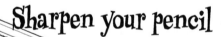

Sharpen your pencil

Which one of these is a valid call to the `pizzaOrdered` function defined above? In all cases, we are assuming the type of pizza being ordered is Hawaiian and the count is 7.

A `pizzaOrdered("Hawaiian", 7)`

B `pizzaOrdered(pizza: "Hawaiian", count: 7)`

C `pizzaOrdered(Hawaiian, 7)`

D `pizzaOrdered(pizza: Hawaiian, count: 7)`

Writing the body of the function

The **body** of the function is where the magic (or, in this case, the reusable piece of logic) happens. In the case of our `pizzaOrdered` function we need to do **two** things—the same two things the *fine* code earlier was doing:

```
func pizzaOrdered(pizza: String, count: Int) {
    if(count > 5) {
        print("Because more than 5 pizzas were ordered, a
            discount of 10% applies to the order.")
    }


    print("\(count)x \(pizza) pizzas were ordered.")
}
```

❶ Discount

First, we check to see if `count`, which is one of the parameters that the function has, is greater than 5. if it is, we print the discount message.

❷ Pizzas

Second, we print the `count` and the `pizza` that was ordered.

> The typed count and pizza values only exist inside the { body } of the function.

Functions allow you to take redundant code, or code that needs to be used over and over again with minimal differences, and store it in a place where you can reuse it.

> Like a phone (remember them?), you can call your functions (which is just a fancy way of saying you'll be making use of them).

Sharpen your pencil
Solution

The valid call to the `pizzaOrdered` function is B. This is only answer that includes the two parameters (`pizza` and `count`) and their arguments correctly ("Hawaiian" is a string and needs to be presented as such, which was not done in answers C and D).

> You'll learn about calling your functions on the next page.

Using functions

Going back to our messy, convoluted pizza ordering code from earlier, because of the function we've written we can replace the entire page of code we had earlier with this instead:

```
var pizzaOrdered = "Hawaiian"
var pizzaCount = 7
```

← This is the same as the original code. We're just defining some variables to serve as the pizza order.

```
func pizzaOrdered(pizza: String, count: Int) {
    if(pizzaCount > 5) {
        print("Because more than 5 pizzas were ordered,
            a discount of 10% applies to the order.")
    }

    print("\(count)x \(pizza) pizzas were ordered.")
}
```

The function declaration and the body of the function are the same as on the previous spread.

```
pizzaOrdered(pizza: pizzaOrdered, count: pizzaCount)
```

Here we call our function.

We pass the argument pizzaOrdered (which is a string variable, defined earlier) in to the parameter pizza (which expects a string).

And we pass the argument pizzaCount (which is an integer variable, defined earlier) in to the parameter count, which expects an integer.

We could also just pass the values in directly as arguments, without having to create or use intermediate variables to represent them. For example, this code is valid too and does exactly the same thing:

```
pizzaOrdered(pizza: "Hawaiian", count: 7)
```

Argument labels and **parameter names** are actually two different things. The argument labels and parameter names happen to be the same when we define our function like this:

```
func pizzaOrdered(pizza: String, count: Int) { }
```

← pizza and count are the argument label and parameter name.

But we can also independently specify argument labels and parameter names:

```
func pizzaOrdered(thePizza pizza: String, theCount count: Int) { }
```

Our function would then be called as follows, noting that the body of the function would still be working with the same names (the parameter names) internally:

thePizza and theCount are the argument labels for the parameter names pizza and count.

```
pizzaOrdered(thePizza: "Hawaiian", theCount: 7)
```

> I thought Swift was meant to be easy to read and neat and tidy. Having pizza as a parameter name and also as part of the function name seems silly!

We can make functions cleaner by thinking about their names and the argument labels for their parameters.

In the case of our `pizzaOrdered` function, because pizza is in the name of the function, we might want to omit the requirement to label that first parameter. Swift likes to encourage you to write functions and code that are mostly readable as plain English. Read this call to our `pizzaOrdered` function out loud:

```
pizzaOrdered(pizza: "Vegetarian", count: 5)
```

Notice how you say *"pizza ordered pizza."* That second *"pizza"* is superfluous to understanding what the function does. We can remove it by updating the function definition to look like this:

```
func pizzaOrdered(_ pizza: String, count: Int) {
    if(pizzaCount > 5) {
    print("Because more than 5 pizzas were ordered,
            a discount of 10% applies to the order.")
    }

    print("\(count)x \(pizza) pizzas were ordered.")
}
```

This means you can call the function like this, instead:

```
pizzaOrdered("Vegetarian", count: 5)
```

If you read that out loud, you'll understand why it's preferable like this for clarity.

The use of the underscore _ instead of an argument label allows for it to be omitted. You can include the underscore in as many of the parameters as you want.

Function parameters are constants.

You cannot change the value of a function parameter from the body of a function. For example, if you have a parameter named `pizza`, *and* "Hawaiian" *is passed in to the function via that parameter, the pizza that exists within the function is a constant with the value* ""Hawaiian". *It can't be changed.*

Functions deal in values

Whether you're familiar with the way other programming languages work or are just trying to get to grips with what happens when a function is called in Swift, it's important to acknowledge that **nothing you pass in to a function will modify the original value** unless you ask for it to be modified. You can test this yourself:

❶ Create a function that performs some simple math

Let's make a function that multiplies a number by 42:

```
func multiplyBy42(_ number: Int) {
    number = number * 42
    print("The number multiplied by 42 is: \(number)")
}
```

❷ Test out your function

Calling your function with a value should print the result of that value being multiplied by 42:

```
multiplyBy42(2)
```

This should print out `"The number multiplied by 42 is: 84"`.

❸ Create a variable

Create a variable to test the function with:

```
var myNumber = 3
```

myNumber

❹ Call the function, passing the variable as the value

Call the `multiplyBy42` function, passing the variable `myNumber` as the value:

```
multiplyBy42(myNumber)
```

The value that's stored in `myNumber` (in this case, 3) is copied into the parameter of the function. `myNumber` is never modified.

This should print out `"The number multiplied by 42 is: 126"`.

❺ Check that your variable is unmodified

Add a call to `print`, to check that the original `myNumber` is unmodified:

```
print("The value of myNumber is: \(myNumber)")
```

What if I want to make a function that modifies the value of the variable passed to it?

You can create a special kind of parameter that allows you to modify the original value.

If you need to write a function that does modify the original value, you can create an **inout** parameter.

If you wanted to write a function that takes a string variable as its sole parameter, and turns that string variable into the string "Bob", you would do it like this:

```
func makeBob(_ name: inout String) {
        name = "Bob"
}
```

You could then use any string variable, like this one:

```
var name = "Tim"
```

And, by passing it in to the makeBob function, make it into a Bob:

```
makeBob(&name)
```

The ampersand placed in front of the variable's name when you pass it into the function indicates that it can be modified by the function.

Now, the value inside name will be "Bob". You can check this by printing name:

```
print(name)
```

The use of an inout parameter means your parameter can never have a constant or a literal value passed to it.

Bullet Points

- Precede an inout parameter's type with the keyword **inout** in the function definition.

- Precede an inout parameter with an ampersand (&) in function calls.

- In function calls, inout arguments must be variables—they can't be expressions or constants.

Brain Power

Rewrite the `multiplyBy42` function from earlier so that rather than returning a value, the argument is an inout parameter.

Many happy returns (from your functions)

The functions you've made so far haven't returned anything. That is to say, they've done stuff, but they haven't sent anything back to where they were called from. Functions can do that too. You can define a function with a return type. That tells Swift what kind of value the function will return. This value can then be used, or stored, as needed.

Take a look at the following function:

This syntax defines the return type. In this case, a string.

```
func welcome(name: String) -> String {
    let welcomeMessage = "Welcome to the Swift Pizza shop, \(name)!"
    return welcomeMessage
}
```

This line returns the current value of the constant, welcomeMessage (which is a string, as per the return type we defined).

But Swift is meant to make things simple...

So you can combine the creation of the message and the return into a single line, like this:

```
func welcome(name: String) -> String {
    return "Welcome to the Swift Pizza shop, \(name)!"
}
```

Or you can make things even simpler with very simple functions, and take advantage of Swift's implicit return feature. If the entire body of a function is a single expression, then it's just returned for you:

```
func welcome(name: String) -> String {
    "Welcome to the Swift Pizza shop, \(name)!"
}
```

Brain Power

See if you can finish the following function. When it's done, update it to return a String, instead of directly printing.

```
func greet(name: String, favoriteNumber: Int, likesKaraoke: Bool) {

}
greet(name: "Paris", favoriteNumber: 6, likesKaraoke: true)
Hi, Paris! Your favorite number is 6, and you like karaoke.
```

I like things to be very predictable. Can I make a function with a default value for each parameter, so I only have to change it if I absolutely have to? I love sensible defaults.

You can provide a default value for any parameter in a function.

When you define your function, you can provide a default value for any of the parameters. If we wanted to add a default value to the `welcome` function we created on the previous page, it would look like this:

This is the default value for the name, inside the function.

```
func welcome(name: String = "Customer") -> String {
    let welcomeMessage = "Welcome to the Swift Pizza shop, \(name)!"
    return welcomeMessage
}
```

When a function has a default value, you can omit the parameter when you call the function if you like.

Sharpen your pencil

What do the following calls to the newly updated `welcome` function return? If they're not valid calls, why not?

☐   `welcome(name: "Paris")`

☐   `welcome("Tim")`

☐   `welcome(Michele)`

☐   `welcome(name: String = "Mars")`

Answers on page 119.

A variable number of parameters (Variadic parameters)

There are times when it is useful to write a function that can take a variable number of parameters. For example, you could write a function that takes a list of numbers, and calculates their average. That function would be far more flexible if you could list as many or as few numbers as you wanted every time you called it.

Sometimes you need three cookies, sometimes you only need one.

This feature is available in Swift—it's called a ***variadic parameter***. Here's how we could use it to implement a function to calculate the average of a list of numbers:

```swift
func average(_ numbers: Double...) -> Double {
    var total = 0.0
    for number in numbers {
        total += number
    }
    return total / Double(numbers.count)
}
```

These three dots (called an ellipsis) indicate that this parameter can have any number of arguments.

Inside the function, the variadic parameter's arguments are available as an array called **numbers** (from the parameter name). We use a **for** loop to iterate through that array, calculating the total as we go, and at the end, we divide the total by the count of numbers in the array to return the average.

You've already seen some looping and array code. We'll get to them in more detail in some upcoming chapters.

We could call our function like this:

```swift
let a = average(10, 21, 3.2, 16)
print (average(2, 4, 6))
```

a gets set to 16.625

prints out 4.0

Watch it!

A variadic can have zero elements.

A variadic can be "empty" at the call site, and you need to ensure your code can handle this correctly. Try calling the average *function above with no arguments to see what happens. In future chapters you'll learn about optionals and throwing errors—two different ways you could handle this.*

Bullet Points

- Use an ellipsis to indicate that a parameter is a variadic.

- A function can only have one variadic parameter, but it can appear anywhere in the parameter list.

- Any parameters defined after a variadic parameter must have argument names.

- When you call a function with a variadic, all of its parameters have to be of the same type.

Fireside Chats

Tonight's talk: **What's in a name?**

The Swift Teacher:

So you may have guessed this by now, but did you realize that function names have to be unique?

Except that's actually not quite true...

That's because technically, it's the function's *signature* that has to be unique—not its name.

A function's signature is a combination of its *name*, plus its *argument names* and *types*, plus its *return type* (if it has one).

Certainly. Here are two functions with the same name but with different signatures:

```
func addString(a: String, to b: String)
func addString(_ a: String, to b: String)
```

No! The argument names for the first function are `a:` and `to:`, but the argument names for the second function are `_:` and `to:`.

Student:

Yes Teacher, that makes sense! Otherwise how could I, or Swift, distinguish between them?

But Teacher! How could it be otherwise? Look—I've even tried it just now, and if I use the same function name twice, Swift says I have an "invalid redeclaration."

Its *signature*? What's *that*?

Can you give me an example, Teacher?

Well, I can see that they're *slightly* different, but aren't the argument names the same?

Huh! That's right—I had forgotten that the argument name is the same as the parameter name when only one is specified! But you mentioned that the *signatures* have to be different, and I'm still not sure what that means.

The Swift Teacher:

I'm glad you're paying attention, Student. As I said, the signature is a combination of the *function name*, the *argument names* and *types*, and the *return type*. So the signature of the first of those example functions is:

```
addString(a: String, to: String)
```

```
addString(_: String, to: String)
```

So even though the function *names* are the same, the *signatures* are different.

Yes—in these examples, there is no return value so technically the return type is **Void**.

Yes. Since the return type differs from the other two examples, your new function has a different signature, and Swift will still be happy.

Absolutely not!

That's true, but to have a function named **addString** that takes two **Float** parameters breaks the unwritten rule of good taste. A function's name should reflect what it does, or how it interacts with its arguments. And you, Student, should reflect on your lessons!

STUDENT!

Student:

OK, and the other one?

Ah—I get it...I think! And parameter names aren't part of the signature. You mentioned that the return type *is* part of the signature though. Is that correct?

So I could have another function in the same file with a different signature, like this, and it would be OK?

```
addString(a: String, to: String) -> Bool
```

The penny has dropped, Teacher! So that also means I could write another function like this:

```
addString(a: Float, to: Float) -> Bool
```

Huh? Now I really am confused, Teacher! The signatures are different!

Yes Teacher! You'll get no *argument* from me!

What can you pass to a function?

The short answer is: you can pass literally anything to a function. The slightly longer answer is: you can pass anything you might need to a function. **Any Swift value can be passed as a parameter**, including a string, a Boolean, an integer, an array of strings...anything:

```swift
func doAThingWithA(string: String, anInt: Int, andABool: Bool) {
    print("The string says '\(string)',
          the integer is \(anInt),
              and the Boolean value is \(andABool)")

}
```

Just a sampling of types, passed as a parameter...

```swift
doAThingWithA(string: "I am a string!", anInt: 7, andABool: true)
```

But it's not just values that are fair game as parameters for your functions. **Expressions work as well:**

```swift
var name = "Bob"


doAThingWithA(string: "Hello, \(name)!", anInt: 20+22, andABool: true)
```

The results of these expressions will be passed in here in the appropriate place.

You can also pass variables and constants in to your functions as parameters, which is actually what you'll be doing most of the time. Here are some calls to the same function, doAThingWithA, using variables and constants instead of just values:

```swift
var myString = "I love pizza."
var myInt = 42
let myBool = false


doAThingWithA(string: myString, anInt: myInt, andABool: myBool)
```

This is the same as calling doAThingWithA(string: "I love pizza.", anInt: 42, andABool: false) with literal values, instead of variables and constants.

Every function has a type

When you define a function, you're also defining a function type. A function type is made up of the parameter types of the function as well as the return type of the function.

These are all examples of function types:

```
(Int, Int) -> Int
(String, Int) -> String
(Int) -> Void
() -> String
```

This type is for a function that takes two integer parameters and returns an integer.

This takes a string parameter and an integer parameter, and returns a string.

This one takes one integer parameter, and has no return value.

And this has no parameters, and returns a string.

My type is take two integers and return a string. What's your type?

(Int, Int) -> String

My type just returns an integer. That's all.

() -> Int

You're definitely my type, but I need this function to return a string!

Sharpen your pencil

Take a look at the following functions. Do they work? What do they do? If they don't work, what's wrong with them?

A
```swift
func addNumbers(_ first: Int, _ second: Int) -> Int {
    return first + second
}
```

B
```swift
func multiplyNumbers(_ first: Int, _ second: Int) -> Int {
    return first * second
}
```

C
```swift
func sayHello() {
    print("Hello, friends!")
}
```

D
```swift
func welcome(user: String) -> String {
    print("Welcome, \(user)!")
    return "User '\(user)' has been welcomed."
}
```

E
```swift
func checkFor42(_ number: Int) -> Bool {
    if(number == 42) {
        return true
    } else {
        return false
    }
}
```

Answers on page 119.

Behind the Scenes

This era started with the debut of the C programming language.

In the early days of programming, people went a bit over the top using functions for everything they could possibly think of. This led to very modular but very hard-to-read programs.

Try to strike a balance. If you're coming to Swift from another programming language, you probably already have your own personal baseline for how modular you go with functions. If that's working for you, bring it to Swift!

You don't need to modularize anything, and Swift's functions are not particularly expensive. You'll know the right balance when you see it. Keep functions to doing only one thing.

> I don't understand why a function needs a type. What's the point of a function type? How do I use them?

Function types work like every other type.

Because a function type is just a type, as far as Swift is concerned, you can use them just like any other type.

It's particularly useful to be able to define a variable of a certain function type:

```swift
var manipulateInteger: (Int, Int) -> Int
```

And then create a function that matches that function type:

```swift
func addNumbers(_ first: Int, _ second: Int) -> Int {
        return first + second
}
```

Assign the function to the variable:

```swift
manipulateInteger = addNumbers
```

and you can then use the assigned function via the variable you assigned it to: *This will result in 10 and 90 being added, for a result of 100.*

```swift
print("The result is: (manipulateInteger(10,90))")
```

Because the `manipulateInteger` variable can store any function with the same type, you can reassign it:

```swift
func multNumbers(_ first: Int, _ second: Int) -> Int {
        return first * second
}
```

This will result in 2 and 5 being multiplied, for a result of 10.

```swift
manipulateInteger = multNumbers
print("The result is: (manipulateInteger(2,5))")
```

Because this is just a type like any other, you can let Swift infer the function type when you create the variable, too:

```swift
var newMathFunction = multNumbers
```

Swift's type system will infer the type of the variable newMathFunction to be (Int, Int) -> Int.

Sharpen your pencil
Solution

From page 111.

☑   `welcome(name: "Paris")`

         This will work fine, and return the welcome message.

☒   `welcome("Tim")`

         This won't work, because you're not specifying that the parameter is called name.

☐?   `welcome(Michele)`

This will attempt to pass a variable named Michele in. If that's not a
String variable or constant that exists, then it won't work.

☒   `welcome(name: String = "Mars")`

         This won't work, as you don't need to say that name is a String (the
type annotation is not relevant or correct here).

Sharpen your pencil
Solution

From page 117.

```
func addNumbers(_ first: Int, _ second: Int) -> Int {
```
A   `return first + second` ⟵ This adds the two numbers
                                passed in, and works fine.
```
}
func multiplyNumbers(_ first: Int, _ second: Int) -> Int {
```
B   `return first * second` ⟵ Multiplies the two numbers
                                passed in, and works fine.
```
}
func sayHello() {
```
C   `print("Hello, friends!")` ⟵ Prints a hello message, and
                                works fine.
```
}
func welcome(user: String) -> String {
```
                              Prints a welcome message, and
D   `print("Welcome, \(user)!")` ⟵ returns a confirmation. Works!
```
        return "User '\(user)' has been welcomed."
}
func checkFor42(_ number: Int) -> Bool {
        if(number == 42) {
```
                            Checks if a number is 42 and
E   `return true`   returns a Bool accordingly. It
```
        } else {
```
                            works fine.
```
                return false
        }
}
```

Function types as parameter types

As you might have picked up on, function types are just types as far as Swift is concerned. This means that you can use a function type as the parameter type when you're creating a function.

Building on what you did previously, consider the following function:

This parameter is named, and is of type (Int, Int) -> Int.

```
func doMathPrintMath(_ manipulateInteger: (Int, Int) -> Int, _ a: Int, _ b: Int) {
    print("The result is: \(manipulateInteger(a, b))")
}

doMathPrintMath(addNumbers, 5, 10)
```

The function that's passed to the manipulateInteger parameter is used to print the result, called with the other two parameters.

By calling this new function with the addNumber function we made on the previous page as the first parameter, the new function can add numbers and print the result.

Brain Power

Consider how function types work as parameter types, and write some of your own.

Consider the following function:

```
func doMathPrintMath(_ manipulateInteger: (Int, Int) -> Int, _ a: Int, _ b: Int){
    print("The result is: \(manipulateInteger(a, b))")
}
```

Write three new functions to pass in as manipulateInteger. Your functions should take two integers, and return an integer.

What do your functions do?

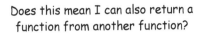

Does this mean I can also return a function from another function?

Again: function types work like every other type.

<u>Function types</u> are **types** in every way:

```
typealias Pizza = String

func makeHawaiianPizza() -> Pizza {
    print("One Hawaiian Pizza, coming up!")
    print("Hawaiian pizza is mostly cheese, ham, and pineapple.")
    return "Hawaiian Pizza"
}

func makeCheesePizza() -> Pizza {
    print("One Cheesey Pizza, coming up!")
    print("Cheesey pizza is just cheese, more cheese, and more cheese.")
    return "Cheese Pizza"
}

func makePlainPizza() -> Pizza {
    print("One Plain Pizza, coming up!")
    print("This pizza has no toppings! Not sure why you'd order it.")
    return "Plain Pizza"
}

func order(pizza: String) -> () -> Pizza {
    if (pizza == "Hawaiian") {
        return makeHawaiianPizza
    } else if (pizza == "Cheese") {
        return makeCheesePizza
    } else {
        return makePlainPizza
    }
}

var myPizza = order(pizza: "Hawaiian")
print(myPizza())
```

Excuse me...I'm a busy function, and I want to send back two things when I return. Help a function out?

Multiple return types

Great idea. Anything for a busy function.

A function can return a tuple containing as many values as needed. For example, if you needed a greeting function for your pizza shop that took a name and returned hello and goodbye messages/greetings as strings, you could do this:

```
func greetingsFor(name: String) -> (hello: String, goodbye: String) {
    var hello = "Welcome to the pizza shop, \(name)!"
    var goodbye = "Thanks for visiting the pizza shop, \(name)!"

    return (hello, goodbye)
}
```

There's no need to name the return values here since the names are specified earlier, as part of the return type.

You'd then be able to call the function, and access the hello greeting as follows:

```
print(greetingsFor(name: "Bob").hello)
```

You can access the hello component of the return using the dot notation on the function call.

Crazy! Thanks. I can return anything I want now!

Brain Power

How do you think you'd access the goodbye part of the returned tuple? Write some code to print it out.

One you've done that, update the function to return three values: add a return message asking the customer to wait for their order while it's cooking.

Fireside Chats

Tonight's talk: **The Order of Things**

The Swift Teacher:

I believe you have a question, Student...

Student:

Yes, Teacher. If I write a function where every parameter has an argument name, why can't I call it with the arguments in any order I want?

How quickly you forget, Student!

Forget? Have you taught me about this already, Teacher?

Yes, Student. We have talked about this in the past. I thought at the time that you fully grokked the lesson.

That I *fully grokked the lesson*? Teacher! What have I told you about *not* trying to fit in with the apprentices?

I don't recall, Student—I'm a better teacher than I am a student. But back to your question: when you call a function, the compiler first determines what its *signature* must be, and then calls the function with that signature.

And if I switch the argument order, I'm using a signature for a function *that isn't defined*! I get it now!

Yes Student, but do you *grok* it?

TEACHER!!

Brain Power

Write a `billSplit` function to help calculate how to evenly split a dining bill. The function should take parameters for the total cost of the meal (a Double), a tip percentage (an Int), and a number of diners (an Int). It should print how much each diner will need to pay.

Functions don't have to stand alone

All of the examples of functions that we've considered in this chapter have been what are called **standalone** or **global** functions. They're defined at **global scope** and can be called from anywhere else in your program.

You may recall, though, that we hinted at the start of this chapter that functions can also be defined as part of a class. When we define functions in this way, they're sometimes referred to as **methods**. And using functions (or methods) as part of a class is one of the hallmarks of object-oriented programming. Swift goes where some other languages don't by also allowing you to define functions as part of structures and enumerations.

Everything we've covered in this chapter in relation to functions also applies when they are defined in those other contexts. You don't have to unlearn anything—the syntax, use of argument and parameter names, variadics, and the inout annotation all apply equally with functions that are part of a class, structure, or enumeration.

Nested functions

Functions can also be defined inside other functions. This can be a convenient way to simplify an otherwise overly complex function that requires a lot of repeated code or expression evaluation, without the need to declare another function at global scope.

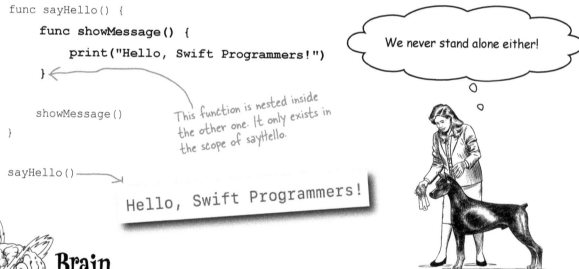

```swift
func sayHello() {
    func showMessage() {
        print("Hello, Swift Programmers!")
    }

    showMessage()
}

sayHello()
```

This function is nested inside the other one. It only exists in the scope of sayHello.

We never stand alone either!

Hello, Swift Programmers!

Brain Power

Write a better version of the `billSplit` function to help calculate how to evenly split a dining bill.
This time, the function should have sensible defaults for some of the values: 2 diners, 20% tip.
It should still print how much each diner will need to pay.

Hmmm...I play a lot of board games. It would be great if I could understand how I might represent the state of those games in Swift.

Enums allow you to create groups of related values.

When you're playing a complex board game, you might need to represent multiple states a player could be in. For example:

```
var playerState: String
playerState = "dead"
playerState = "blockaded"
playerState = "winner"
```

This is sub-par, and hard to manage, and potentially unsafe or fragile if you mistype one of the strings you're using to represent state. Basically, it's terrible. Meet enums!

```
enum PlayerState {
    case dead
    case blockaded
    case winner
}
```

Now, when we talk about a player state, we can use the enum instead of the potentially fragile string:

```
func setPlayerState(state: PlayerState) {
    print("The player state is now \(state)")
}

setPlayerState(state: .dead)
```

Anatomy of an Enum

Defining an enum

```
enum Thing {

}
```

Associated values and enums

```
enum Response {
    case success
    case failure(reason: String)
}
```

This is called conforming to a protocol—here, the CaseIterable protocol. In this case, it makes an enum iterable. More on protocols later.

An iterable enum

```
enum Fruit: CaseIterable {
    case pineapple
    case dragonfruit
    case lemon
}

for fruit in Fruit.allCases {
    print(fruit)
}
```

Initializing from a raw value

```
case Hat: Int {
    case top = 1
    case bowler
    case baseball
}
var hat = Hat(rawValue: 3)
```

Adding cases to an enum

```
enum Fruit {
    case apple
    case banana
    case pear
}
```

Implicitly assigned raw values

```
enum Planet: Int {
    case mercury
    case venus
    case earth
    case mars
    case jupiter
    case saturn
    case uranus
    case neptune
}
```

Raw values

```
case Suit: String {
    case heart = "Red Hearts"
    case diamond = "Red Diamonds"
    case club = "Black Clubs"
    case spade = "Black Spades"
}
var card: Suit = .heart
print(card.rawValue)
```

Switching with enums

`switch` statements and enums are a match made in heaven. You can match individual enumeration values with a `switch` statement. It's very useful:

If we set a PlayerState, using our PlayerState enum with associated values...

```
var playerOneState: PlayerState = .dead(cause: "crop failure")
```

...we can then switch on it.

```
switch(playerOneState) {
    case .dead(let cause):
        print("Player One died of \(cause).")
    case .blockaded(let byEnemy):
        print("Player One was blockaded by \(byEnemy).")
    case .winner(let score):
        print("Player One is the winner with \(score) points!")
}
```

You can extract the associated values during the switch by placing one or more constant or variable declarations inside the switch.

```
Player One died of crop failure.
```

Remember that switch statements must be exhaustive.

If you're switching on an enum value, then you must have a case for each of the enumeration in question's cases. In other words, the `switch` *statement will ideally have a case matching each of the enumeration's cases.*

Alternatively, you can make the `switch` *statement exhausive by providing a default case, and omit any cases that are not relevant:*

```
enum Options {
        case option1
        case option2
        case option3
    }

    var option: Options = .option1
    switch(option) {
        case .option1:
            print("Option 1")
        default:
            print ("Not Option 1")
    }
```

An enumeration can have either raw values or associated values, but not both.

 ## Exercise

Create a new enumeration to represent movie genres. It should contain a handful of movie genres, of your choice Once you've created it, make a `switch` statement, and switch on a variable storing a genre (maybe call it favoriteGenre?). Print out a sassy comment for each genre.

With that working, try creating a new enumeration that represents cocktails. For each cocktail, store a raw string value describing the cocktail.

With that done, iterate through the cases of the enum using a loop, and print the description of each cocktail.

⟶ Answers on page 131.

Anatomy of a Function

Defining a function

The func keyword tells Swift we're about to define a function.

This function is named welcomeCustomers.

The code that gets run when you <u>call</u> the function (using its name) goes here. It's the body of the function.

```
func welcomeCustomers {
}
```

The body of a function

```
func welcomeCustomers {
    print("Welcome to the pizza shop!"
}
```

Functions can have parameters and return values of any type

This function takes one parameter called name, which is a string.

And returns a string.

```
func sayHello(name: String) -> String {
    print("Hello, \(name)! Welcome to the pizza shop!")
    return "'\(name)' was welcomed."
}
```

A function with a variable number of parameters and multiple return types

```
func biggestAndSmallest(numbers: Int...) -> (smallers: Int, biggest: Int) {
    var currentSmallest = numbers[0]
    var currentBiggest = numbers[0]
    for number in numbers[1..<numbers.count] {
        if number < currentSmallest {
            currentSmallest = number
        } else if number > currentBiggest {
            currentBiggest = number
        }
    }
    return (currentSmallest, currentBiggest)
}
```

Functioncross

Let's give your left brain a break, and try out a quick crossword. All of the solutions are related to concepts covered in this chapter!

Across

1) A type of parameter that can support multiple values.
5) Inside a function, a parameter is _____.
6) The external name for a function parameter.
7) A function defined inside another function is said to be
_____.
8) How Swift uniquely identifies a function.
10) The maximum number of variables a function can have.
11) Character to supress an argument name.
13) Statement to define a block of code to be executed later.

Down

2) Assign a value to a parameter in a function definition to make it a _____ value.
3) Parameter that can be modified inside a function.
4) The sort of entity that has to be passed as an inout parameter.
5) A keyword that can't be deferred
9) Return type for a function that doesn't return anything.
12) Ensure code is executed before function ends.

⟶ Answers on page 132.

Exercise Solution

From page 128.

```
enum Genres {
    case scifi
    case thriller
    case romcom
    case comedy
}

var favoriteGenre: Genres = .scifi

switch(favoriteGenre) {
case .comedy:
    print("Comedy is fine, as long as it's British.")
case .romcom:
    print("It had better star Hugh Grant.")
case .thriller:
    print("Only Die Hard counts.")
case .scifi:
    print("Star Trek is the best.")
}

enum Cocktails: String, CaseIterable {
    case oldfashioned = "Sugar, bitters, and whisky."
    case manhattan = "Bourbon, sweet vermouth, and bitters."
    case negroni = "Gin, red vermouth, and Campari."
    case mojito = "White rum, sugar, lime juice, soda water, and mint."
}

for drink in Cocktails.allCases {
    print(drink.rawValue)
}
```

Functioncross Solution

From page 130.

```
                                    ¹V  A  R  I  A  ²D  I  C
                                               E
                                               F
              ³I              ⁵C  O  N  S  T  A  N  T
         ⁴V   N                  O              U
         A    O                  N              L
      ⁶A  R  G  U  M  E  N  T                  ⁷N  E  S  T  E  D
         I   T                  T
         A                      I
         B           ⁸S  I  G  N  A  T  U  R  E
    ⁹V   L                      U
   ¹⁰O  N  E      ¹¹U  N  ¹²D  E  R  S  C  O  R  E
    I                      E
    D              ¹³D  E  F  E  R
                           E
                           R
```

5 closures

Fancy, Flexible Functions

> Functionality wrapped into a variable? I really hope this chapter gives me some <u>closure</u> on the matter...

Functions are useful, but sometimes you need more flexibility.

Swift allows you to **use a function as a type**, just like an integer or string. This means **you can create a function and assign it to a variable**. Once it's assigned to a variable, you can call the function using the variable, or pass the function to other functions as a parameter. When you create and use a function in this manner, it's called a **closure**. Closures are useful because they can **capture references** to constants and variables from the context in which they are defined. This is called **closing over a value**, hence the name.

Meet the humble closure

This is a **closure**:

Our function is assigned to the constant, pizzaCooked.

This is the start of the function. It hasn't got a name.

```
let pizzaCooked = {
        print("Pizza is cooked.")
}
```

This is the body of the function.

This is the end of the function.

You can call **pizzaCooked()** just like a regular function:

```
pizzaCooked()
```

Pizza is cooked.

This doesn't seem very useful. What's the deal?

At first glance, you might think a closure is just <u>another way to write a function</u>.

You'd be *kind of* correct, but closures allow you to do a lot of things that functions alone aren't suited for. You'll understand the power in a few pages.

Closures are like functions that you can pass around as variables. That's the starting point to their usefulness, and it only goes up from there!

I don't get it. It's a function, but it's a variable. Why not just use a function?!

Closures are definitely a little bit confusing.

It's normal to be a bit confused about closures, how they work, and why they're useful, even if the rest of programming, broadly, doesn't confuse you. Don't panic! You'll understand by the end of this book, and you'll be a bit more confident by the end of this chapter.

Closures are really useful when you want to store some functionality and use it later, or use it again.

Particular occasions when you often need to store some functionality include:

✳ When you want to wait some time, then run code afterward

✳ When you have a user interface, and you need some sort of animation or interaction to finish before you run code

✳ When you are performing some sort of indeterminately long network operation (like a download) and want your code to run when it's done

Test Drive

Try these closures. Some of them are valid, some of them aren't. What do you think is missing from them, if they're invalid? The easiest way to try them out is to run them in a Playground, and then call them. Once you've figured out which ones are valid and which ones aren't, try writing a valid closure of your own and calling it.

```swift
var closureMessage = {
    print("Closures are pretty similar to functions!")
}
let bookTitle = {
    print("Head First Swift")
}
var greeting() = {
    print("Hello!")
}
```

Closures are better with parameters

Closures are not particularly useful without parameters. Sure, it's fun to create and assign a nameless function to a variable or a constant, but they truly come into their own once you start to realize the possibilities of parameters.

The small wrinkle in this plan is that ***closures don't accept parameters the same way as regular functions do***. Imagine the closure we assigned to the `pizzaCooked` constant earlier was a regular function.

If we wanted to add a parameter to specify which specific pizza kind was cooked, the function definition might look a little bit like this:

```
func cooked(pizza: String, minutes: Int) {
        print("\(pizza) Pizza is cooked in \(minutes) minutes.")
}
```

A call to this `cooked` function would then look like this:

```
cooked(pizza: "Hawaiian", minutes: 7)
```

If we wanted to write the same functionality as a closure, it might look like this:

```
let pizzaCooked = { (pizza: String, minutes: Int) in
        print("\(pizza) Pizza is cooked in \(minutes) minutes.")
}
```

And calling this closure would look like this:

```
pizzaCooked("Hawaiian", 7)
```
We suspect you can guess what this will output.

Behind the Scenes

The reason that closures take their parameters inside the curly braces and use the `in` keyword to mark the end of the parameter list (and the start of the closure's body) is because if we wrote them in what might seem like a more intuitive way, like this:

```
let pizzaCooked = (pizza: String, minutes: Int)
```

It would to look more like we're trying to create a tuple, and the Swift compiler might get confused. Placing the parameters inside the braces clearly shows that the entire closure is a block of data stored in a variable (or constant). The `in` keyword delineates where the body starts, because there's no second set of braces.

So, when I create a function I can make it return values. Can I do that with closures?

Closures can return values, just like functions.

Much of the functionality of closures is identical to functions, but the syntax for setting it up is slightly different. To create a closure that can return a value, you define the return type before the in keyword, like this:

```
let hello = { (name: String) -> String in
        return "Hello, \(name)!"

}
```

The syntax used to declare the return type is the same as for functions.

We can use this closure like this, running it and printing its return value:

```
let greeting = hello("Harry")
print(greeting)
```

Brain Power

Write a closure that takes a single integer as its parameter, and returns that integer multiplied by itself inside a string.

Write some code to use that closure, by passing in the value 10 (it should print "The result is 100" or similar).

Now, update the closure and make it take two integers as parameters. Test that closure with 10 and 50 (it should return "The result is 500" or similar).

Sharpen your pencil

Take a look at the closures below. What do you think the type is for each of them? Think back to the function types from the previous chapter, if you're stuck.

A
```
let pizzaCooked = { (pizza: String, minutes: Int) -> String in
        return "\(pizza) Pizza is cooked in \(minutes) minutes."
}
```

B
```
let pizzaCooked = { (pizza: String, minutes: Int) -> String in
        var message ="\(pizza) Pizza is cooked in \(minutes) minutes."
        print(message)
        return(message)
}
```

C
```
let pizzaCooked = { (pizza: String) in
        print("\(pizza) Pizza is cooked in 10 minutes.")
}
```

D
```
let pizzaCooked = { (minutes: Int) in
        print("Hawaiian Pizza is cooked in \(minutes) minutes.")
}
```

➤ Answers on page 140.

Bullet Points

- Closures are blocks of code that you can pass around and use, just like variables.

- A closure can have any number of parameters, including no parameters at all.

- Every single closure has a type which includes the type of the closure's parameters.

- Closures are useful for code that you want to run at a certain time, like when something has completed, or when you need to pass around a block of code that does something and use it in different contexts.

- Closures mostly work just like functions. Mostly.

> I may not be a programmer, but it looks to me like you could replace that pizza ordering system you made with something using closures, no?

Closures can be used as parameters.

Earlier, when you were learning about functions, you made an order function that took a pizza name, as a String, and returned a function of the type `() -> Pizza` (Pizza was a `typealias` for `String`).

Our observant pizza chef is correct: we could make a similar set of functionality using closures. To start with, our order function might look something like this:

```
func order(pizza: () -> Void) {
        print("# Ready to order pizza! #")
        pizza()
        print("# Order for pizza placed! #")
}
```

Each pizza would have a closure defined. For the Hawaiian pizza it might look like this:

```
let hawaiianPizza = {
        print("One Hawaiian Pizza, coming up!")
        print("Hawaiian pizza is cheese, ham, & pineapple.")
}
```

You could then order a Hawaiian pizza like this:

```
order(pizza: hawaiianPizza)
```
← *What do you suppose this prints out?*

Brain Power

The closure for a Hawaiian pizza is written above. What do you think the closures for Cheesey pizza and Plain pizza would look like? Check back to the section "Function types as parameter types" on page 120 in the previous chapter for the pizza chef's recipes for them, and then write their closures. Test the closures out by passing them in to the order function.

Hang on. Can I use a closure with parameters as a parameter?

Closures with parameters can, themselves, be used as parameters.

It's already a little fiddly to figure out what's going on when you use a closure as a parameter, but things take a further turn for the inaccessible when you also need to use a closure that takes parameters as a parameter for something else.

Don't worry, it's a little confusing to unpack sometimes, but you'll get there.

There's nothing magic to closures. They may have a scary-sounding name, but they're really just functions. You already know how to pass a function as a parameter, and it's the same with closures. (Because they're just functions!)

Sharpen your pencil
Solution

From page 138.

A   (String, Int) -> String

B   (String, Int) -> String

C   (String) -> Void

D   (Int) -> Void

Serious Coding

Let's try out some more closures and parameters. It's slightly tricky to get your head around, but this is a concept that comes up regularly in the Swift world.

Consider the following function:

It's named performWithPiano.

As a parameter, it takes a closure, which it refers to as song.

```
func performWithPiano(song: (String) -> String) {
    var performance = song("Piano")
    print(performance)
}
```

That closure takes a String as a parameter, and also returns a String.

If you had a closure that met this requirement of taking a String and returning a String, perhaps named neverGonnaGiveYouUp, you could then call the performWithPiano function as follows:

```
performWithPiano(song: neverGonnaGiveYouUp)
```

```
'Never Gonna Give You Up' on Piano
```

What might the closure neverGonnaGiveYouUp look like, so that it would meet the requirements and end up with performWithPiano printing the correct output?

We've started you off, but try to complete it, and test the closure in your own Playground.

```
var neverGonnaGiveYouUp = {
```

Once you've got it working, try creating another closure, for a different song.

OK...So can we code a pizza ordering system where we can modify the pizzas...using closures?

Closures actually have quite a few perfect uses, as you'll find out by the end of the book...

We most certainly can! This a perfect use for a closure.

Earlier we implemented a function called order that took a closure as a parameter. We can modify that function to take a closure that has its own parameters.

The order function could look like this:

This function takes a customer name, a String.

We indicate the closure's parameter type using parentheses.

```
func order(customer: String, pizza: (Int) -> String){
    // Order the pizza

}
```

But it also takes a pizza type, which is a closure of a type that takes an Int and returns a String.

What the order function does with the closure is up to it. This function can accept any sort of closure as the pizza, as long as that closure takes a single integer parameter and returns a string.

The way we envisaged it might work is that the integer parameter would be the quantity of that specific pizza, and the returned string would be a confirmation message with details of the quantity and type of pizza ordered—but it could be anything.

Because a closure is nice, neat box of functionality, the power is in replacing the box: the order function doesn't need to care how the closure that represents a specific pizza works, so if the chef invents a really complex pizza (they do this all the time) in the future, we can write a new closure that deals with that recipe.

All it needs to do is take an integer and return a string.

That's (Int) -> String, in case you had already forgotten...

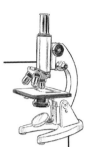

Anatomy of a Closure

A closure expression

A *closure expression* is a way to express (which is just a fancy way to say write) a closure in a simple, straightforward, often inline syntax:

Parameters can be inout (but cannot have a default value), and a variadic parameter can be used as long as it has a name.

The start of a closure's body is designated by the in keyword.

```
{ ( parameters ) -> return type in
    statements
}
```

You can have as many or as few statements as you want inside the closure.

Trailing closures

If a closure is the last, or only, parameter for a function (or another closure), you can use the *trailing closure* syntax to pass the closure in.

For example, if you had a function like this, which takes a closure as its last or only parameter:

```
func saySomething(thing: () -> Void)
{
        thing()
}
```

you could use the trailing closure syntax to pass the closure in like this:

```
saySomething {
        print("Hello!")
}
```

It's called a trailing closure because it trails the function. It is written after the function call's parentheses, even though it's still an argument to the function.

If you didn't want to use the trailing closure syntax, you'd instead need to write something like this:

```
saySomething(thing: {
        print("Hello!")
})
```

Basically, it's just a nice, clean syntax!

Boiling it all down to something useful

The problem

We want to write some code to take an array of integers and boil it down to a single integer. We want to be able to change the way it's boiled down.

We have an array of integers. We want to boil it down to a single integer.

The solution

We could write a special function that takes an array of integers and returns an integer, and create a single function per operation we want performed: one for multiplying all the integers together to create our final number, one for adding, and so on.

Or we could use closures.

❶ Create a function to operate on an array

First parameter is an array of integers.

Second parameter is a closure (or function) of the type that takes two integers, and returns an integer.

```
func operateOn(_ array: [Int], operation: (Int, Int) -> Int) -> Int
{
        // code goes here
}
```

And the function itself returns an integer.

❷ Implement the function

```
func operateOn(_ array: [Int], using operation: (Int, Int) -> Int) -> Int {
    var cur = array[0]

    for item in array[1...] {
        cur = operation(cur, item)
    }
    return cur
}
```

var cur = array[0] ← Store the first element of the passed-in array.

Iterate through the array from the next (1) element, updating the current number by passing it plus the current item in the array iteration through the operation closure that's been passed in.

return cur ← Return the current number.

Reducing with closures

❸ Create an array to test it out with

```
let numbers = [7, 14, 6, 1, 8]
```

❹ Test the function

This is a constant to store the result in.

We assign the result of the operateOn function to our constant.

```
let test = operateOn(numbers, operation: {(total: Int, next: Int) in
            return total * next
})
```

And pass in the numbers array for the first parameter.

And it returns the total, multiplied by the next integer.

For the second parameter, we pass in a closure as a closure expression.

The closure takes two parameters (total and next, both integers).

❺ Check the result

```
print(test)
```

Behind the Scenes

Swift operators are actually functions! This means that if we want to reduce an array using our operateOn function and add all the elements together, we can actually just supply the built-in Swift operator +, like this:

```
let sumResult = operateOn(numbers, operation: +)
```

Try *, −, and / too!

So, a closure is just...a variable
that can hold some code in it?

Spot on.

You're pretty familiar with storing integers, floats, strings, Booleans, dictionaries, and arrays. A closure is just another data type.

A closure is a variable (or a constant) that stores some code. Just as there's nothing mysterious with this:

```
var myNumber = 100
```

There's also nothing mysterious with this:

```
let myClosure = {
        print("Hello!")
}
```

It's just a closure.

Brain Power

Instead of passing a closure expression in to your operateOn function, create a closure that's assigned to a variable and pass that in.

Your closure should sum the numbers for the reduce (taking a bunch of integers that are in the array and reducing them to a single number, in this case the total of all the numbers added together).

Test your closure (assuming it's called sumClosure) by running it like so:

```
let sumTest = operateOn(numbers, operation: sumClosure)
```

Right, I can see how you can pass those around like every other variable, but why is it called a "closure"? It's a strange name...

It's a weird name, we'll give you that.

Closures are called closures because they capture—or *close over*—variables from outside their scope.

If you create the following integer variable:

```
var count = 5
```

And then create a closure immediately afterward that looks like this:

```
let incrementer = {
        count +=1
}
```

The closure will have no problems incrementing count, because both count and incrementer (the closure) were created in the same scope.

Changes to count are the same inside or outside the closure. The closure, incrementer, has captured—closed over—count.

Brain Power

What do you suspect count might equal if you coded the above in a Playground, and then called incrementer 10 times in a row?

Capturing values from the enclosing scope

Because closures behave like this, we can make useful things like this counting function:

= super useful

It's named counter. It has no parameters.

It returns a closure. The returned closure has no parameters, and returns an integer.

```
func counter() -> () -> Int {
    var count = 0
    let incrementer: () -> Int = {
        count += 1
        return count
    }
    return incrementer
}
```

The closure returned increments the internal count variable each time it's called.

And each time the overall function is called, you get a different counter.

With this function in place, you can then use it like this:

```
let myCounter = counter()
myCounter()
myCounter()
myCounter()
```

1

2

3

You can independently work with any number of counters!

Brain Power

Create another counter:

```
let secondCounter = counter()
```

Increment the original counter a few more times:

```
myCounter()
```

```
myCounter()
```

```
myCounter()
```

What happens if you also increment the second counter?

Are we sure closures are reliable? I've heard they can escape?! Nothing escapes me...

A closure can escape the function it was passed to.

If a closure lives longer than the function it was called by, then it's said to be an ***escaping closure***. It's escaped the function, get it?

More simply: if a closure is called after the function that it was passed in to returns, then it's an ***escaping closure.***

A closure is marked as escaping when you use the **@escaping** keyword before the parameter's type. This tells Swift that the closure is allow to escape the bounds of the function.

The most common way a closure escapes is when it's stored in a variable that's been defined outside the scope of a function.

Even if you store the closure in a variable defined outside the function, you still need the @escaping keyword on the parameter.

What came first, the <u>function or the closure?</u>

It's sometimes difficult to figure out what order something is going to happen in, especially when closures get involved (and even more so when the closures are escaping).

It's time to bust out our dear friend, the **contrived example**!

The cast of characters for our contrived example in this case includes an *array of closures* and a *function* that takes an escaping closure of type () -> Void as its only parameter. **❶** **❷**

When the function is called, it prints a message saying that the function was called, appends the closure that got passed in to the array of closures, runs the closure, then returns.

Then, *when we call the function, we pass a closure in*: in this case, that's going to be a trailing closure that prints a message saying that the closure was called. **❸**

Confused? Let's go over the steps in more detail.

Escaping closures: the <u>contrived example</u>

➊ An array of closures

```
var closures:[()->()] = []
```
← This array can store closures.

To mark a closure as escaping, the @escaping keyword is used.

➋ A function

```
func callEscaping(closure: @escaping () -> Void) {
    print("callEscaping() function called!")
    closures.append(closure)
    closure()
    return
}
```

The closure that's passed in to the function is stored in the array which was defined outside the function.

Because of this, the closure needs to escape the function.

➋ A call to the function

It's passed to the callEscaping function using the trailing closure syntax.

```
callEscaping {
    print("closure called")
}
```

This closure does nothing but print that it was called.

Sharpen your pencil

If you coded the above Swift program, escaping closure and all, in a Playground, what do you think the output woud be?

A

```
callEscaping() function was called!
closure called!
```

B

```
closure called!
callEscaping() function was called!
```

Why do you think that might be the case? What's going on?

Hint: there's nothing magical about closures, so if you patiently and carefully trace your way through the program, you'll get the right answer. We'll discuss what happened on the next page.

> When my workers are cooking, they sometimes forget what they're meant to do next. Looks like closures can help me there...

Closures make great <u>completion handlers</u>.

A completion handler is a term for some code—usually a function or a closure—that's called when some other code—also usually a function or a closure—has completed its task.

So, if you have a `cookPizza` function, and you want the pizza to be delivered to the customer afterward, you could do something like this:

```
func cookPizza(completion: () -> ()) {
    print("The pizza is cooking!")
    print("The pizza is cooked!")
    completion()
    print("Pizza cooked & everything is done.")
}
```

And then define a closure to serve as the completion handler (serving the pizza to the customer):

```
var servePizza = {
    print("Delivered pizza to the customer!")
}
```

This would make it trivial to change what happens after cooking (to, say, allow the pizza to be boxed for delivery instead of served):

```
cookPizza(completion: servePizza)
```

↑
You could also use the trailing closure syntax to do something entirely new!

Sharpen your pencil
Solution
The answer is A. The function will print its message first, then the closure. This seems like it's straightforward, but there's a lot going on under the hood in Swift to make sure it all works right.

Because the array of closures, `closures`, was created outside of the function `callEscaping`, the closure from inside `callEscaping` needs to escape the function in order to be stored in it.

Behind
the Scenes

Under the hood, the completion handler's execution steps look something like this:

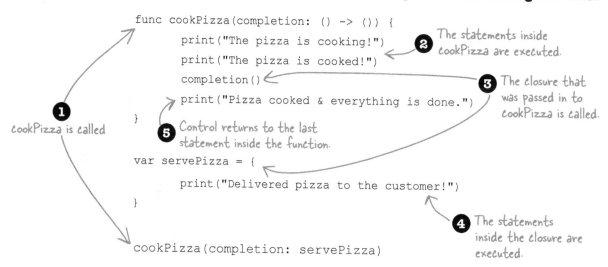

```
func cookPizza(completion: () -> ()) {
    print("The pizza is cooking!")
    print("The pizza is cooked!")
    completion()
    print("Pizza cooked & everything is done.")
}

var servePizza = {
    print("Delivered pizza to the customer!")
}

cookPizza(completion: servePizza)
```

2 The statements inside cookPizza are executed.

3 The closure that was passed in to cookPizza is called.

1 cookPizza is called

5 Control returns to the last statement inside the function.

4 The statements inside the closure are executed.

Watch it!

Closures are reference types.

We think it's important to point out that closures are reference types.

So if you create a closure:

```
var myClosure = {
    print("Amazing!")
}
```

And you assign it to another variable:

```
var coolClosure = myClosure
```

Then both coolClosure *and* myClosure *refer to the same closure.*

Autoclosures provide flexibility

The situation

You've got a function that is used to serve a pizza. It takes two parameters, a Bool that dictates whether the pizza should be boxed and the pizza name as a String:

```
func servePizza(box: Bool, pizza: String) {
    if box {
        print("Boxing the pizza '\(pizza)'")
    } else {
        print("We're all done.")
    }
}
```

This is pretty straightforward, and easy to call:

```
servePizza(box: true, pizza: "Hawaiian")
```

You also have another function, representing a random pizza, that returns a String, like this:

```
func nextPizza() -> String {
    return "Hawaiian"
}
```

You could use that function when calling servePizza:

```
servePizza(box: true, pizza: nextPizza())
```

But what would happen if the pizza isn't being boxed, and your call looks like this?

```
servePizza(box: false, pizza: nextPizza())
```

The problem

The problem is that even if you don't actually need nextPizza to be called, as in that example, it's going to be called anyway. That's a waste of resources. We can fix this with closures. If we update the function definition:

```
func servePizza(box: Bool, pizza: () -> String)
```

Then this call to servePizza() won't compile at all, because the pizza parameter can only ever be a closure that returns a string (but calling nextPizza() will return a String):

```
servePizza(), pizza, nextPizza(), String
```

This won't compile now!

...and we obviously cannot just pass a String anymore, either.

```
String
```

The solution

The solution is an autoclosure! By adding the `@autoclosure` attribute to the parameter, we can avoid this problem entirely. If we update the function definition:

```
func servePizza(box: Bool, pizza: @autoclosure () -> String)
```

We can now pass in anything, as long as it results in a String:

```
servePizza(box: true, pizza: nextPizza())

servePizza(box: false, pizza: "Vegetarian")

servePizza(box: true, pizza: "Meaty Meat Surprise")
```

So an autoclosure...
automatically makes
a closure from an
expression?

**That's exactly right. An autoclosure
turns the expression into a closure.**

The code you write for the expression is not a
closure, but it becomes a closure. This gives you
the flexibility to mix and match what you're doing.

Watch it!

**It's unlikely you'll
regularly need to use
autoclosures.**

*They're really powerful,
and useful for setting things up
if you're writing code that other
people's code will use, but they can
make your code hard to read if you
overuse them. Use autoclosures
sparingly!*

You've convinced me. Fine. What else can I do with closures?

Closures are really important for networking, user interfaces, and complex behaviors that require timing.

You'll learn more about user interfaces in a few chapters, but before then it's important you get the basics of closures down.

The final useful thing you can do with closures (at least, the final thing you'll be doing in this chapter) is using them to sort collections.

If you have an array of numbers, like this:

```
var numbers = [1, 5, 2, 3, 7, 4, 6, 9, 8]
```

...you can use a closure to sort it!

Swift's collection types have a `sort(by:)` method, and it takes a closure. Because Swift's operators are actually functions, you can just pass a < or > in to this, if you want:

```
numbers.sort(by: <)
numbers.sort(by: >)
```

← These will do the same thing.

But you can also pass your own inline closure in to `sort(by:)`:

```
numbers.sort(by: { a, b in
        return a < b

})
```

Brain Power

Create a new closure to sort your `numbers` array with. Define it like this:

Put your sorting logic here. It needs to return a Boolean.

```
let sortClosure = { (a: Int, b: Int) -> Bool in


}
```

See how the different possibilities behave by sorting the `numbers` array (or some new `numbers` arrays) with your custom sort closure. You can pass it in to `sort(by:)` like this (instead of using a closure expression, like we were doing earlier):

```
numbers.sort(by: sortClosure)
```

Shorthand argument names

When you're working with an inline closure, you can skip naming the arguments and refer to the values by using $0, $1, $2, $3, and so on. So, for our `numbers` array sorting example from the previous page, you could actually pass your own inline closure in like this, using the shorthand argument names:

```
numbers.sort(by: { $0 < $1 } )
```

You also get to omit →
the in keyword.

Ready Bake
Code

Who Does What?

Match each closure-related term to its description. You should be familiar with all of these terms; check the solution if you're having trouble, or just skim back through the previous pages.

Autoclosure	A self-contained block of code that can be passed around
Completion handler	Passing a function as an argument after a function call's parentheses, when the closure is the last or only parameter
Function type	Some code (usually a closure) that's called after something else (usually a function) is done
Closure expression	A constant or variable captured by a closure from the surrounding context
Captured value	Let you refer to the first, second (and so on) arguments in an inline closure with numbers, like $0 and $1
Escaping closure	A type definition for a function or a closure that shows the parameter types and return types
Trailing closure	A simple syntax for writing inline closures
Shorthand argument names	A closure that is called (or continues existing) after a function returns
Implicit return	A closure that's automatically created from an expression
Closure	Omitting the return keyword from single-expression closures
Non-escaping closure	A closure that's not called outside the function it's used in

→ Answers on page 160.

 # Closurecross

Test your zeal for closures with this crossword. It closes over (get it?) concepts from this chapter.

Across

1) This keyword is used to mark the end of the parameter list for a closure.

2) A function that's assigned to a variable or constant.

3) When a closure lives longer than the function it was passed to, this is called an _____ closure.

7) Closures can _____ values, just like functions.

9) Closures can _____ variables from the enclosing scope.

10) A closure is a _____ type, not a value type.

11) An automatically created closure from a closure expression.

13) _____ handlers are a great use for a closure.

Down

1) _____ returns mean you can omit the return keyword from single-expression closures.

4) A closure can be used as a _____ for another closure (or a function).

5) You can use _____ argument names to refer to closure arguments by number.

6) Just like variables, closures have a _____.

8) A closure _____ is a simple inline syntax for closures.

12) _____ closures are closures that are the last, or only, parameter to a function.

→ Answers on page 159.

BE the Swift Compiler

Each of the Swift code snippets on this page represents something about closures. Your job is to play Swift compiler, and determine whether each one is valid.

A

```swift
var createPizza(for name: String) = {
     print("This pizza is for: \(name)")
}
createPizza(for: "Bob")
```

B

```swift
var deliverPizza() {
     print("The pizza is delivered!")
}
```

C

```swift
let cookPizza = {
     print("The pizza is cooking!")
}
cookPizza()
```

D

```swift
let boxPizza = {
     print("The pizza is in the box!")
}
boxPizza()
```

E

```swift
eatPizza = {
     print("Now eating!")
}
```

F

```swift
let pizzaHawaiian {
     print("Delicious pineapple on it!")
}
pizzaHawaiian()
```

G

```swift
eatPizza: String = {
     print("Now eating!")
}
```

H

```swift
var slicePizza = {
     print("Slicing into 8 pieces.")
}
slicepizza()
```

I

```swift
let garlicBread() = {
     print("Making garlic bread!")
}
upgrade()
```

→ Answers on page 160.

Closurecross Solution

From page 157.

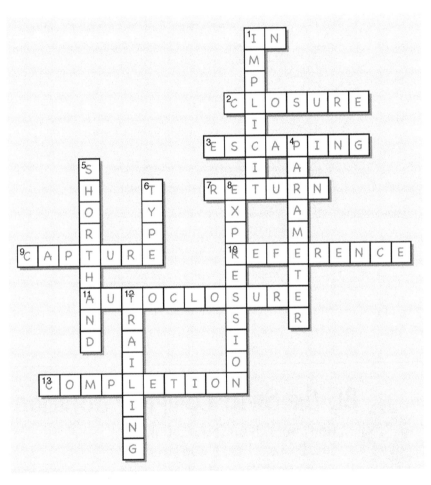

Who Does What? Solution

From page 156.

Autoclosures — A self-contained block of code that can be passed around

Completion handler — Passing a function as an argument after a function call's parentheses, when the closure is the last or only parameter

Function type — Some code (usually a closure) that's called after something else (usually a function) is done.

Closure expression — A constant or variable captured by a closure from the surrounding context

Captured value — Let you refer to the first, second (and so on) arguments in an inline closure with numbers, like $0 and $1

Escaping closure — A type definition for a function or a closure, that shows the parameter types and return types

Trailing closure — A simple syntax for writing inline closures

Shorthand argument names — A closure that is called (or continues existing) after a function returns

Implicit return — A closure that's automatically created from an expression

Closure — Omitting the return keyword from single-expression closures

Non-escaping closure — A closure that's not called outside the function it's used in

BE the Swift Compiler Solution

From page 158.

A won't work, B won't work, C works fine, D works fine, E won't work, F won't work, G won't work, H will work, I won't work.

6 structures, properties, and methods

Custom Types and Beyond

We don't go anywhere without our custom types! Nobody who's anybody will take you seriously without at least one thing that's yours and yours alone...

Working with data often involves defining your own kinds of data.

Structures—often shortened to their Swift language keyword, **structs**—allow you to create your own **custom data types** (just like String and Int are data types) by **combining other types**. Using structs to represent the data that your Swift code is working with allows you to step back and consider how the data that flows through your code fits together. **Structs can hold variables and constants** (which are called **properties** when they're inside a struct) **and functions** (which are called **methods**). Let's add some structure to your world, and dive into structs.

We've been making a lot of pizzas! Is it possible to make some sort of useful Pizza type that defines a pizza and use that instead of a String?

Like String, Int, etc.

You can make your own types in Swift.

The most common way of doing this is with a feature called structures, or **structs** for short. This might be surprising if you've used another language, where people can be stuck in their classy ways.

Structs give you the phenomenal power to *contain variables, constants, and functions within a type of your own choosing*!

This is a Pizza type, defined as a struct:

```swift
struct Pizza {

    var name: String

}
```

Variables that are inside structs are referred to as properties.

After defining your Pizza struct, you can then create an **instance** of Pizza like this:

```swift
var myPizza = Pizza(name: "Hawaiian")
```

And access (and print) its name *property* (a String) like this:

```swift
print(myPizza.name)
```

Because the name property is a variable, you can manipulate it just like any other variable:

This pizza's name property is now "Meatlovers".

```swift
myPizza.name = "Meatlovers"
print(myPizza.name)
```

You're not actually changing it, you're copying the struct except for the new value. But the end result is that it changes.

Let's make a pizza, in all its glory...

The chef made a great point on the previous page: it would be really useful to have a **type** for our pizzas, so we didn't have to keep using strings to represent them.

A struct represents a collection of properties and methods. Coincidentally, we could also represent a pizza as a collection of properties and methods.

What properties and methods does representing a pizza require? We're thinking about a pizza as a concept, not as a specific pizza attached to someone's order (so size doesn't matter right now).

A Pizza struct

A pizza has a name, like "Hawaiian".

```
struct Pizza {
    var name: String
    var ingredients: [String] = []
}
```

A pizza has a number of ingredients.

The <u>name</u> and <u>ingredients</u> variables are called <u>stored properties</u> because they are properties of the thing represented by the struct. There is another type of property called a <u>computed property</u>, which runs some code to get its value instead of just having a value stored in it.

Sharpen your pencil

Can you figure out how to create an instance of this new Pizza struct? On the previous page, we made a Pizza struct that only had the pizza's name as a property, but this one also takes an array of strings as ingredients.

What would the statement be to initialize a new instance of our Pizza struct as a Hawaiian pizza (which has Cheese, Pineapple, Ham, and Pizza Sauce as ingredients)?

What about a Vegetarian Special pizza (Cheese, Avocado, Sundried Tomato, Basil)?

And a BBQ Chicken pizza (Chicken, Cheese, BBQ Sauce, Pineapple)?

→ Answers on page 165.

> Hang on...how does Swift know how to initialize a Pizza like that? Passing in the values for properties of a struct looks a lot like calling a function to me...

An initializer lets you create new instances of something.

Swift's structs come with a synthesized memberwise initializer.

A **_memberwise initializer_** is a special kind of function that exists inside the struct. It's called an initializer because it helps you initialize a new instance of that struct.

The memberwise initializer that you use to create an instance of a struct is actually *synthesized* for you, and accepts values for each of the struct's properties, which also make up the parameter labels.

So, if you have a Pizza struct with three properties:

```swift
struct Pizza {
    var name: String
    var ingredients: [String]
    var dessertPizza: Bool
```

Synthesized, in this case, just means that it's automagically created for you.

The initializer **_requires_** three parameters—name, ingredients, and dessertPizza:

```swift
var rockyRoadPizza = Pizza(name: "Rocky Road",
                    ingredients: ["Marshmallows",
                            "Peanuts", "Chocolate",
                            "Sugar"],
                    dessertPizza: true)
```

But if you provide a **default value** for any of the properties, the synthesized initializer also knows about it, which makes it your choice whether you provide it:

```swift
struct Pizza {
    var name: String
    var ingredients: [String]
    var dessertPizza: Bool = false
}
```

We've provided the default value of false to the dessertPizza Bool (it's more likely that pizzas are not dessert pizzas, so this reduces typing when creating a pizza in the most typical case).

Then you can create a new instance with or without that parameter supplied:

```swift
var cheesePizza = Pizza(name: "Cheese", ingredients: ["Cheese"])
var candyPizza = Pizza(name: "Candy",
                    ingredients: ["Gummie Bears", "Nerds"],
                    dessertPizza: true)
```

Bullet Points

- Structs (or "structures") are constructs that allow you to create your own types in Swift.

- You can include variables and constants of other types inside structs. When a variable or constant is inside a struct, it's called a property (because it's a property of the piece of data that the struct represents).

- A struct comes with an automatically synthesized memberwise initializer that allows you to create an instance of the struct by passing in values of all the struct's properties.

- A property can have a default value supplied in the struct's definition, which means it won't be required in the automatically synthesized initializer.

Sharpen your pencil Solution

From page 163.

To create an instance of a Hawaiian pizza (which has Cheese, Pineapple, Ham, and Pizza Sauce as ingredients) using our struct, you need to call the automatically generated initializer, passing appropriately typed values to each named property. A Pizza needs a name string, and a string array for the ingredients.

```
var hawaiianPizza =
      Pizza(name: "Hawaiian",
            ingredients: ["Cheese", "Pineapple", "Ham", "Pizza Sauce"])
```

And here's how you'd create an instance of a Vegetarian Special pizza (Cheese, Avocado, Sundried Tomato, Basil):

```
var vegetarianSpecialPizza =
      Pizza(name: "Vegetarian Special",
            ingredients: ["Cheese", "Avocado", "Sundried Tomato", "Basil"])
```

And a BBQ Chicken pizza (Chicken, Cheese, BBQ Sauce, Pineapple):

```
var bbqChickenPizza =
      Pizza(name: "BBQ Chicken",
            ingredients: ["Chicken", "Cheese", "BBQ Sauce", "Pineapple"])
```

Under the hood...

In Swift, something can be a value type or a reference type.

Structs are **value types**. This means that if you assign a struct to another variable or constant, you're **creating a copy with the current value**, and *not* referring to the original.

For example, if you take the Rocky Road Pizza from the previous page:

```
var rockyRoadPizza =
        Pizza(name: "Rocky Road",
        ingredients: ["Marshmallows", "Peanuts",
                         "Chocolate", "Sugar"],
        dessertPizza: true)
```

Structures are value types. A value type is a type whose instances are copied on assignment.

And then *assign* it to a new variable:

```
var anotherRockyRoadPizza = rockyRoadPizza
```

Then modify that variable:

```
anotherRockyRoadPizza.name = "Fury Road"
```

You'll end up with *two different instances of* `Pizza`, one with the `name` property set to Fury Road, and one with the `name` property set to Rocky Road.

You can check this using the print statement:

```
print(rockyRoadPizza.name)
print(anotherRockyRoadPizza.name)
```

Being a value type means that each instance keeps a unique copy of the data within it.

A value type will copy its data when an assignment, initialization, or argument pass occurs. Most of Swift's built-in data types are value types (in most cases, this is a side effect of them being implemented as structs under the hood): Array, String, Dictionary, Int, and beyond are all implemented as structs, and are all value types.

A reference type means that that there is an implicitly shared instance of the data, and multiple variables can refer to a single instance of the data concerned. You haven't encountered a reference type yet, but you will soon. **Structs are always value types.**

It might not just be a dream!

If only I could create my own initializer. It would be so useful to be able to set up my structure data types the way I wanted...but it's just a dream.

DIY Initializers

This syntax is the same as creating a function. So, because the initializer we created here doesn't need to take any parameters, we don't pass any in.

It's actually really easy to make your own initializers.

You can replace the synthesized initializer with your own. It's very similar to making a function, but the function has no name and starts with the **init** keyword, instead of the func keyword.

So, if you wanted all pizzas, at the point of creation, to default to Cheese, you could do this:

```
struct Pizza {
    var name: String
    var ingredients: [String]
    var dessertPizza: Bool

    init() {
        name = "Cheese"
        ingredients = ["Cheese"]
        dessertPizza = false
    }
}
```

Your initializers must ensure that every property of the struct has a value by the end of the initializer.

You can then create a new Pizza without passing any values:

```
var pizza = Pizza()
```

Because of the initializer (which provides a value for every property), any Pizza created does not (and cannot) take parameters, and will always be a Cheese Pizza.

Watch it!

You can't use the synthesized initializer any more if you create your own.

The initializer you create replaces the synthesized initializer. This means that you can no longer create a Pizza by specifying a name, list of ingredients, and dessert pizza status. All pizzas are created as Cheese, without any choice.

Of course, because the properties of Pizza are variables, you can update them after:

```
pizza.name = "Margherita"
pizza.ingredients.append("Tomato")
```

The initializer behaves just like a function

You can do most things that a function can do with the initializer. You can accept parameters and use them to set the properties, if you want.

This initializer replicates the functionality of the synthesized initializer that we were using before:

```
struct Pizza {
    var name: String
    var ingredients: [String]
    var dessertPizza: Bool

    init(name: String, ingredients: [String], dessertPizza: Bool) {
        self.name = name
        self.ingredients = ingredients
        self.dessertPizza = dessertPizza
    }
}
```

Brain Power

The chef is considering branching out in their strictly pizza-only pizza shop and also serving garlic bread (they've heard something about a rapidly encroaching chain of pizza restaurants called "Pizza Yurt" and have some concerns).

The chef has been paying attention to all the Swift you've been coding, and has had a crack at implementing a structure to represent the new garlic bread product:

```
struct GarlicBread {
    var strength: Int
    var vegan: Bool
}
```

Using your knowledge of initializers and structures, write a custom initializer for the GarlicBread struct that sets the vegan Bool to false (the chef isn't yet ready to offer vegan garlic bread, but plans to in the future) and accepts a strength value.

The chef would also like the initializer to print out a message that states "New Garlic Bread of strength x created!" each time a GarlicBread is initialized.

Surely you could have more than one initializer, right? You should be able to create a Pizza any way you need to...

You can have as <u>many</u> initializers as you need.

You can add initializers that do anything you need done, so you can update your Pizza struct to the following version to get the original functionality of the synthesized initializer back, plus the functionality of the first initializer you deliberately created:

```
struct Pizza {
    var name: String
    var ingredients: [String]
    var dessertPizza: Bool

    init() {
        name = "Cheese"
        ingredients = ["Cheese"]
        dessertPizza = false
    }

    init(name: String, ingredients: [String], dessertPizza: Bool) {
        self.name = name
        self.ingredients = ingredients
        self.dessertPizza = dessertPizza
    }
}
```

The only requirement of an initializer is that all properties have a value assigned before the initializer ends.

Brain Power

Revisit the GarlicBread struct you were working with earlier:

```
struct GarlicBread {
    var strength: Int
    var vegan: Bool
}
```

The chef would like to update the struct to include an integer to represent how spicy the GarlicBread is, and would like the option to initialize a GarlicBread in any one of the following ways:

With no parameters (a strength value of 1, a spicy value of 0, not vegan)

With only a strength parameter passed in (a spicy value of 0, not vegan)

With a strength parameter and a spicy parameter passed in (not vegan)

With a strength parameter, a spicy parameter, and the vegan status passed in

Code as many initializers for GarlicBread as are necessary to support this.

Bullet Points

- The most common way to make your own types in Swift is with structs.

- A struct lets you combine variables, constants, and functions into your own custom type. Variables and constants in a struct are called properties, and functions in a struct are called methods.

- A struct automatically synthesizes an initializer for you, called a memberwise initializer. It allows all the properties of the struct to be given a value when an instance of the struct is created.

- Structs in Swift are value types. This means if you assign an instance of one to another variable, you're creating a brand new copy of it with all the same data stored.

- Instead of relying on a synthesized memberwise initializer, you can create as many of your own initializers as you like, as long as your initializers always end with every property of the struct being assigned a value.

- Once you've written an initializer of your own for a struct, the synthesized initializer is no longer available.

Static properties make structures more flexible

You can declare a property to be **static** when you create a struct. This tells Swift that you want it to **share the value** of that property across **all** instances of that specific struct.

If you wanted to add a count for how many Pizza types had been initialized, you could do this:

```
struct Pizza {
    var name: String
    var ingredients: [String]
    var dessertPizza: Bool
    static var count = 0

    init() {
        name = "Cheese"
        ingredients = ["Cheese"]
        dessertPizza = false
        Pizza.count += 1
    }

    init(name: String, ingredients: [String], dessertPizza: Bool) {
        self.name = name
        self.ingredients = ingredients
        self.dessertPizza = dessertPizza
        Pizza.count += 1
    }
}

var pizza1 = Pizza()
var pizza2 = Pizza()
print(Pizza.count)
```

A static property is declared by using the static keyword. This property represents the count of Pizzas initialized.

In the initializer, the static property gets incremented. You refer to the struct using the struct's name to get a handle on the count property.

The count needs to be incremented in both possible initializers, so it's an accurate representation of what it's counting.

The count property belongs to the struct, not the instances of the struct, so we access it using the struct Pizza.

Brain Power

Which of the following examples of a static property are valid? If it's not valid, why isn't it? See if you can figure it out.

☐
```swift
struct Car {
    static let maxSpeed = 150
    var color: String
}
```

☐
```swift
struct Job {
    var title: String
    var location: String
    static salary = 60000
}
```

☐
```swift
struct Spaceship {
    static let ships = [Spaceship]()
    init() {
        Spaceship.ships.append(self)
    }
    static func testEngines() {
        for _ in ships {
            print("Testing engine!")
        }
    }
}
```

☐
```swift
struct Cactus {
    static var cactuses = 0
    var type: String
    init(cactusType: String) {
        type = cactusType
        cactuses += 1
    }
}
```

Access control and structs

When you create a structure, by default there is nothing stopping you from accessing any of the properties held by the struct directly.

So, if your Pizza struct looked like this:

```
struct Pizza {
        var name: String
        var chefsNotes: String
}
```

And you created a Pizza:

```
var hawaiian = Pizza(name: "Hawaiian",
             chefsNotes: "A tasty pizza, but pineapple
                              isn't for everyone!")
```

There would be nothing stopping you from accessing the chefsNotes property of an *instance* of the structure, and doing anything you like with it:

```
print(hawaiian.chefsNotes)
```

Access control gives you the capability to restrict access to a property or method inside your structs.

If you apply the **private** keyword to a property (or method), it can't be accessed from outside the struct.

So, if you updated the definition of chefsNotes to this:

```
private var chefsNotes: String
```

...then you might expect everything to work, except for accessing the chefsNotes property from outside the structure—but adding the private keyword means that you can't access chefsNotes as part of the automatically synthesized initializer, so you'll need to create your own.

'Pizza' initializer is inaccessible due to 'private' protection level

Brain Power

Use your knowledge of access control, structures, and creating your own initializers to complete the code segment below.

We need to add an initializer that allows us to define the chef's note when an instance of the Pizza struct is created, because of the access control on the `chefsNotes` property.

```
struct Pizza {
    var name: String
    private var chefsNotes: String

    init(_____) {
        _____ = _____
        _____ = _____
    }
}
```

With the initializer in place, create a few new instances of Pizza, and test out your ability (or inability) to access the `chefsNotes` property.

```
print(hawaiian.chefsNotes)
```

'chefsNotes' is inaccessible due to 'private' protection level

Bullet Points

- Structures are value types. This means that a struct's value is copied around on assignment, initialization, or argument passing.

- Most of Swift's built-in types (String, Array, and so on) are also value types.

- Any type you create with a struct is a value type, too.

- You can create your own initializers for the types you create with structs using the `init` keyword.

- You can have as many initializers as you like. The only requirement is that all properties of the struct have a value by the time the initializer ends.

- The synthesized initializer is no longer available if you decide to create your own.

- A property can be flagged using the `static` keyword. This means that property shares its value across all instances of the struct.

- A property can also be flagged using the `private` keyword. This means it canot be accessed from outside the struct in question.

~~Functions~~ ⌄inside structures
Methods

Functions are great; you already know that. But what's even better is putting functions inside your structures. When a function is inside a structure it's referred to as a **method**.

Methods are declared with the same keyword as functions, `func`, and are otherwise exactly the same as functions. You just *refer to them as methods when they're in a struct*.

Functions are discrete units of code. Functions inside something else are methods of the thing they're inside.

Sharpen your pencil

Think about everything you've learned about functions, and apply that to adding a method to a Pizza struct.

Take your simple Pizza struct and add a method named `getPrice` that takes no parameters and returns the total cost of the pizza as an integer.

```
struct Pizza {
    var name: String
    var ingredients: [String]

    _____
    _____
    _____
    _____
    _____
    _____
    _____
}
```

> I like to keep it simple... my pizzas cost $2 per ingredient. Good deal, right?

Once you've implemented your method, create a few Pizzas and test it with them:

```
var hawaiian = Pizza(name: "Hawaiian", ingredients: ["Ham", "Cheese", "Pineapple"])
var meat = Pizza(name: "Meaty Goodness",
          ingredients: ["Pepperoni", "Chicken", "Ham", "Tomato", "Pulled Pork"])
var cheese = Pizza(name: "Cheese", ingredients: ["Cheese"])
```

⟶ Answer on page 178.

Changing properties using methods

This is all part of Swift's commitment to safety.

If you want to create ***a method that changes a property*** inside a struct, you need to do a tiny bit of extra work to allow it.

Consider the following Pizza struct:

```
struct Pizza {
        var name: String
        var ingredients: [String]
}
```

If you wanted to write a method to allow the name to be updated, it's nice and straightforward to add one inside the struct:

```
func setName(newName: String) {
        self.name = newName
}
```

But if you do this, you'll find that it won't work. You'll get an error.

Mark method 'mutating' to make 'self' mutable

The error will tell you exactly what you need to do: you need to mark your method as **mutating** in order to make things in the self scope mutable (that is, make them able to be modified).

Update the method:

```
mutating func setName(newName: String) {
        self.name = newName
}
```

A mutating method cannot call a non-mutating method. It can call other mutating methods, though.

And take the brand new setName method out for a spin:

```
var hawaiian = Pizza(name: "Hawaiian", ingredients: ["Pineapple", "Ham", "Cheese"])
hawaiian.setName(newName: "Pineapple Abomination")
```

Just using the mutating keyword will stop Swift from letting you use the method on constant structs.

Swift takes your word that it's a mutating method. So even if the method doesn't touch properties at all, you won't be able to call it on a struct that's created as a constant.

Sharpen your pencil
Solution

From page 176.

```swift
struct Pizza {
    var name: String
    var ingredients: [String]

    func getPrice() -> Int {
        return ingredients.count * 2
    }
}


var hawaiian = Pizza(name: "Hawaiian", ingredients: ["Ham", "Cheese",
    "Pineapple"])
var meat = Pizza(name: "Meaty Goodness", ingredients: ["Pepperoni",
    "Chicken", "Ham", "Tomato", "Pulled Pork"])
var cheese = Pizza(name: "Cheese", ingredients: ["Cheese"])

var hawaiianPrice = hawaiian.getPrice()

var meatPrice = meat.getPrice()

var cheesePrice = cheese.getPrice()


print("The hawaiian costs \(hawaiianPrice), the meat costs \(meatPrice),
and the cheese costs \(cheesePrice)")
```

Computed properties

The properties you've created so far have been **stored properties**, because they're stored values within the entity.

Computed properties are another kind of property: *computed properties can run code to determine their value.*

> Again, I'm no programmer, but it sounds like you could use these computed property thingies to make it easier for me to tell if a pizza is lactose free?

The chef is correct, you could make checking if a pizza is lactose free easier using a computed property.

Imagine you have a simple Pizza struct (it should look very familiar by now), and you've added a nice Bool, which you'll use to flag if a pizza contains cheese or not:

```
struct Pizza {
    var name: String
    var ingredients: [String]
    var lactoseFree: Bool
}
```

This makes it easy to say whether a Pizza is lactose free or not:

```
var hawaiian = Pizza(name: "Hawaiian",
            ingredients: ["Pineapple", "Ham", "Cheese"],
    lactoseFree: false)
```

But it's still reliant on whoever ends up coding instances of the Pizzas to remember to use the `lactoseFree` flag correctly. That's not what programming is all about! Especially Swift programming.

Enter **computed properties**.

Anatomy of a Computed Property

Computed properties are **properties that compute their value** when they're accessed.

```
struct FavNumber {
    var number: Int

    var isMeaningOfLife: Bool {
        if number == 42 {
            return true
        } else {
            return false
        }
    }
}
```

❶ Declare a property

Computed properties have a name and a type, just like stored properties do.

❷ Provide some code to set the value

The code needs to set the value of the property. It does this by returning the value. Looks a bit like a closure, doesn't it?

Go on then. Make it work for checking if a pizza is lactose free.

Exercise

Modify the `lactoseFree` property of your Pizza struct to automatically determine whether the pizza is lactose free or not, using a computed property.

Test out your newly modified Pizza struct with the following Pizzas and print statements:

```
var hawaiian =
    Pizza(name: "Hawaiian",
        ingredients: ["Pineapple","Ham","Cheese"])
print(hawaiian.lactoseFree)

var vegan =
    Pizza(name: "Vegan",
        ingredients: ["Artichoke", "Red Pepper",
                        "Tomato", "Basil"])
print(vegan.lactoseFree)
```

→ Answer on page 185.

Sometimes **it's useful to run some code** *before* **or** *after* **a property changes.**
Property observers are the Swift magic that lets you do just that.

Imagine your Pizza struct also comes with a quantity:

```
struct Pizza {
    var name: String
    var ingredients: [String]
    var quantity: Int
}
```

It would be useful if, every time the quantity changed, a message was displayed telling the chef how many pizzas of that type were left.

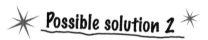 **Possible solution 1** ⟵ *This one is more of a red herring than a possible solution, if we're being honest.*

You could write a method that can be used to set the `quantity` property, and inside that method you could print out the current quantity. This would be fine, but kind of defeats the point of Swift's easily accessible properties.

✳ Possible solution 2 ✳

You could also use a property observer. Property observers let you define some code that runs either before or after a property changes. Clean and Swifty.

Possible solution 2 is the winner, in this case.

Creating a property observer

Property observers are defined using the `didSet` or `willSet` keyword. `didSet` lets you define code that gets run after a property has changed, and `willSet` lets you define code that gets run before a property has changed.

If you update the `quantity` property definition to include `didSet`, you'll get a nice message every time the quantity changes:

```
var quantity: Int {
    didSet {
        print("The pizza \(name) has \(quantity) pizzas left.")
    }
}
```

Now when you create a Pizza, and then change its quantity, you'll get a nice message: *The property observer won't be called when you create an instance of the struct only when it's modified after creation.*

```
var hawaiian = Pizza(name: "Hawaiian",
                ingredients: ["Pineapple", "Ham", "Cheese"], quantity: 10)
hawaiian.quantity -= 1
hawaiian.quantity -= 1
```

The pizza Hawaiian has 9 pizzas left.
The pizza Hawaiian has 8 pizzas left.

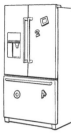

Code Magnets

See if you can assemble the magnets into some useful code. Be careful; a few extra magnets got mixed in, and some might get used more than once.

```
let blueTeamScore: Int {
```

```
struct BoardGame {
```

```
int redTeamScore: Int {
```

```
print("Blue Team increased score!")
```

```
didSet {
```

```
print("Red Team increased score!")
```

```
int blueTeamScore: Int {
```

```
let redTeamScore: Int {
```

```
}
```

A property observer always responds to changes in a property's value. This means property observers will trigger even if the newly set value is exactly the same as the previously set (current) value.

→ Answer on page 192.

Relax

You might not ever need to use willSet. *It's far more likely that you'll use* didSet.

Which keyword you use depends on whether you want to do something after a change to your property has happened (didSet) or before (willSet). The things you'll find yourself doing will, more than likely, involve reacting to a change, not taking action before the change has happened (no matter how inevitable the change is).

For example, if you're updating some sort of user interface, or saving something, it's likely to be more useful to do that after whatever is changing has changed.

You might find yourself using willSet if you need a before and an after state of a value in order to do something: you can use willSet to capture and preserve the before state in order to do something with it afterward. This is particularly useful in user interface animation, for example.

Getters and setters for computed properties

Computed properties have another trick up their proverbial sleeves: **getters and setters**. Taking a detour from pizza for a moment, consider a struct representing temperatures.

```
struct Temperature {
    var celsius: Float = 0.0
    var fahrenheit: Float {
        return ((celsius * 1.8) + 32.0)
    }
}
```

This is a stored property, representing the celsius value.

This is a computed property, like you've made before, that calculates fahrenheit based on the celsius value.

It can be used as follows:

```
var temp = Temperature(celsius: 40)
print(temp.fahrenheit)
```

The fahrenheit computed property could also be expressed in this form, using the **get** keyword:

```
struct Temperature {
    var celsius: Float = 0.0
    var fahrenheit: Float {
        get {
            return ((celsius * 1.8) + 32.0)
        }
    }
}
```

The get keyword (and the computed property syntax by default) makes the computed property readable, and gives you the opportunity to provide code that computes its values.

You can calculate fahreinheit given celsius by multiplying the value by 1.8 and adding 32.

Bullet Points

- Getters use the get keyword. Getters let you read a property from elsewhere.

- You can also provide syntax that computes the value of a property inside the getter syntax.

- Setters use the set keyword. Setters let you write to a property from elsewhere.

Implementing a setter

A setter can also be added to any computed property, using the `set` keyword:

```
struct Temperature {
    var celsius: Float = 0.0
    var fahrenheit: Float {
        get {
            return ((celsius * 1.8) + 32.0)
        }
        set {
            self.celsius = ((newValue - 32) / 1.8)
        }
    }
}
```

The set keyword makes the computed property writable.

You can pass a local name inside parentheses after the set keyword, or use the default name: newValue.

It can then be used as follows:

```
var temp = Temperature(celsius: 40)
print(temp.fahrenheit)
temp.fahrenheit = 55
print(temp.celsius)
```

We're looking at you, Java.

Watch it!

Other programming languages have "getters" and "setters" everywhere. Swift's are different.

In Swift, getters and setters are not the same as in most other languages. In some languages, when you have an instance variable (a property, to speak in Swift terms at this point in your learning), you often need to create special methods to access and modify those instance variables. These are what many other programming languages call getters and setters. Swift takes care of that for you.

Exercise
Solution

From page 180.

Modify the `lactoseFree` property of your Pizza struct to automatically determine whether the pizza is lactose free or not, using a computed property:

```
struct Pizza {
    var name: String
    var ingredients: [String]
    var lactoseFree: Bool {
        if ingredients.contains("Cheese") {
            return false
        } else {
            return true
        }
    }
}
```

You learned about the `contains` method, available on arrays, back in Chapter 3. Of course, this assumes that cheese is the only possible lactose-containing ingredient...

You can test out your newly modified Pizza struct with the following Pizzas and print statements:

```
var hawaiian =
    Pizza(name: "Hawaiian",
        ingredients: ["Pineapple","Ham","Cheese"])
print(hawaiian.lactoseFree)

var vegan =
    Pizza(name: "Vegan",
        ingredients: ["Artichoke", "Red Pepper",
                        "Tomato", "Basil"])
print(vegan.lactoseFree)
```

Behind
the Scenes

Swift Strings are actually structs

We mentioned it earlier, but it's important to emphasize that Swift's Strings are actually implemented as structs. ***Structs are really lightweight***, under the hood. This means it's easy to create them, destroy them, and forget about them as much as you want without getting stressed about performance.

Swift's String has lots of useful methods that do useful things, including `count`, `uppercase`, and `isEmpty`.

Because a String is implemented as a struct, all the functionality for these myriad **instance methods** can be encapsulated within the implementation of String. It's nice and neat this way.

```
352    public struct String {
353        public // @SPI(Foundation)
```

Who Does What?

Match the output to the line that produced it:

var myString = "Pineapple belongs on pizza"

PINEAPPLE BELONGS ON PIZZA	myString.hasPrefix("p")
true	myString.uppercased()
26	myString += "!"
false	myString.contains("Pineapple")
Pineapple belongs on pizza!	myString.count

⟶ Answers on page 190.

The case for lazy properties

Sometimes it's useful to be lazy. Lazy properties are properties that are only created when needed, instead of when the type defined by the struct they're in is initialized.

Consider a Pizza struct, with a computed property that represents how long the pizza takes to cook:

```
struct Pizza {
    var cookingDuration = getCookingTime()
}

func getCookingTime() -> Int {
    print("getCookingTime() was called!")
    return 100
}


var hawaiian = Pizza()


print(hawaiian.cookingDuration)
```

This method just returns 100 here, but imagine if it needed to perform lots of complex work to figure out a cooking time. That could be resource-intensive.

Let's walk through what happens in this code:

1 The Pizza struct is defined.

2 A getCookingTime() method is defined, which displays a message and returns an integer.

3 An instance of Pizza named hawaiian is created, which causes the getCookingTime() method to be called because it's needed to store a value inside the cookingDuration property required by this new instance of the Pizza struct.

4 The cookingDuration of the hawaiian instance of the Pizza struct is printed.

This is a bit inconvenient when what we really need is the cookingDuration to be calculated when it's accessed, rather than on the creation of an instance of the struct; it makes more sense like that if cookingDuration is used when the customer is on the way to the restaurant.

Using lazy properties

If we actually would prefer the `cookingDuration` to be computed when, for example, the customer is about to arrive at the shop (to prevent burning the pizza), or if the process of computing the `cookingDuration` was resource-intensive, we might want it to be deferred until it's needed.

We can do this by adding the **lazy** keyword to the property:

```
struct Pizza {
    lazy var cookingDuration = getCookingTime()
}


func getCookingTime() -> Int {
    print("getCookingTime() was called!")
    return 100
}


var hawaiian = Pizza()


print(hawaiian.cookingDuration
```

Let's walk through what happens in this version of the code:

1 As before, the Pizza struct is defined.

2 As before, a `getCookingTime()` method is defined that displays a message and returns an integer.

3 An instance of Pizza named `hawaiian` is created. The property `cookingDuration` is not computed because it's marked as **lazy**.

4 The `cookingDuration` of the `hawaiian` instance of the Pizza struct is printed. This causes the `cookingDuration` to be computed, which in turn causes the `getCookingTime()` method to be called.

The lazy keyword means that it's only created and computed when it's accessed.

Brain Power

Run the above code, with and without the **lazy** keyword on the `cookingDuration` property.

When does the print statement inside `getCookingTime` get executed?

How is that impacted by the use of the `lazy` keyword?

Observe how the `lazy` keyword impacts when Swift creates the `cookingDuration` property (and thus calls the `getCookingTime` method).

Structcross

We've strategically incorporated all the key points you've learned about Swift structures into this crossword. Use it as a palate cleanser before continuing.

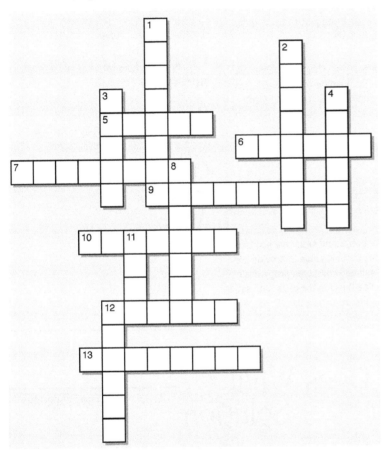

Down

1) A property _____ lets you run code before or after a property changes.
2) A _____ method can change the value of a struct's property.
3) This type copies its data around.
4) _____ properties have a value inside them.
8) A _____ value is one that is predefined inside the struct.
11) This keyword is used to create an initializer inside a struct.
12) This built-in Swift type represents some characters and is implemented as a struct.

Across

5) This built-in Swift type represents an unordered set of things, and is implemented using a struct.
6) We call functions this when they're inside a struct.
7) _____ properties run code to determine their value.
9) This type shares a single copy of its data.
10) The keyword we use to invoke the access control system and prevent a property or method being used outside of the structure it's in.
12) A property that shares its value across all instances of the struct it's within.
13) We call variables this when they're inside a struct.

⟶ Answers on page 191.

there are no
Dumb Questions

Q: What's the point of access control when I'm writing my own code? Why can't I just enforce access to things based on what I access? I could turn off the access control if I wanted to, so why have it at all?

A: Well, the first and most obvious answer is that sometimes code you write won't only be used by you. But that's a bit of an easy out. Realistically, access control lets you control and determine how, for example, a certain value might be used. If something needs careful treatment, access control makes sure you treat it carefully. You may not always be alert when dealing with your own code, or even remember your exact thought process when you wrote it.

Q: Why are lazy properties called lazy?

A: It's about when the property is computed—they're lazy because computation is deferred until the value is needed. "Lazy" is short for "on demand."

Q: Is everything just a struct under the hood in Swift?

A: Not everything, but most things, yes. Structs in Swift are far more powerful than they are in other languages, and Swift makes extensive use of them.

Q: What about classes?

A: We'll get to that, but almost everything you might have used a class for in another language can be a struct in Swift.

Q: So, getter and setter are just the Swift terms for being able to provide code that can set/read computed properties? They aren't subject to the getter and setter requirements from, say, Java?

A: That's right. Getters and setters in Java are when you write methods that let you access a variable inside something, or set a variable's value inside something. Swift automatically makes that possible, so a getter and setter in Swift refer to something a little different.

Q: Why are functions called methods inside structs?

A: Because they're methods of operating on something. They're not just discrete pieces of functionality anymore.

Q: What's with all the pineapple on the pizzas?

A: It's great, isn't it?

Who Does What?
Solution

From page 186.

Match the output to the line that produced it:

```
var myString = "Pineapple belongs on pizza"
```

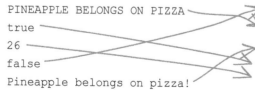

```
PINEAPPLE BELONGS ON PIZZA        myString.hasPrefix("p")
true                              myString.uppercased()
26                                myString += "!"
false                             myString.contains("Pineapple")
Pineapple belongs on pizza!       myString.count
```

structures, properties,

Structcross Solution

From page 189.

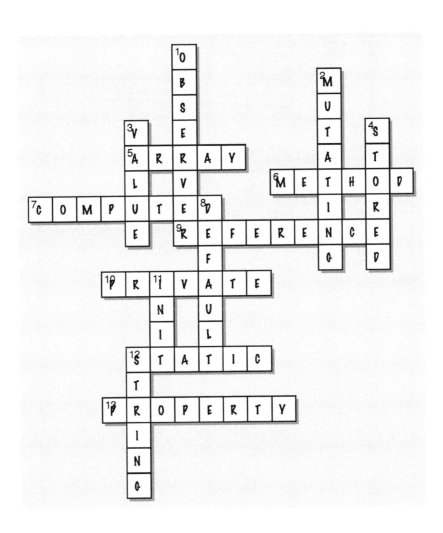

Code Magnets Solution

From page 182.

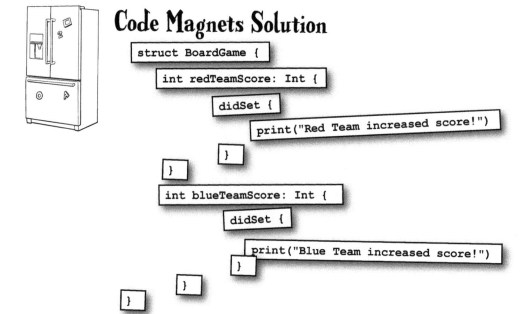

```
struct BoardGame {
    int redTeamScore: Int {
        didSet {
            print("Red Team increased score!")
        }
    }
    int blueTeamScore: Int {
        didSet {
            print("Blue Team increased score!")
        }
    }
}
```

7 classes, actors, and inheritance

Inheritance Is Always a Thing

Sometimes inheritance is more trouble than it's worth. There's always tinkering to fix things and make them work.

Structs showed us how useful it can be to build custom types.

But Swift has a number of other tricks up its sleeve, including **classes**. Classes are **similar** to structs: they let you make **new data types that have properties and methods** within them. However, in addition to being **reference types**—instances of a specific class share a single copy of their data (unlike structs, which are value types and get copied)—**classes support inheritance**. Inheritance allows one class to build upon the features of another.

A struct by any other name (that name: a class)

A **class** is very similar to a struct, with a few important differences:

This means you have to create your own initializer when you make a class.

✳ A class does not come with a memberwise initializer, and a struct does.

Structs cannot inherit.

✳ A class can inherit from another class. This gives it access to its properties and methods.

It can only inherit from a class. There's also no multiple inheritance, if you've come from another language.

A class is a reference type. A struct is a value type.

✳ A copy of a class just points to the same set of shared data. A copied struct is a unique duplicate.

A struct cannot have a deinitializer, and doesn't need one.

✳ A class has a deinitializer, which gets called when it is destroyed. A struct does not.

✳ A variable property in a constant class can be modified, but not in a constant struct.

This is a class. It represents a pizza and stores a name (as a String) and a list of ingredients (Strings).

```
class Pizza {
    var name: String
    var ingredients: [String]

    init(name: String, ingredients: [String]) {
        self.name = name
        self.ingredients = ingredients
    }
}
```

It has an initializer, because classes require you to provide an initializer.

This is a struct. It represents a pizza as well, and stores a name (as a String) and a list of ingredients (Strings).

```
struct Pizza {
    var name: String
    var ingredients: [String] = []
}
```

So I always need to write an initializer for my classes?

If your class has properties, then you must create an initializer. So, yes, if it has properties.

When you're writing your class, *if you include any properties at all, then you need to provide an initializer*.

So, if you wrote a class to represent types of plants, like this:

```
class Plant {
    var name: String
    var latinName: String
    var type: String

    init(name: String, latinName: String, type: String) {
        self.name = name
        self.latinName = latinName
    }
}
```

— Defining an initializer.

You could then create instances of that class like this:

```
let bay = Plant(name: "Bay laurel",
                latinName: "Laurus nobilis",
                type: "Shrub")
```

This looks exactly the same as what you'd do for a struct.

The rules for creating an initializer are the same as for a struct. You just have to have one.

Inheritance and classes

Sometimes you need to create similar but slightly different things, or objects that share some properties and methods, but are a little bit different. ***Inheritance* is a feature of Swift's classes that allows you to create a class that's *based* on an existing class, and *adds* its own features.**

Our Plant class lets us create a variety of Plants:

```
class Plant {
    var name: String
    var latinName: String
    var type: String


    init(name: String, latinName: String, type: String) {
        self.name = name
        self.latinName = latinName
        self.type = type
    }
}
```

But we can *specialize* it by creating a new class called Succulent. Our Succulent class inherits all the properties from Plant, as well as its initializer, so it doesn't even need any code inside:

Succulent is the child class.

Plant is the parent class.

```
class Succulent: Plant {


}
```

No code is needed here. Everything is inherited from the parent class.

```
let americanAloe = Succulent(name: "American aloe",
                             latinName: "Agave americana",
                                      type: "Succulent")
```

Bullet Points

- A class can inherit from another class. This is called inheritance, or subclassing.

- A class that is being inherited from is called a parent class, or superclass.

- A class that inherits from a class is called a child class.

- All properties and methods, including initializers, are inherited by the child class.

- A child class cannot access private variables or methods.

I'm assuming it's not a dream to be able to provide an initializer within the child class. That seems sensible at this point. But can I really do that?

DIY Initializers

(Again)

It's actually really easy to make your own initializers.

We can give Succulent its own initializer, but we don't have to unless it requires it.

If a child class introduces new elements that would need to be initialized, then it needs it own initializer. Another reason we might want to give it its own initializer is to provide values to the parent class's properties based around the fact that it's a Succulent.

Because we know the `type` will always be `"Succulent"`, we can create a new initializer for Succulent that only requires a `name` and a `latinName`, and then use that information (plus the already known `type`) to call `super.init()`, which calls the parent class's initializer:

The type is preset, and passed through to the parent class's initializer.

```
class Succulent: Plant {

    init(name: String, latinName: String) {

        super.init(name: name, latinName: latinName, type: "Succulent")

    }
}
```

You must always call the parent class's initializer from child classes.

You can then create a new Succulent without having to pass in a type:

```
let americanAloe = Succulent(name: "American aloe", latinName: "Agave americana")
```

Watch it!

Classes in Swift do not come with a memberwise initializer.

You always have to provide your own initializer when you create a class, unlike a struct.

Classes in Swift do not have a memberwise initializer because of their inheritance features: if you built a class that inherited from another class, and then that class later had some additional properties added, the code in the child class might no longer work.

The rule here is simple: if you make a class, you must always write the initializer yourself. Thus, you're always aware of, and responsible for, updating the initializer to reflect any changes to the class's properties.

The exception to this rule is if you subclass something and don't need an initializer because the parent's initializer has you covered.

Brain Power

Practice making some new instances of Succulent. Create the following Succulents using our Succulent child class:

- Elephant's foot (Beaucarnea recurvata)
- Calico hearts (Adromischus maculatus)
- Queen victoria (Agave victoria regina)

Once you've done that, create a new child class to represent a Tree. A Tree's type is always "Tree", and its name always has "tree" suffixed to the end of it:

```
class Tree: Plant {



                  }
```

Once you've created a new Tree child class, create some instances of Tree. Create the following Trees using your new Tree child class:

- European larch (Larix decidua)
- Red pine (Pinus resinosa)
- Northern beech (Fagus sylvatica)

~~Replacing~~ Overriding methods

The initializer is not the only method you can replace when you create a subclass: you can also replace any of the methods in the parent class. When you do this, it's called **overriding**.

Here's our Plant class:

```
class Plant {
    var name: String
    var latinName: String
    var type: String

    init(name: String, latinName: String, type: String) {
        self.name = name
        self.latinName = latinName
        self.type = type
    }

    func printInfo() {
        print("I'm a plant!")
    }
}
```

The Plant class has a method, printInfo, that prints some info saying it's a plant.

Here's our Succulent child class, overriding a method of the parent:

```
class Succulent: Plant {
    init(name: String, latinName: String) {
        super.init(name: name, latinName: latinName, type: "Succulent")
    }

    override func printInfo() {
        print("I'm a Succulent!")
    }
}
```

You could also then call the parent's implementation of printInfo() by calling super.printInfo(), if you wanted.

We override the printInfo method of the parent class. This changes the implementation of this specific method when it's used from the child class.

Relax

You have to use the override keyword when you want to override a method.

There's no risk of you accidentally overriding a method by creating something with the same name.

If you accidentally wrote a method in a child class that had the same name as a method in the parent class, and you didn't use the override keyword, Swift would give you an error:

```
func printInfo() {

    Overriding declaration requires an 'override' keyword
```

You'll also get an error if you try to override something that doesn't exist in the parent class:

```
override func printDetails() {

    Method does not override any method from its superclass
```

Sharpen your pencil

Here's a class representing a (space) alien. It has a method that can be called to drink.

```
class Alien {
    func drink() {
        print("Drinking some alien wine!")
    }
}
```

Create a new child class, for a Klingon (a type of alien), and override the drink method to make a Klingon do something Klingon-y when it drinks (like shouting "ragh!" and drinking some blood wine).

⟶ **Answers on page 205.**

Brain Power

You can also override any of the properties in the parent class, if you need to. Add a new computed property to the Plant class to store a description:

```
var description: String {
    return "This is a \(name) (\(latinName)) \(type)."
}
```

Then, update the Succulent child class to include an `age` property that belongs to it:

```
var age: Int
```

Next, your turn:

> You'll need to update the initializer in the Succulent class to take an age as a parameter. Then use the value passed in to update `self.age` (the new `age` property you just added).

> Once you've done that, in the Succulent class, override the `description` property using the same override syntax as we used for methods, and return a new description that takes into account the Succulent's `age` property.

You might find it helpful to know that you can access the properties of the superclass as follows:

```
super.name
```

Once you're done, you should be able to create a Succulent:

```
let americanAloe =
    Succulent(name: "American aloe",
              latinName: "Agave americana",
                  age: 5)
```

And then print its `description` property, and see the age included:

```
print(americanAloe.description)
```
        ↘
```
This is a American aloe (Agave americana)
    Succulent. It is 5 years old.
```

Under the hood...

Classes are reference types. A reference type is a type whose instances always point to the same object in memory.

In Swift, something can be a value type or a reference type.

Classes are **reference types**. This means that if you assign them to another variable or constant, you're **referring to the same object in memory**, and *not* creating a copy.

For example, if you take the American aloe Succulent from the previous page:

```
let americanAloe =
        Succulent(name: "American aloe",
                    latinName: "Agave americana")
```

And then *assign* the reference to a new variable:

```
var anotherAloe = americanAloe
```

Then modify that variable:

```
anotherAloe.name = "Sentry plant"
```

You have modified *the original and only instance of* Succulent, which now has the name property set to "Sentry plant".

You can check this using the print statement:

```
print(americanAloe.name)
print(anotherAloe.name)
```

Brain Power

Try reimplementing Succulent as a struct. Once you've done that, create some instances of the new struct-powered Succulent, then assign it to a new variable, then modify that variable. What happens to the original instance? This is the difference between value and reference types.

Watch it!

Value types vs. reference types can be confusing.

The copying behavior of value types (like structs) is one of the primary reasons that Swift encourages you to use structs for the majority of your custom types. There's something to be said for each area of your program having its own copy of data, and not risking it changing or becoming inconsistent.

Final classes

Sometimes it's useful to prevent a class from being inherited from. The **final** keyword lets you do this. Final classes ***cannot*** have child classes, so they cannot have their methods overridden. Final classes need to be used the same way they're written.

```
final class Garden {
    var plants: [Plant] = []

    init(plants: [Plant]) {
        self.plants = plants
    }

    func listPlants() {
        for plant in plants {
            print(plant.name)
        }
    }
}
```

Final classes lock a class down, so it can't be subclassed. It's a good way of avoiding code drama.

If you try to inherit from a final class, Swift will give you an error.

```
    class RooftopGarden: Garden {
```

Inheritance from a final class 'Garden'

```
    }
```

There's a persistent rumor that final classes perform better in Swift.

This used to be true: marking a class final meant the Swift compiler knew it would never be changed, so it could perform some optimizations that otherwise wouldn't be possible.

This is sometimes true, but unless your code needs every millisecond to count, it's not important since Swift 5. A final class just cannot be subclassed.

From page 201.

Sharpen your pencil
Solution

```
class Alien {
        func drink() {
                print("Drinking some alien wine!")
        }
}


class Klingon: Alien {
        override func drink() {
                print("Drinking blood wine! Ragh!")
        }
}


let martok = Klingon()
martok.drink()
```

Swift also has a thing called an Actor, which looks a lot like a Class.

Actors are a little beyond the scope of this book, but they basically function like a Class, except they are safe to use in a concurrent environment. What's that mean? It means that Swift does its best to make sure nothing can try and change data inside an Actor at the same time as something else is trying to do the same thing. That's a bit problem in concurrency. This is a valid actor, defining a Human with a maximum age:

```
actor Human {
    var maximumAge = 107

    func printAge() {
        print("Max age is currently \(maximumAge)")
    }
}
```

Actors are just like classes and structs, and can have properties and methods. And they're reference types, like classes, so they're more similar to a class than a struct.

We'll revisit them again, in a moment...

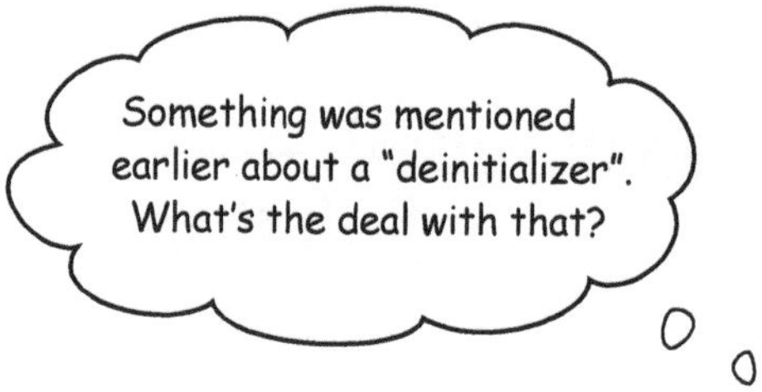

> Something was mentioned earlier about a "deinitializer". What's the deal with that?

Right. Classes can have deinitializers.

A deinitializer is code that gets run when an instance of a class gets destroyed.

A deinitializer is created using the **deinit** keyword, and otherwise works just like an initializer (without any parameters):

```
class Plant {

    var name: String

    var latinName: String

    var type: String


    init(name: String, latinName: String, type: String) {

        self.name = name

        self.latinName = latinName

        self.type = type

    }


    deinit {

        print("The plant '\(name)' has been deinitialized.")

    }

}
```

You can check that the deinitializer is run by using the _ keyword and creating a Plant (which will be immediately destroyed because of the way the _ works):

```
var _ = Plant(name: "Bay laurel",

              latinName: "Laurus nobilis", type: "Evergreen Tree")
```

    The plant 'Bay laurel' has been deinitialized.

So, why don't structs have a deinit?

Classes are a lot more complex than structs. That's the short answer.

The longer anwer is that classes have more complicated copying behavior, and several copies of a class could exist in your program, but all point to the same underlying instance. This means it's very hard to tell when a class instance has been destroyed (it's destroyed when the final variable that points to it has gone).

A deinitializer tells Swift when a class instance is destroyed. For a struct, that's easy to figure out: a stuct is gone when whatever owns it is no longer around.

Structs don't need deinitializers because each struct has its own copy of its data, and nothing magical needs to happen when a struct is destroyed.

Are we going to look at Actors again?

Sure, let's go back to Actors.

Remember the `Human` with the `maximumAge` from a few pages ago. It was an `Actor`, but we didn't really do anything `Actor`-specific with it.

Imagine if it needed to update the `maximumAge`, based on another `Human` who had lived longer. Here's what we'd add to do it safely, with an actor:

```
func updateMaximumAge(from other: Human) async {

    maximumAge = await other.maximumAge

}
```

You probably won't need to use Actors much at this stage. But it's worth knowing they exist.

The `aysnc` and `await` keywords basically tell Swift we want to send a quick message to the other instance of `Human` and ask it to let us know what its maximum age is at its earliest possible convenience. That might be immediate, or might be a long time in the future. This way we can safely work with it.

Automatic reference counting   ➚**ARC**

Behind the Scenes

Under the hood, Swift uses a process called **automatic reference counting**, or **ARC**.

<u>ARC keeps track of every single instance of a class that is created</u>. This is how Swift knows when to call the deinitializer.

Every time a copy of a class instance is made, *ARC adds 1 to its reference count*. Every time a copy of a class instance is destroyed, *ARC subtracts 1 from its reference count*.

Because of this, when the reference count hits 0, ARC can be sure that nothing is referring to that class any more, and Swift can call the deinitializer, which will destroy the object.

```swift
class Thing {
    let name: String
    init(name: String) {
        self.name = name
        print("Thing '\(name)' is now initialized.")
    }

    deinit {
        print("Thing '\(name)' is now deinitialized.")
    }
}

var object1: Thing?
var object2: Thing?
var object3: Thing?

object1 = Thing(name: "A Thing")
object2 = object1
object3 = object1
object1 = nil
object2 = nil
object3 = nil
```

1 Our class, Thing, has a name, and an initializer and a deinitializer which print out when they're called.

2 These three optional Things can be used to store a Thing, or `nil`.

3 We create a Thing instance, and assign it to `object1`. There is a strong reference from `object1` to the new Thing instance.

—Reference count for our instance of Thing is 1.

`Thing 'A Thing' is now initialized.`

4 At this point, there are now three strong references to our Thing instance (from `object1`, `object2`, and `object3`).

Reference count is 3.

5 Now we break two of the strong references (because we assign nil to two of the optional Things we created). Our Thing instance won't go away because there is still a strong reference from `object3`.

Reference count is 1.

6 With the last strong reference set to nil, there are no strong references left. So the instance of Thing will go away.

Reference count is 0.   `Thing 'A Thing' is now deinitialized.`

Beware
Mutability

It's important to remember **mutability** when you're dealing with classes.

A variable property in a struct that's declared as a constant cannot be changed.

However, **a constant class with a variable property will allow the property to be changed at any time**:

```
class Plant {
    var name: String

    init(name: String) {
        self.name = name
    }
}

let myPlant = Plant(name: "Vine")
print(myPlant.name)
myPlant.name = "Strawberry"
print(myPlant.name)
```

To prevent this, you'd need to make the property a constant using the let keyword.

This is an instance of our class, Plant, stored as a constant.

`Vine`

`Strawberry`

And, unlike structs, classes don't need the `mutating` keyword on methods that change properties.

Bullet Points

- Variable classes can have variable properties modified.

- Constant classes can have variable properties modfied.

- Variable structs can have variable properties modified.

- Constant structs cannot have variable properties modified.

- Actors are like Classes but are designed for concurrency and safety.

- Using async and await keywords, Actors can safely request data from other Actors in a concurrency-friendly way.

- If you make an Actor, you can do anything you like with its own properties and methods, but if you need to talk to another type you'll need to use async and await to get hold of it safely.

- That's because Actors guarantee they'll be safe during concurrency.

Swift Safety
Today's Lesson

Identity operators

As we've learned, classes in Swift are reference types. This means **it's possible for multiple variables or constants to refer to the same specific instance** of a class.

Because of this, it's useful to be able to:

1 Check whether two instances are the same instance, using the `===` operator. This operator checks if the two instances are identical, not equal. Equality is still checked using the == operator.

2 Check whether two instances are the same instance, using the `!==` operator. This operator checks if the two instances are not identical, not not equal, which is still checked using the ! = operator.

Again, we'll use our simple Plant class...

```
var plantOne = Plant(name: "Bay tree")
var plantTwo = Plant(name: "Lemon tree")
var plantThree = plantOne
```
...and a few Plants.

We can use === to check if two instances are the same.

1
```
if (plantOne === plantThree) {
    print("plantOne and plantThree ARE the same instance of Plant")
}
```

We can use !== to check if two instances are not the same.

2
```
if (plantOne !== plantTwo) {
    print("plantOne and plantTwo ARE NOT the same instance of Plant")
}
```

The identity and equality operators are quite different, despite the similar symbols used.

Watch it!

Identity is === (and !==) and equality is == (and !=). Identical means that the two variables or classes are exactly the same class instance. Equal means that two instances are equal in value.

there are no
Dumb Questions

Q: I used to program in another language. In that language, I had to create two separate files when I made custom classes (and structures): one for the interface, which defined what properties and methods the class had, and one for the implementation of those properties and methods. I don't seem to have to do that with Swift. What's up with that?

A: When you create a structure or a class in Swift, you do it in a single file. Swift automatically creates an external interface for other code to use. So, the short answer is: you don't need to make two files in Swift.

Q: Is an instance of a class an object? You don't seem to talk about objects much in Swift.

A: A instance of a class could be referred to as an object, but thst isn't very Swifty. Because structures and classes in Swift are pretty similar, it's more correct and more Swifty to refer to instances in Swift, not objects.

Q: What can classes do that structures can't?

A: Only classes can inherit. Structs can conform to protocols, but they can't inherit (you'll learn about protocols soon). Classes can be typecast, which lets you check the type of a class instance at runtime, but structs cannot. Classes can also have deinitializers, and structs cannot.

Q: Does using the `final` keyword on a class do anything other than stopping other classes from inheriting from it?

A: Nope, that's it.

Q: If two variables point at the same instance of a class, are they really both pointing to the same thing?

A: Yes. If you point two variables to the exact same instance of a class, then they're both pointing to the same place in memory, which means changing one will change the other. Because they're the same thing.

Q: It looks like I can modify variable properties in classes, even if the instance of the class it's in is a constant. Is that right?

A: Yes, that's correct. Classes don't behave the same way as structs when it comes to variable properties and constant instances.

Who Does What?

Test your knowledge of the keywords used for classes and inheritance, and match each keyword on the left to what it does on the right.

super   I can prevent a class being inherited from.

init   I declare a class is being defined.

final   I'm called when a class instance is removed from memory.

class   I can replace a method or property in a parent class with a new implementation.

override   I'm called to create a new class instance.

deinit   I'm used to refer to things in the parent class.

➤ Answers on page 218.

Fireside Chats

Tonight's talk: **So, should I use a struct or a class?**

Student:

Teacher:

So, Teacher, should I use a structure or a class? It's hard to tell the difference, and it's even harder to tell which one I should use. Can you give me your wisdom?

Use structures. Goodbye, Student.

Uh, Teacher, can you be a little more informative? That's helpful, but not as helpful as you think it might be.

Use structures, but learn about classes so you know that you should use structures. Goodbye, Student.

Teacher, please. You need to give me a little more than that.

Fine, Student, you win. Use structures by default. Structures are better for representing common kinds of data, and Swift's structures actually behave a lot like classes in other programming languages. Things like stored and computed properties, methods, and more are all the domain of classes in other languages. Not so in Swift.

That's very convincing, Teacher. Thank you. Is there anything else I should know?

Yes, never run with scissors. But seriously, structures make it a lot easier for you to consider the state of your program, without having to consider the entire program's state—structures, being value types, are just simpler. Don't modify structs a lot, though, as you can consume all the memory. Each modification is a copy, remember!

Classes are not always the best way to do things in Swift.

While it's very common to construct your programs using classes and inheritance in other programming languages, Swift's structures are so powerful that you'll rarely have a good reason to use a class instead.

Additionally, as you'll learn soon, Swift has yet another trick up its sleeve that makes inheritance seem less important: protocols.

BE the Swift Compiler

Each of the Swift code snippets on this page represents a complete Playground. Your job is to play Swift compiler, and determine whether each of these will run or not. If they run, what do they do?

A

```swift
class Airplane {
    func takeOff() {
        print("Plane taking off! Zoom!")
    }
}

class Airbus380: Airplane { }

let nancyBirdWalton = Airbus380()
nancyBirdWalton.takeOff()
```

B

```swift
class Sitcom {
    func playThemeSong() {
        print("<generic sitcom theme>")
    }
}

class Frasier: Sitcom {
    override func playThemeSong() {
        print("I hear the blues are calling...")
    }
}

let show = Frasier()
show.playThemeSong()
```

C

```swift
class Appliance { }

class Toaster: Appliance {
    func toastBread() {
        print("Bread now toasting!")
    }
}

let talkieToaster = Toaster()
talkieToaster.toastBread()
```

⟶ Answers on page 216.

Pool Puzzle

Your **job** is to take lines of code from the pool and place them into the blank lines in the Playground. You may **not** use the same line more than once, and you won't need to use all the lines. Your **goal** is to make the code that will generate the output shown.

```
class Dog {

    var age: Int
    var breed: String
    init(name: String, age: Int, breed: String) {
        self.name = name
        self.age = age


    }

        print("\(name) the  \(breed) barks loudly!")
    }
}
class Greyhound        {
                                    {

    }
                    bark() {
        print("\(name) the greyhound doesn't care to bark.")
    }
}
var baggins =
        Dog(name: "Bilbo Baggins", age: 12, breed: "Poodle")
var trevor = Greyhound(name: "Trevor", age: 10)


trevor.bark()
```

Bilbo Baggins the Poodle barks loudly!
Trevor is a greyhound, and doesn't care to bark.

↑ Output

Note: each thing from the pool can only be used once!

```
                     : Dog
    override func
                  let name: String
    super.init(name: name, age: age, breed: "Greyhound")
                          func bark()          baggins.bark()
    init(name: String, age: Int)
                          self.breed = breed
```

Answers on page 216.

Classcross

It's time to test your brain. Gently.

This is just a normal crossword, but all the clues relate to concepts we covered in this chapter. How closely were you paying attention?

Across

3) A _____ class cannot be inherited from.

4) This keeps track of every single instance of a class that is created.

7) Classes do not come with a _____ initializer. But structs do.

9) The === operator.

11) You can _____ methods in the parent class.

12) A class can _____ from another class.

Down

1) A struct is a _____ type.

2) If a class has _____, then it requires you to provide an initializer.

5) A class can have a _____, which gets called when it's destroyed.

6) A class is a _____ type.

8) Like a class, but not.

10) The child class inherits from this.

→ Answers on page 217.

Pool Puzzle Solution

From page 214.

```
class Dog {
    let name: String
    var age: Int
    var breed: String
    init(name: String, age: Int, breed: String) {
        self.name = name
        self.age = age
        self.breed = breed
    }
    func bark() {
        print("\(name) the  \(breed) barks loudly!")
    }
}
class Greyhound: Dog {
    init(name: String, age: Int) {
        super.init(name: name, age: age, breed: "Greyhound")
    }
    override func bark() {
        print("\(name) the greyhound doesn't care to bark.")
    }
}
var baggins =
        Dog(name: "Bilbo Baggins", age: 12, breed: "Poodle")
var trevor = Greyhound(name: "Trevor", age: 10)
baggins.bark()
trevor.bark()
```

BE the Swift Compiler Solution

From page 213.

They will all print something:

A prints "Plane taking off! Zoom!"

B prints "I hear the blues are calling..."

C prints "Bread now toasting!"

 Classcross
Solution

From page 215.

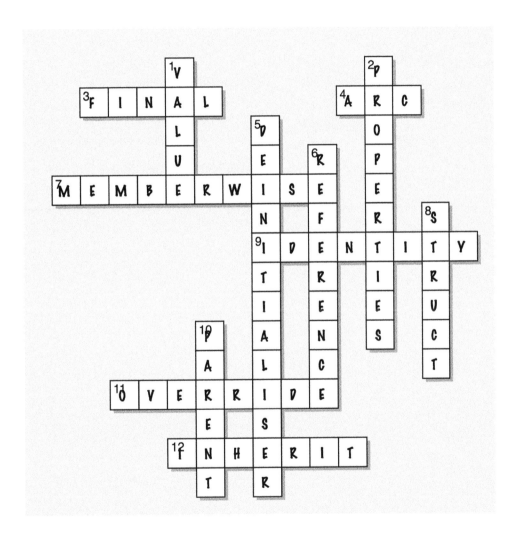

Who Does What? Solution

From page 211.

super ——————————————— I can prevent a class being inherited from.

init ——————————————— I declare a class is being defined.

final ——————————————— I'm called when a class instance is removed from memory.

class ——————————————— I can replace a method or property in a parent class with a new implementation.

override ——————————————— I'm called to create a new class instance.

deinit ——————————————— I'm used to refer to things in the parent class.

8 protocols and extensions

↓

A Swift Lesson in Protocol

You will also extend your knowledge! Get it? No? ↗
You will soon.

We're very focused on protocols. Conforming to them is an important part of every day. Knowing what to expect is vital.

You know all about classes and inheritance, but Swift has a few more tricks for structuring programs, and they're a lot Swiftier. Meet protocols and extensions. **Protocols in Swift let you define a blueprint specifying methods and properties** that are required for some purpose, or some piece of functionality. **A protocol is adopted** by a class, structure, or enumeration, and the actual implementation happens there. Types that provide the functionality needed, and adopt a protocol, are referred to as **conforming** to that protocol. **Extensions** simple let you **add new functionality to existing types**.

> I like classes and inheritance. I can see the power, but what if I need some functionality in all my subclasses, but it doesn't make sense for it to be in the parent class?

That's a fabulous question, and we're glad you asked.

Swift has a whole other way of building related logic and objects, using protocols and extensions. It's very *Swifty*, and it's kind of unique.

Protocols let you define a set of functionality that something can *conform* to, without having to provide the implementation until you conform something to it.

A protocol is kind of like a contract: if you define a protocol that requires something to have a property called `color`, storing a String representing a color, then any type that conforms to that protocol absolutely must, under penalty of not compiling, have a String property called `color`. A type can conform to more than one protocol to say that it will implement multiple sets of features.

Got it? You will.

Extensions allow you to add fully implemented new methods and properties to existing types, without having to modify the type's implementation itself.

Extensions are a great way to add useful functionality to classes and structs you *didn't* write (like, say, Swift's built-in types), as well as a great way to cleanly separate and lay out your own code.

We'll start with **protocols**.

Anatomy of a Protocol

Defining a protocol

A protocol starts with the protocol keyword...

...then a name. This protocol is named MyProtocol.

specialNumber must be gettable and settable.

The protocol specifies one property, named specialNumber (an Int).

```
protocol MyProtocol {
    var specialNumber: Int { get set }
    func secretMessage() -> String
}
```

And the protocol specifies one method, named secretMessage, which takes no parameters and returns a String.

Conforming to a protocol

Define a struct (or class). This one is named MyStruct.

Declare that you'll be conforming to a protocol by using its name.

Define any required properties from the protocol.

```
struct MyStruct: MyProtocol {
    var specialNumber: Int
    func secretMessage() -> String {
        return "Special number: \(specialNumber)"
    }
}
```

Define any required methods from the protocol. The specific implementation of the method is up to the struct or class, as long as it takes the parameters and returns what the protocol defines.

The Robot Factory

The problem:

We need to write some code that can represent all the different kinds of robots the Robot Factory can make. The issue is that there's a lot of variation between the types of robots.

Some robots have two legs, and two antennae.

Some robots have no legs, two antennae, two arms, and are stationary.

Some robots have one wheel, two arms, and two antennae.

Some robots have a laser gun, and two wheels.

Some robots have two arms, and three wheels.

Robots are by iconcheese from the Noun Project!

A solution:

It's a solution, not <u>the</u> solution, because there are many other ways you could solve this.

If we figure out all the features a robot can have, we can implement a protocol for each robot feature and use those protocols to implement types for the robots. There are a million different ways we could structure this kind of code, but this is a particularly *Swifty* way.

① Figure out all the possible robot features

Once we've identified possible robot features, we make a list.

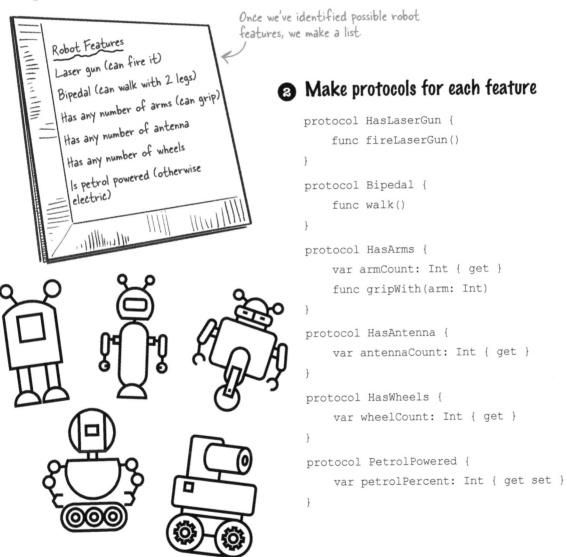

Robot Features
Laser gun (can fire it)
Bipedal (can walk with 2 legs)
Has any number of arms (can grip)
Has any number of antenna
Has any number of wheels
Is petrol powered (otherwise electric)

② Make protocols for each feature

```
protocol HasLaserGun {
    func fireLaserGun()
}

protocol Bipedal {
    func walk()
}

protocol HasArms {
    var armCount: Int { get }
    func gripWith(arm: Int)
}

protocol HasAntenna {
    var antennaCount: Int { get }
}

protocol HasWheels {
    var wheelCount: Int { get }
}

protocol PetrolPowered {
    var petrolPercent: Int { get set }
}
```

❸ Make the robot types

For each type of robot we create a struct, adhering to each protocol as needed. Then we can create individual instances of robots.

```
struct RobotOne: Bipedal, HasAntenna {
    var antennaCount: Int

    func walk() {
        print("Robot is now walking, using its legs.")
    }
}

var myFirstRobot = RobotOne(antennaCount: 2)
myFirstRobot.walk()
```

This robot is bipedal, and has antennae.

```
struct RobotTwo: HasArms, HasAntenna, PetrolPowered {
    var armCount: Int
    var antennaCount: Int
    var petrolPercent: Int

    func gripWith(arm: Int) {
        print("Now gripping with arm number \(arm)")
    }
}

var mySecondRobot = RobotTwo(armCount: 2,
                             antennaCount: 2,
                             petrolPercent: 100)
mySecondRobot.gripWith(arm: 1)
```

This robot has arms, antennae, and is petrol powered.

This robot has wheels, arms, and antennae.

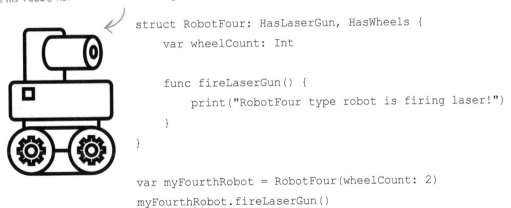

```
struct RobotThree: HasWheels, HasArms, HasAntenna {
    var wheelCount: Int
    var armCount: Int
    var antennaCount: Int

    func gripWith(arm: Int) {
        print("A RobotThree type robot is
                      now gripping with arm number \(arm)")
    }
}

var myThirdRobot = RobotThree(wheelCount: 1,
                               armCount: 2,
                               antennaCount: 2)
myThirdRobot.gripWith(arm: 2)
```

This robot has wheels and a laser gun.

```
struct RobotFour: HasLaserGun, HasWheels {
    var wheelCount: Int

    func fireLaserGun() {
        print("RobotFour type robot is firing laser!")
    }
}

var myFourthRobot = RobotFour(wheelCount: 2)
myFourthRobot.fireLaserGun()
```

```
struct RobotFive: HasArms, HasWheels {
    var armCount: Int
    var wheelCount: Int

    func gripWith(arm: Int) {
        print("Now gripping with arm number \(arm)")
    }
}

var myFifthRobot = RobotFive(armCount: 2, wheelCount: 3)
myFifthRobot.gripWith(arm: 2)
```

This robot has wheels and arms.

Brain Power

Implement the Robot protocols, and then create structs for the following robots:

- A robot that has has a laser gun, wheels, arms, and is petrol powered.
- A robot that is petrol powered and has arms.
- A robot that has a laser gun and is bipedal.
- A robot that has wheels and antennae.
- A robot that is petrol powered and has wheels.

Create an instance of each of these robots.

Create a brand new robot feature protocol, and add it to one of your existing robots.

Protocol inheritance

Remember this robot? RobotOne.

We had to conform to these two protocols to get the functionality we wanted.

```
struct RobotOne: Bipedal, HasAntenna {
    var antennaCount: Int

    func walk() {
        print("Robot is now walking, using its legs.")
    }
}

var myFirstRobot = RobotOne(antennaCount: 2)
myFirstRobot.walk()
```

And use its features like this.

Which means we could instantiate copies of this robot like this.

It's actually possible to take protocols one level deeper, and build protocols that inherit from other protocols.

Sometimes it can be easier to declare a protocol...

...that conforms to a bunch of other protocols.

```
protocol ReportingRobot: Bipedal, HasAntenna { }
```

We could specify additional required features of this new AssemblyRobot protocol, but in this case we don't need any, so we leave it empty.

```
struct RobotOne: ReportingRobot {
    var antennaCount: Int

    func walk() {
        print("Robot is now walking, using its legs.")
    }
}

var myFirstRobot = RobotOne(antennaCount: 2)
myFirstRobot.walk()
```

You can then just conform to the new protocol that inherits from the others., and away you go. Nice and clean.

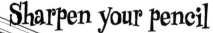

Sharpen your pencil

Given the following collection of protocols—for different vehicular capabilities, create a new vehicle, as a struct, that adheres to all four protocols and thus can fly, float, and move on land, and is petrol powered:

```
protocol Aircraft {
        func takeOff()
        func land()
}


protocol Watercraft {
        var buoyancy: Int { get }
}


protocol PetrolPowered {
        var petrolPercent: Int { get set }
        func refuel() -> Bool
}


protocol Landcraft {
        func drive()
        func brake() -> Bool
}
```

Answers on page 231.

Bullet Points

- Protocols let you describe a set of properties and methods that a struct or class must have.

- A struct or class can adopt any number of protocols, requiring it to implement the properties and methods the protocols it adheres to describe.

- Protocols are not used directly. They're just descriptions of something that can be created.

- A protocol can inherit from one or more other protocols. This is called protocol inheritance.

Mutating methods

If you need to specify a method that will modify the instance it belongs to in your protocol, you can use the `mutating` keyword.

Define a protocol.

```
protocol Increaser {
    var value: Int { get set }
    mutating func increase()
}
```

Add the mutating keyword to any methods that will modify instances of any type that conforms to the protocol.

```
struct MyNumber: Increaser {
    var value: Int
```

Declare you'll be conforming to the protocol.

```
    mutating func increase() {
        value = value + 1
    }
}
```

Conform to the protocol and implement the mutating method. It should modify the instance (i.e., modify some of the properties).

```
var num = MyNumber(value: 1)
num.increase()
```

Enums can also conform to protocols, and also need the mutating keyword in this case, but we'll get to that later.

The mutating keyword only applies to structs.

If you declare a protocol instance method to be mutating, you only need to use the `mutating` *keyword on structs that conform to the protocol.*

Classes can still adopt the protocol, but don't need to use the `mutating` *keyword.*

It looks like protocols can be used as types, kind of? How does that work? When can I use a protocol as a type?

You can use protocols as types.

Even though protocols don't actually implement functionality, you can use them as types. When you use a protocol as a type, any instance of something that conforms to the protocol can be used.

```
protocol ReportingRobot: Bipedal, HasAntenna { }
```
Remember the ReportingRobot?

```
struct SecurityBot: ReportingRobot {
    Implementation goes here.
}
struct FoodMonitorBot: ReportingRobot {
    Implementation goes here.
}
```
Consider a situation where you have two different robots that conform to ReportingRobot, but are used to do different things: security, and making sure food doesn't overcook.

```
class Situation {
    var robot: ReportingRobot

    init(robot: ReportingRobot) {
        self.robot = robot
    }

    func observeSituation() {
        robot.walk()
    }
}
```
If you use the protocol ReportingRobot as a type...

You'll know certain functionality will always be available.

```
var securityRobot = SecurityBot(antennaCount: 2)
var foodmonitorRobot = FoodMonitorBot(antennaCount: 1)
var securityMonitoring = Situation(robot: securityRobot)
var cookingMonitoring = Situation(robot: foodmonitorRobot)
securityMonitoring.observeSituation()
cookingMonitoring.observeSituation()
```
Regardless of the situation it's used in.

Sharpen your pencil
Solution

From page 228.

```
struct FutureVehicle: Aircraft, Watercraft, PetrolPowered, Landcraft {

    var buoyancy: Int  = 0
    var petrolPercent: Int = 0

    func takeOff() {
        print("Taking off!")
    }

    func land() {
        print("Landing!")
    }

    mutating func refuel() -> Bool {
        petrolPercent = 100
        return true
    }

    func drive() {
        print("Driving!")
    }

    func brake() -> Bool {
        print("Stopped!")
        return true
    }
}

var futureCar: FutureVehicle = FutureVehicle(buoyancy: 10, petrolPercent: 100)
futureCar.drive()
```

Protocol types and collections

Because protocols behave like types, you can
use them as the type in a collection:

= super useful

```
protocol Animal {          ← This protocol, named Animal, requires a variable of type String.
    var type: String { get }
}


struct Dog: Animal {       ← This type is a Dog, and it conforms to the Animal protocol.
    var name: String
    var type: String

    func bark() {
        print("Woof!")
    }
}


struct Cat: Animal {       ← This type is a Cat, and it conforms to the Animal protocol as well.
    var name: String
    var type: String

    func meow() {
        print("Meow!")
    }
}
```

We can now make some Dogs and Cats.

```
var bunty = Cat(name: "Bunty", type: "British Shorthair")
var nigel = Cat(name: "Nigel", type: "Russian Blue")
var percy = Cat(name: "Percy", type: "Manx")
var argos = Dog(name: "Argos", type: "Whippet")
var apollo = Dog(name: "Apollo", type: "Lowchen")


var animals: [Animal] = [bunty, nigel, percy, argos, apollo]
```

Because both Cat and Dog conform to the Animal protocol, we can make an array of
Animals, and store both Dogs and Cats in it. Super useful!

Brain Power

Make a loop that iterates through the animals in our Animal array, and see if you can figure out how to call either bark or meow, depending on whether the item in the array is a Dog or a Cat.

Once you've done that, create a new animal that conforms to the Animal type . Give it a method named after the sound it makes, add it to the Animal array, and make it work with the loop.

Is there something I can do if I want to make a protocol that can only be conformed to by types I specify?

You can make a protocol that's only able to be used by classes (and not structs, or anything else).

To force a protocol to be limited to class types only, you can add the AnyObject protocol to its inheritance list:

```
protocol SecretClassFeature: AnyObject {
    func secretClassFeature()
}
```

If you try to adopt the SecretClassFeature protocol with anything but a class, you'll get an error:

```
struct NotAClass: SecretClassFeature {

}
```

Non-class type 'NotAClass' cannot conform to class protocol 'SecretClassFeature'

```
class AClass: SecretClassFeature {
    func secretClassFeature() {
        print("I'm a class!")
    }
}
```

Protocols seem useful. But it would be handy to be able to add methods to existing types. How can I make classes and structs do things they weren't originally coded to do?

Funnily enough, Swift has a feature for this: extensions.

Extensions allow you to **add brand new functionality to existing classes, structures, and protocols**. You can use extensions to add computed properties, methods, or initializers, or make something conform to a protocol.

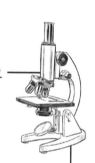

Anatomy of an Extension

Declaring an extension

An extension is declared with the extension keyword.

The type you want to extend is specified. This extension extends Int.

The functionality you want to add goes inside the extension.

```
extension Int {
    func cubed() -> Int {
        return self * self * self
    }
}
```

Using functionality from an extension

```
var number: Int = 5
number.cubed()
```

Create something of the same type you extended.

Use the functionality you added—in this case, a method named cubed.

Sharpen your pencil

See if you can figure out if each of the following is a valid Swift extension. If it's not, why not? If it is, what does it do?

☐
```swift
extension Int {
    var even: Bool {
        return self % 2 == 0
    }
}
```

☐
```swift
extension String {
    override func makeHaha() -> String {
        return "Haha!"
    }
}
```

☐
```swift
extension Int {
    func cubed() -> Int {
        print(self*self*self)
    }
}
```

☐
```swift
extension Bool {
    func printHello() {
        print("Hello!")
    }
}
```

───────────────→ Answers on page 237.

Bullet Points

- Extensions let you add features to types that you did not create.

- Anything you add to a type with an extension is treated exactly the same way as if it was built into the original type.

- Extensions can add methods and computed properties, but not stored properties.

- Extensions are also useful for organizing your code. Separating your code and the features of a type you've created using extensions can help make your code easier to read and understand.

Computed properties in extensions

Remember when we added a `lactoseFree` computed property to our Pizza struct, back when we were helping out the pizza chef?

What if we forgot to do that, and didn't have access to the code any more, but needed to interface with it and add the `lactoseFree` property? Computed properties can be added via an **extension**.

Here's our Pizza struct, missing the `lactoseFree` property:

```
struct Pizza {
    var name: String
    var ingredients: [String]
}
```

And here are some Pizzas:

```
var hawaiian = Pizza(name: "Hawaiian", ingredients: ["Pineapple", "Ham", "Cheese"])
var vegan = Pizza(name: "Vegan", ingredients: ["Red Pepper", "Tomato", "Basil"])
```

We'll implement the `lactoseFree` property using an extension.

❶ Declare an extension

```
extension Pizza {
    var lactoseFree: Bool {
        if(ingredients.contains("Cheese")) {
            return false
        } else {
            return true
        }
    }
}
```

❷ Use functionality from our extension

```
print(hawaiian.lactoseFree)
print(vegan.lactoseFree)
```

```
false
true
```

Sharpen your pencil
Solution

From page 235.

See if you can figure out if each of the following is a valid Swift extension. If it's not, why not? If it is, what does it do?

☑
```
extension Int {
    var even: Bool {
        return self % 2 == 0
    }
}
```
Works fine. Allows you to query the <u>even</u> property to see if an integer is even.

☒
```
extension String {
    override func makeHaha() -> String {
        return "Haha!"
    }
}
```
Does not work. String doesn't normally have a makeHaha function, so you can't override it.

☐?
```
extension Int {
    func cubed() -> Int {
        print(self*self*self)
    }
}
```
Functionally, it's mostly OK, but because it's meant to return an Int and doesn't, it won't work.

☑
```
extension Bool {
    func printHello() {
        print("Hello!")
    }
}
```
Works fine. Lets you print a hello message from a Boolean, for some reason.

Useful extensions and you

Sometimes it's a little hard to see the usefulness of extensions, or to figure out how they fit into the code you need to write. We're here to help.

Useful initializers

```
struct Size {
    var w = 0
    var h = 0
}
```

Consider these structs, which can be used to represent a rectangle.

```
struct Point {
    var x = 0
    var y = 0
}
```

```
struct Rectangle {
    var origin = Point()
    var size = Size()
}
```

```
var smallSquare =
    Rectangle(
        origin: Point(x: 15, y: 5),
            size: Size(w: 2, h: 2)
    )
```

size
origin

Adding an initializer (with an extension)

We can use an extension to create a new initializer for the Rectangle struct, supplementing its memberwise initializer, that allows us to create new Rectangle instances that will represent a rectangle of a specific size that starts at a specific center point, instead of from a corner origin:

```
extension Rectangle {
    init(center: Point, size: Size) {
        let origin_x = center.x - (size.w/2)
        let origin_y = center.y - (size.h/2)
        self.init(origin: Point(x: origin_x, y: origin_y), size: size)
    }
}
var bigSquare =
    Rectangle(
        center: Point(x: 10, y: 10),
        size: Size(w: 10, h: 10)
    )
```

size
center
origin

Sharpen your pencil

Consider the following code. It has a few missing bits. Can you figure out what they are?

Fill them in and run the code. For extra credit, add some more methods and properties to the type we're extending.

What else can you make this type do?

```
extension _____ {

    var square : Int{

        _____

    }

    _____ -> Int{
        return self * self * self
    }

    _____ func incrementBy10() {

        _____

    }

    _____ {
        return "This Int contains the value \(self)"
    }
}

var myInt: Int = 100
print(myInt.square)
print(myInt.cube())
myInt.incrementBy10()
print(myInt.description)
```

⟶ Answers on page 242.

Extending a protocol

You can also use an extension to outright add implemented methods, computed properties, and initializers to protocols. Remember our Animal protocol?

```
protocol Animal {
    var type: String { get }
}
```

We could use an extension to extend the Animal protocol directly, adding a new method called `eat`. When you extend a protocol, you can define behavior in the protocol itself, instead of in each type that conforms to it:

```
extension Animal {
    func eat(food: String) {  ⟵
        print("Eating \(food) now!")
    }
}
```

We provide an implementation here, even though this extension is for a protocol. All types that conform to this protocol get this method without needing to implement it themselves.

Now, when we have a type that conforms to the protocol we extended—in this case, Animal:

```
struct Horse: Animal {
    var name: String
    var type: String
}
```

...we give all conforming types the method implementation, without having to write it inside the type:

```
var edward = Horse(name: "Edward", type: "Clydesdale")
edward.eat(food: "hay")
```

Eating hay now!

You cannot make a protocol extend or inherit from another protocol using extensions.

If you want to make a protocol inherit from another protocol, that's fine, but you need to do it in the protocol itself.

Protocol composition

Useful protocols and you

It's sometimes really useful to be able to require something to conform to multiple protocols at once.

As you did earlier, you could make a new protocol that conforms to several other protocols:

```
protocol ReportingRobot: Bipedal, HasAntenna { }
```

But you can also just specify several protocols as a single type requirement:

The robot parameter requires something that conforms to both HasArms and HasLaserGun.

```
func doSomethingWith(robot: HasArms & HasLaserGun) {
    print("Gripping with arm!")
    robot.gripWith(arm: 1)
    print("Firing laser!")
    robot.fireLaserGun()
}
```

Because we know robot is guaranteed to conform to the HasArms protocol, we can call gripWith.

Likewise, because we know robot is guaranteed to conform to HasLaserGun, we can call fireLaserGun.

You can also create a typealias using protocol composition:

```
typealias RobotQ = Bipedal & PetrolPowered
```

```
func doSomethingElseWithA(robot: RobotQ) {
    print("Walking!")
    robot.walk()
    print("Petrol percent is \(robot.petrolPercent)")
}
```

As long as the type that's passed in to the methods conforms to both the required protocols, then it will work.

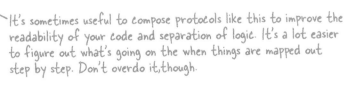

It's sometimes useful to compose protocols like this to improve the readability of your code and separation of logic. It's a lot easier to figure out what's going on the when things are mapped out step by step. Don't overdo it, though.

Sharpen your pencil
Solution

From page 239.

```
extension Int {

    var square : Int{
        return self*self
    }

    func cube() -> Int{
        return self * self * self
    }

    mutating func incrementBy10() {
        self = self + 10
    }

    var description: String {
        return "This Int contains the value \(self)"
    }
}

var myInt: Int = 100
print(myInt.square)
print(myInt.cube())
myInt.incrementBy10()
print(myInt.description)
```

Off the Path

We've got some great news. You can.

Using an extension, you can conform an existing type to a protocol. This isn't any particular magic: an extension can add properties and methods to types, which means any requirements a protocol may require can be adhered to.

Using extensions is a great way to organize your code for readability.

```
struct Dog {
    var name: String
    var age: Int
}
```
This struct represents a Dog.

```
var argos = Dog(name: "Argos", age: 7)
```
This is a Dog, using our new type.

```
protocol Bark {
    func bark()
}
```
This protocol, Bark, requires a method, bark.

```
extension Dog: Bark {
    func bark() {
        print("Woof!")
    }
}
```
This extension to Dog conforms to the Bark protocol, and adds the features of the Bark protocol to Dog.

```
argos.bark()
```
And now our Dog can bark.

Brain Power

What do you think might happen if you use an extension to conform to a protocol, but the type you're extending already conforms to the requirements of the protocol (even if it didn't explicitly conform to the protocol before you created the extension)? Give it a try.

Conforming to Swift's protocols

Sequences

Swift provides lots of useful protocols you can conform to, allowing you to add extra features to your own types.

For example, when you're iterating through a collection (like an array) using a `for-in` loop, Swift is using a special under-the-hood system called an iterator to map the `for-in` loop that you created to a hidden `while` loop that has an iterator. Swift uses that iterator, repeatedly, until the iterator sends back nil and the `while` loop ends. The iterator is responsible for iterating through the collection.

You can implement the same protocols Swift uses under the hood to provide this functionality in its own collection types.

There are two that you'll need to work with: Sequence, which is something that can be looped over in a sequence, and IteratorProtocol, which is something that itself can iterate over a sequence. Having a single type conform to both of them means you need to implement a next method, which can return whatever the next sensible value is for your sequence.

Conforming to Sequence and IteratorProtocol:

```
struct MySequence: Sequence, IteratorProtocol {
    var cur = 1

    mutating func next() -> Int? {
        defer {
            cur = cur * 5
        }
        return cur
    }
}
```

Our MySequence type conforms to Sequence and IteratorProtocol....

...which means we need to provide a next method, returning the next entry.

Wrapping this in defer { } means that Swift will do it when the current scope ends. This has the effect of returning cur, then updating cur to be cur times 5.

Using your new sequence:

```
var myNum = 0
let numbers = MySequence()
for number in numbers {
    myNum = myNum + 1
    if myNum == 10 {
        break
    }
    print(number)
}
```

```
1
5
25
125
625
3125
15625
78125
390625
```

You can find all of the built-in protocols available to conform to (and what's required to conform) by looking through the Swift documentation.

Equatable

Another useful built-in protocol is Equatable. It enables objects made from your custom types to be compared using the == operator.

The problem

```
enum DogSize {
    case small          ← A DogSize enum, representing sizes of dogs.
    case medium
    case large
}
struct Dog {            ← A Dog struct, representing
    var breed: String     specific dogs, or types of dogs.
    var size: DogSize
}

                        ┌─ Some Dogs...
var whippet = Dog(breed: "Whippet", size: .medium)
var argos = Dog(breed: "Whippet", size: .medium)
var trevor = Dog(breed: "Greyhound", size: .large)
var bruce = Dog(breed: "Labrador", size: .medium)


if(whippet == argos) {           A problem!
    print("Argos is a whippet!")
}
```

Binary operator '==' cannot be applied to two 'Dog' operands

Swift's default implementation of Equatable will check every single property of the type. So if you only want to check some of them, or some of your properties are not already Equatable, you'll need to implement your own ==.

Conforming to Equatable:

```
struct Dog: Equatable {
    var breed: String
    var size: DogSize
}
```

Conforming our Dog type to
Equatable makes it...equatable!

```
if(whippet == argos) {
    print("Argos is a whippet!")
}
```

Argos is a whippet!

Implementing ==

```
struct Dog: Equatable {
    var breed: String         ┌─ We only want to
    var size: DogSize         │  compare sizes, not
                              │  the breed.
                              ↓
    static func ==(lhs: Dog, rhs: Dog) -> Bool {
        return lhs.size == rhs.size
    }
}
if(bruce == argos) {
    print("Argos and Bruce are the same size!")
}
```

Argos and Bruce are the same size!

Code Magnets

A Swift program is all scrambled up on the fridge. Can you rearrange the code snippets to make a working program that produces the output listed on the next page? The code uses concepts we've discussed in detail, as well as a few that we haven't.

Rearrange these magnets to make the program work.
↓

```
var myCollection = GameCollection(gamesList: videoGames)
```

```
var videoGames = ["Mass Effect", "Deus Ex", "Pokemon Go",
"Breath of the Wild", "Command and Conquer", "Destiny 2",
"Sea of Thieves", "Fallout 1"]
```

```
myCollection.
enumerateCollection()
```

```
struct GameCollection: EnumerateCollection {
```

```
videoGames.describe()
```

```
var gamesList: [String]
```

```
extension Collection {
    func describe() {
        if count == 1 {
            print("There is 1 item in this collection.")
        } else {
            print("There are \(count) items in this collection.")
        }
    }
}
```

```
}
```

```
func enumerateCollection() {
    print("Games in Collection:")
    for game in gamesList {
        print("Game: \(game)")
    }
}
```

```
protocol EnumerateCollection {
    func enumerateCollection()
}
```

Code Magnets, cont.

Organize code magnets from the previous page here.

```
There are 8 items in this collection.
Games in Collection:
Game: Mass Effect
Game: Deus Ex
Game: Pokemon Go
Game: Breath of the Wild
Game: Command and Conquer
Game: Destiny 2
Game: Sea of Thieves
Game: Fallout 1
```

This is the output. Can you get the code snippets in the right order? Every snippet is used.

Answer on page 251.

Protocolcross

Here lies a fabulous excuse for doing a crossword.

Across

1) This keyword is used to mark an initializer implementation when using a protocol initializer on a conforming class.

3) A protocol can be used as a _____ in your code, as a parameter _____, a return _____, and more (the three blanks are the same word).

7) _____ implementations are used to provide a preexisting implementation of a method or property.

9) This keyword is used to signify properties in protocols that can be written.

10) An _____ provides the ability to add methods and properties to preexisting types.

11) A method that modifies the instance it belongs to is a _____ method.

12) This type of property can be added to existing types using extensions.

Down

2) Protocol _____ is when you build protocols on top of other protocols.

4) You can add _____ to protocol extensions that conforming types must satisfy.

5) This keyword is used to signify properties in protocols that can be read.

6) Protocol-_____ programming is a style of programming using protocols instead of classes and inheritance.

7) This is used to respond to certain actions without needing to know the underlying type of the source of the action.

8) A _____ provides a set of methods and/or properties for a type to conform to.

———————➤ Answers on page 252.

BE the Swift Compiler

Each of the snippets on this and the following page represents some Swift code. Your job is to play Swift compiler, and determine whether each of these will run or not. If they will not compile, how would you fix them?

A

```swift
protocol Starship {
    mutating func performBaryonSweep()
}

extension Starship {
    mutating func performBaryonSweep() {
        print("Baryon Sweep underway!")
    }
}
```

B

```swift
struct Hat {
    var type: String
}

var bowler = Hat(type: "Bowler")

protocol Wearable {
    func placeOnHead()
}

extension Hat: Wearable {
    func placeOnHead()  {
        print("Placing \(self.type) on head.")
    }
}

bowler.placeOnHead()
```

C

```swift
protocol Clean { }
protocol Green { }

typealias EnvironmentallyFriendly =
    Clean & Green

struct Car: EnvironmentallyFriendly {
    func selfDrive() {
        print("Beep boop")
    }
}
```

——————⟶ Answers on page 252.

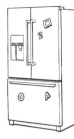

Code Magnets Solution

From page 247.

```
extension Collection {
    func describe() {
        if count == 1 {
            print("There is 1 item in this collection.")
        } else {
            print("There are \(count) items in this collection.")
        }
    }
}
protocol EnumerateCollection {
    func enumerateCollection()
}
struct GameCollection: EnumerateCollection {
    var gamesList: [String]

    func enumerateCollection() {
        print("Games in Collection:")
        for game in gamesList {
            print("Game: \(game)")
        }
    }
}
var videoGames = ["Mass Effect", "Deus Ex", "Pokemon Go", "Breath of the
Wild", "Command and Conquer", "Destiny 2", "Sea of Thieves", "Fallout 1"]
videoGames.describe()
var myCollection = GameCollection(gamesList: videoGames)
myCollection.enumerateCollection()
```

```
There are 8 items in this collection.
Games in Collection:
Game: Mass Effect
Game: Deus Ex
Game: Pokemon Go
Game: Breath of the Wild
Game: Command and Conquer
Game: Destiny 2
Game: Sea of Thieves
Game: Fallout 1
```

Protocolcross Solution

From page 249.

Across/Down crossword solution:

- 1. REQUIRED
- 2. INHERITANCE
- 3. TYPE
- 4. CONSTRAINTS
- 5. GETTER
- 6. ORIENTED
- 7. DEFAULT
- 8. PROTOCOL
- 9. SET
- 10. EXTENSION
- 11. MUTATING
- 12. COMPUTED

BE the Swift Compiler Solution

From page 250.

A, B, and C are all valid!

A doesn't print anything as no instances of anything are created.

B prints "Placing Bowler on head."

C doesn't print anything as no instances of anything are created.

9 optionals, unwrapping, generics, and more

It's a funny joke because you can't really avoid optionals.

Nothing Optional About It

Sometimes there's something inside these, sometimes they're empty. You never know until you open them...

Dealing with data that doesn't exist can be challenging.

Thankfully, Swift has a solution. Meet **optionals**. In Swift, an optional allows you to work with a value, or with **the absence of a value**. They're one of the many ways that Swift is designed to be a safe language. You've occasionally seen optionals in your code so far, and now we're going to explore them in more depth. **Optionals make Swift safe** because they keep you from accidentally writing code that would break if it's missing data, or if something can sometimes return a value that isn't actually a value.

Optionals Exposed
Today's interview: the humble Optional

Head First: Thanks for joining us, Optional. We're all very excited to get to know you a bit better.

Optional: No problem at all. I'm very popular these days, but I always make time to talk to people. Do you mind if I make notes about you while we talk?

Head First: About me? I'm talking to you to learn about you! But, I guess, sure. Whatever you need.

Optional: Thanks! What's your favorite number?

Head First: I don't really have one. Sorry. I'm told you're one of Swift's most powerful features. Care to comment on what that means?

Optional: No favorite number, right. Just making a note of that. Powerful—well yeah, I don't know about powerful, but I have certain abilities. I let you represent the absence of some data.

Head First: What sort of data?

Optional: Anything. Anything at all.

Head First: A String?

Optional: Yeah, a String. I can represent a String that's either there, or isn't there at all.

Head First: That's the same as an empty String, right?

Optional: Nope. An empty String is a String that is empty. This is a value that can be a String, which could be an empty String, or the total absence of a String. Got it?

Head First: Uh, yeah, I think so. Any data type can be an optional in Swift, you say?

Optional: Yep! An optional Int might be 5, 10, 1000, or nil—n other words, it might not exist at all.

Head First Swift: So an optional something could be any possible value for that type, or nil?

Optional: Yes. Think of a simple type: a Boolean. It can only be true or false. But an optional Boolean can be true, false, or nil.

Head First: Are you sure you're useful?

Optional: Absolutely sure. You'll understand soon. What's your year of birth?

Head First: Uh, how's that relevant?

Optional: It's not, but you definitely have one, right?

Head First: Yes...

Optional: Good, good.

Head First: Well thanks for chatting!

Optional: You're welcome.

Optional Syntax Up Close

The core of optional syntax is the ? operator. It's used to indicate something is an optional type. For example, to make an optional integer, do this:

```
var number: Int? = nil
```

`number` doesn't hold anything at the moment. Just nil, because it's an optional. If you want to store an integer in `number` at a later point, you can:

```
number = 42
```

Dealing with something that's missing

The problem

You're making a nice Swift program that provides the ability to specify a favorite quote:

```
var favoriteQuote: String = "Space, the final frontier..."

if favoriteQuote != "" {
    print("My favorite quote is: '\(favoriteQuote)'")
} else {
    print("I don't have a favorite quote.")
}
```

Here's a favorite quote, stored as a String.

And here's some code that checks that there is, in fact, a quote, and displays it if there is.

> **Optionals let us cleanly deal with the absence or potential absence of a value.**

I'm going to be honest with you here...I don't really see a problem. This code looks like it will work just fine. What am I missing?

The code will work just fine.
It's perfectly valid.

The problem is that this isn't a very <u>Swifty</u> way of doing things.

If you run this code, exactly as it is, it will work. It will print the favoriteQuote String, and all will be right with the world:

```
My favorite quote is: 'Space, the final frontier...'
```

If there's no favorite quote, and you set the favoriteQuote String to be empty, then it will also work, and it will print:

```
I don't have a favorite quote.
```

This isn't very Swifty. And it's not very safe. An empty String isn't really no favorite quote, it's actually an empty String.

Using optionals allows us solve this by representing the **potential absence** of something.

Brain Power

Create a Playground and try the code on the previous page. It should work fine. What happens if you remove the definition of favoriteQuote entirely? How does the `if`-statement behave then?

Optionals in context   Why you might need an optional

Sometimes it's a little hard to get your head around optionals, or to figure out how they fit into the code you need to write. We're here to help.

A Person

This struct represents a Person.

```
struct Person {
        var name: String
        var coffeesConsumed: Int
}
```

This is Josh. They're a Person.

Josh drinks a lot of coffee. They've already had 5 coffees today (and will probably have more!). Tom doesn't drink coffee at all, so the best we can do is to say they've had zero when we create their struct.

This is Tom. They're also a Person.

This is Josh in the form of our Person struct.

```
var josh = Person(name: "Josh", coffeesConsumed: 5)
```

This is Tom in the form of our Person struct.

```
var tom = Person(name: "Tom", coffeesConsumed: 0)
```

The struct for Josh is good, it represents Josh reasonably well: Josh is named "Josh", and they've consumed 5 coffees.

```
var josh = Person(name: "Josh", coffeesConsumed: 5)
```

Josh

name

5

coffeesConsumed

But the struct for Tom doesn't really represent them. They haven't really consumed 0 coffees; they don't drink it at all.

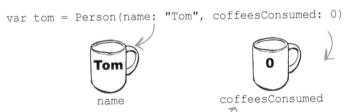

```
var tom = Person(name: "Tom", coffeesConsumed: 0)
```

Tom

name

0

coffeesConsumed

This is technically correct, in that Tom has had zero coffees, but there's a more accurate way of representing Tom.

Brain Power

We could address this by adding a consumesCoffee Boolean property to the struct, or something similar. Have a go at fixing the code by doing this before we look at optionals.

Sharpen your pencil

Take a look at the following list of potential pieces of data. Think about which of these would be good candidates for storing using an optional.

If so, why? If not, why not?

☐ The capital of a country for a user registering in your app

☐ The country code for dialing Australia

☐ A birthdate for a friend in a contacts app

☐ A list of languages spoken by a user

☐ Someone's hair color

☐ The length of someone's name in characters

☐ The age of an adopted dog

☐ The page count of a book

⟶ Answers on page 261.

Optionals and handling missing data

✳ A Person ✳

A small change: coffeesConsumed is now an optional Int.

```swift
struct Person {
    var name: String
    var coffeesConsumed: Int?
}
```

Alex and Tom

Alex is exactly the same. They drink coffee.

```swift
var alex = Person(name: "Alex", coffeesConsumed: 5)

var tom = Person(name: "Tom")
```

Tom doesn't drink coffee, so we don't even need coffeesConsumed at all anymore because it's an optional Int.

> OK, that makes sense, but is it still just an Int? Do I have to do something special to get to coffeesConsumed now that it's an optional?

Yes, to get access to an optional, you have to unwrap it.

Because an optional—let's go with an <u>optional</u> Int, like coffeesConsumed—might contain either an Int, like 5, or nil (that is, nothing at all), you need to **unwrap it before you can use it**.

There's a predictable set of things, like arithmetic operations, for example, that you can do with an **Int**, but you wouldn't be able to do them with nil. It would be unsafe if Swift let you.

So, to get access to the juicy center of an optional you must unwrap it!

Unwrapping an optional is key to being able to use it. You must always unwrap them to use them safely.

Unwrapping optionals Optionals in context

To learn how to <u>unwrap</u> optionals, we can look at our new and improved `Person` struct:

```
struct Person {
    var name: String
    var coffeesConsumed: Int?
}
```

Plus our people, created with it:

```
var alex = Person(name: "Alex", coffeesConsumed: 5)
var tom = Person(name: "Tom")
```

And then consider what happens if we print out the properties of these two instances of our `Person` struct:

```
print("\(alex.name) consumed \(alex.coffeesConsumed) coffees."")
print("\(tom.name) consumed \(tom.coffeesConsumed) coffees.")
```

It's less than ideal that, instead of printing 5, it prints `Optional(5)`. The number we want is still there, but it's wrapped in the word `Optional()`.

> Alex has consumed Optional(5) coffees.
> Tom has consumed nil coffees.

This value is of type `Optional<Int>`, not `Int`. If we want to work with the `Int`, we need to unwrap the optional:

This use of __if let__ unwraps the variable with a condition.

```
if let coffees = alex.coffeesConsumed {
    print("The unwrapped value is: \(coffees)")
} else {
    print("Nothing in there.")
}
```

If there's a value in here that isn't an optional, it will get assigned to coffees.

If there's no value in the thing we're unwrapping, then the else clause will get executed.

Sharpen your pencil
Solution

From page 258.

☑ The capital of a country for a user registering in your app

It's possible that a user might enter a fake country, so the country might not exist. Good candidate for optional.

☒ The country code for dialing Australia

Not a good candidate, this is a thing that always exists.

☑ A birthdate for a friend in a contacts app

You might not know someone's birthday. Good candidate for an optional.

☒ A list of languages spoken by a user

Everyone speaks a language. Not a good candidate.

☑ Someone's hair color

Someone might be bald. A good candidate.

☒ The length of someone's name in characters

Every name has a length. Not a good candidate.

☒ The age of an adopted dog

It definitely has an age. Not a good candidate.

☒ The page count of a book

Every book has some pages. Not a good candidate for optionals.

Bullet Points

- Optionals allow you to work with data that is not actually there.
- Any other type, including types you've created yourself, can be created as an optional version of itself.
- An optional version of something is created using the ? operator.
- An optional type can store anything the regular type could hold, or nil, which represents the absence of any value at all.
- Accessing the data inside an optional requires an extra step, called unwrapping.

Sharpen your pencil

See if you can figure out what each of the following will print, if anything. It it doesn't print anything, what's the smallest change you could make to get it to print?

☐
```
var magicNumber: Int? = nil
magicNumber = 5
magicNumber = nil
if let number = magicNumber {
    if(number == 5) {
        print("Magic!")
    }
} else {
    print("No magic!")
}
```

☐
```
var soupOfTheDay = "French Onion"
if let soup = soupOfTheDay{
    print("The soup of the day is \(soup)")
} else {
    print("There is no soup of the day today!")
}
```

☐
```
let mineral: String? = "Quartz"
if let stone = mineral {
    print("The mineral is \(stone)")
}
```

☐
```
var name: String? = "Bob"
if let person = name {
    if(person=="Bob") {
        print("Bye Bob!")
    }
}
```

Answers on page 265.

Unwrapping optionals with guard

Optionals in context

➊ Sometimes you want to keep using the unwrapped optional

Sometimes you want to be absolutely sure you've gotten an unwrapped value out of an optional, and you want to keep that value around for the rest of the scope in which it's been unwrapped.

➋ Guard lets you do this

Substituting the `guard` keyword for the `if` keyword in the same syntax we used to unwrap an optional a moment ago lets us unwrap an optional, or exit the current scope if we cannot.

Using guard let to unwrap an optional:

```swift
func order(pizza: String?, quantity: Int) {

    guard let unwrappedPizza = pizza else {
        print("No specific pizza ordered.")
        return
    }

    var message = "\(quantity) \(unwrappedPizza) pizzas were ordered."

    print(message)
}
```

We'll bail right out of the order function here if there's no value inside the pizza optional.

Relax

You'll probably want to use `if let` to unwrap optionals most of the time.

`guard let` is most useful to unwrap an optional or three at the beginning of a function or method, so that you know everything after that is good to go, and the method has been bailed out of if any of those optionals didn't actually contain a value. It lets you relax because you know all your values will be there. In other words, `guard let` is for checking if some optional-related conditions are good to go before you continue. `guard let` won't work without the `return` keyword.

Force unwrapping

I've heard tales of a Swift operator that's so dangerous that it...well it shouldn't be used...but I've heard that it's called the "crash operator." What's the story?

The crash operator isn't a myth. It's real.

And it's actually called **force unwrapping**. The operator is exactly what you might expect...it's a !

You can use the force unwrapping operator to skip all the checks and processes you'd normally need to do to get to the juicy value inside an optional.

For example, if you had an optional String:

```
let greeting: String? = "G'day mates!"
```

You could force unwrap it using the ! operator like this:

```
print(greeting!)
```
→ `G'day mates!`

By comparison, if you didn't unwrap it at all, like this, it would still be an optional:

```
print(greeting)
```

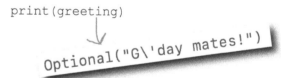

`Optional("G\'day mates!")`

It's nicknamed the crash operator for a reason.

You should only be force unwrapping things if you are absolutely certain that the value is inside, and is usable in the way you intend to use it.

Sharpen your pencil
Solution

From page 262.

☑
```
var magicNumber: Int? = nil          ← Prints "No magic!"
magicNumber = 5
magicNumber = nil
if let number = magicNumber {
    if(number == 5) {
        print("Magic!")
    }
} else {
    print("No magic!") ———→  No magic!
}
```

☒
```
var soupOfTheDay = "French Onion"    ← Doesn't do anything, as it uses if let on
if let soup = soupOfTheDay{              a regular String, not an optional String.
    print("The soup of the day is \(soup)")
} else {
    print("There is no soup of the day today!")    To fix it, make soupOfTheDay
                                                   an optional String.
}
```

☑
```
let mineral: String? = "Quartz"←     — Prints "The mineral is Quartz!"
if let stone = mineral {
    print("The mineral is \(stone)")——→  The mineral is Quartz
}
```

☑
```
var name: String? = "Bob" ←
if let person = name {          Prints "Bye Bob!"
    if(person=="Bob") {
        print("Bye Bob!")
                                  ——→  Bye Bob!
    }
}
```

Swift Safety
Today's Lesson

→ Force unwrapping optionals

A great scenario for when you might actually want to force unwrap an optional is when you're hardcoding a value that you know will always work, and storing it as an optional.

Consider the following code:

```
let linkA = URL(string:"https://www.oreilly.com")
```

URL is a class provided by Apple's Foundation library that lets you represent a URL: for example, a link to a website. In this case, it's storing the URL of a certain well-known publisher of largely animal-themed technical books. This is a validly formed URL (it doesn't matter that it works, and is a real functional URL too): it has slashes, and dots in the right place. It's well formed.

But URL doesn't know that you'll always pass in a string that is a well-formed, correct URL. You could do this:

```
let linkB = URL(string: "I'm a lovely teapot")
```

Because "I'm a lovely teapot" is a perfectly fine string, but not a valid, well-formed URL, this URL will just store nil. Assigning it to linkB means that linkB stores an optional URL (because if URL can return either a URL or nil, then it's sensible for it to return an optional URL).

Thus, if you try to use it, like this:

```
print(linkB)
```
→ `nil`

...you'll see nil, because linkB is storing nil.

But if you try to use linkA, like this:

```
print(linkA)
```
→ `Optional(https://www.oreilly.com)`

...you'll get an optional URL.

If you were to try to force unwrap the URL as you assigned it, you'd get an error:

```
let linkC = URL(string: "I'm a lovely teapot")!
```

> Unexpectedly found nil while unwrapping an Optional value

This is because the use of the ! operator assures Swift that the optional will definitely contain a value, and not contain nil, but this one contains nil.

If you force unwrap a URL containing a valid URL, because you know it's all fine, it'll just work:

```
let linkC = URL(string:"https://www.oreilly.com")!
print(linkC)
```
→ `https://www.oreilly.com`

BE the Swift Compiler

Your job is to play Swift compiler and examine the
following optional-using code to see if it will
compile, or if it will error/crash because of the
way optionals are used or not used. Take your
time. Assume all the snippets run independently,
and have no knowledge of each other.

A

```
typealias Moolah = Int
let bankBalanceAtEndOfMonth: Moolah? = 764
var statementBalance = bankBalanceAtEndOfMonth!
```

B

```
var moolah = 100
func addMoney(amount moolah: Int) -> Int? {
    return nil
}
var myMoney = (moolah + addMoney(amount: 10)!)
```

C

```
func countPasswordChars(password: String?) -> Int {
    let pass = password!
    return pass.count
}
print(countPasswordChars(password: "IAcceptTheRisk"))
```

D

```
struct Starship {
    var shipClass: String
    var name: String
    var assignment: String?
}
let ship1 =
    Starship(shipClass: "GSV", name: "A Very Bad Idea", assignment: "Contact")
let ship2 =
    Starship(shipClass: "GSU", name: "Lack of Morals", assignment: nil)
print("Assignment of \(ship2.shipClass) \(ship2.name) is: \(ship2.assignment!)")
```

——————➤ Answers on page 280.

> So, that's all there is to this so-called crash operator? I was somehow expecting more...

Well, there are other things you do with it, like implicit unwrapping.

Implicit unwrapping lets you define a value that will behave as if it's not optional at all, and not need to be unwrapped, but is still an optional.

You can do this by adding the ! operator after the type during a declaration, like this:

```
var age: Int! = nil
```

When you use an implicitly unwrapped optional, it will behave as if it's already unwrapped, but if you use one when it's nil, you'll get a crash. So be careful:

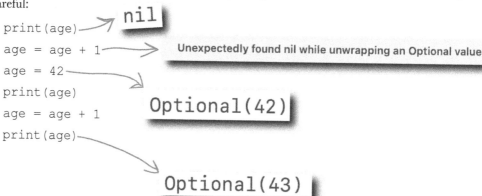

```
print(age)
age = age + 1
age = 42
print(age)
age = age + 1
print(age)
```

`nil`

Unexpectedly found nil while unwrapping an Optional value

`Optional(42)`

`Optional(43)`

Use normal options if you can.

It's very helpful to be able to use implicitly unwrapped optionals if you're absolutely sure it's not going to be a problem, because you'll always be assured that they have a value. But you'll probably be guessing. Be careful, and use regular old optionals and unwrap them yourself whenever you can.

Anatomy of Optional Chaining

Optional chaining is one of the many useful Swift features that is technically kind of a shortcut to functionality you could implement in a slightly longer way.

The problem

You're writing some code that works with arrays of people's attendance at live concerts.

```
var bobsConcerts = ["Queen at Live Aid", "Roger Waters — The Wall"]
var tomsConcerts = [String]()
```

For some reason you want to get the first concert each of these people attended out of the array, and store it as part of a message, but you want it in UPPERCASE. So you do this...

```
var message: String

if let bobFirstConcert = bobsConcerts.first {
    message = "Bob's first concert was \(bobFirstConcert.uppercased())"
}
```

The solution

Optional chaining gives you a shorthand to access optionals that are in between (or chained with) other optionals. To chain optionals, you use the ? operator in the midst of other variables:

```
let bobsFirstConcert = bobsConcerts.first?.uppercased()
let tomsFirstConcert = tomsConcerts.first?.uppercased()
```

Swift will check to see if the middle component of this chain (the return value of calling .first on the concert array) has a value (instead of it being nil). If it's nil, the rest of the chain (calling uppercased(), in this situation) won't run. If it has a value, it will continue as though it's unwrapped.

Optional chaining lets you poke through a number of chained layers of optionals using a cleaner, single line of code. If any of the optional layers ends up being nil, then the whole line will evaluate to nil. Convenient, right?

Serious Coding

Take a look at the following code. It defines some structs that create a Person and a Song. Each Person has a name, a favoriteSong, and a favoriteKaraokeSong. But favoriteKaraokeSong is an optional, because not everyone likes karaoke. We've also created some example people for you.

```
struct Person {
    var name: String
    var favoriteSong: Song
    var favoriteKaraokeSong: Song?
}
```

The ? operator signifies an optional.

```
struct Song {
    var name: String
}
let paris =
    Person(name: "Paris",
            favoriteSong: Song(name: "Learning to Fly — Pink Floyd"),
            favoriteKaraokeSong: Song(name: "Africa — Toto"))


let bob =
    Person(name: "Bob",
            favoriteSong: Song(name: "Shake It Off — Taylor Swift"))


let susan =
    Person(name: "Susan",
            favoriteSong: Song(name: "Zombie — The Cranberries"))
```

Write some code to print out the favoriteKaraokeSong of the three instances of Person we created for you, using an if statement. Print out a message saying that they don't have a favorite karaoke song if they don't have one.

Once you've done that, create some additional people using our Person struct, and see if you can convert your code into a function.

Is there any way I can use optionals to make objects that can fail to be created?

Yes, that's called a failable initializer.

Imagine you're coding a struct to represent a shape. A shape has a number of sides, and that's it.

Your struct has a method, printShape(), that might eventually draw the shape on the screen but for now just prints out how many sides the shape has.

Let's say your Shape struct looks like this:

```
struct Shape {
    var sides: Int
    func printShape() {
        print("Shape has \(sides) sides.")
    }
}
```

But what if we never wanted people to be able to create a Shape that has less than 3 sides? It's hard to make a shape with less you 3 sides anyway, so it's probably something you should prevent.

This is where a failable initializer can help! By adding one to your Shape struct, you can cause it to return nil if someone tries to create a Shape that has less than 3 sides:

```
init?(sides: Int) {
    guard sides >= 3 else { return nil }
    self.sides = sides
}
```

A failable initializer has a ? after the init keyword.

We use a guard statement to return nil if sides is not greater thanor equal to 3.

If we get to this point, it's safe to assign the properties as normal in an initializer.

Now you can safely create valid and invalid shapes:

```
var box = Shape(sides: 4)
var triangle = Shape(sides: 3)
var triquandle = Shape(sides: -4)
```

This will return an Optional<Shape> (with 4 sides).

This will return an Optional<Shape> (with 3 sides).

This will be nil.

Brain Power

Take a crack at modifying the failable initializer to fail if someone tries to make a Shape with more than 9 sides.

Swift Safety
Today's Lesson

→ **Typecasting optionals**

Swift provides a useful keyword, **as?**, that you can use to typecast something and return `nil` if it fails, or the converted type if it doesn't. The `as?` keyword lets us check if something is of a certain optional type; if it is we can make use of it, and if it's not we just get a `nil`.

```swift
class Bird {
    var name: String
```
← A Bird class. With nothing but a name as a property.
```swift
    init(name: String) {
        self.name = name
    }
}
```
— A subclass for singing birds, Singer.
```swift
class Singer: Bird {
    func sing() {
```
— A sing method, for singing Birds.
```swift
        print("\(self.name) is singing! Singing so much!")
    }
}
```
— A subclass for nesting birds, Nester.
```swift
class Nester: Bird {
    func makeNest() {
```
← A makeNest method, for nesting Birds.
```swift
        print("\(self.name) made a nest.")
    }
}
```
— An array of different subclasses of Bird, and regular Birds.
```swift
let birds = [Bird(name: "Cyril"), Singer(name: "Lucy"),
                Singer(name: "Maurice"), Nester(name: "Cuthbert")]
for bird in birds {
```
← And here we want only the Singer birds to sing.
```swift
    if let singer = bird as? Singer {
        singer.sing()
    }
}
```
⌐ So we use the as? keyword to typecast each thing in the array as a Singer. If it's a Singer, we'll get the value, and if it's not, we'll get nil and we won't. Nice and safe.

```
Lucy is singing! Singing so much!
Maurice is singing! Singing so much!
```

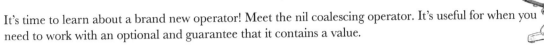

Anatomy of the Nil Coalescing Operator

It's time to learn about a brand new operator! Meet the nil coalescing operator. It's useful for when you
need to work with an optional and guarantee that it contains a value.

The problem

If you have an optional type with some data in it...

```
var dogBreed: String? = "Beagle"
print("Look at that cute \(dogBreed!)!")
```

*...and use the ! operator to force unwrap
it when you use it, things are fine.*

> Look at that cute Beagle!

But if you have an optional type without any value:, it's got nil in it...

```
var dogBreed: String?
print("Look at that cute \(dogBreed!)!")
```

...and if you use the ! operator to force unwrap it when you use it, you have a problem.

Unexpectedly found nil while unwrapping an Optional value

The solution

```
var dogBreed: String?
print("Look at that cute \(dogBreed ?? "doggo")!")
```

*Using the ?? nil coalescing operator will
unwrap the optional, and if it's nil, it will
use the provided value instead.*

> Look at that cute doggo!

```
var dogBreed: String? = "Beagle"
print("Look at that cute \(dogBreed ?? "doggo")!")
```

> Look at that cute Beagle!

Generics

Writing flexible and reusable code is important. Generics are a fantastic contribution to the lofty goals of flexibility and reusability. **Generics allow you to write functions and types that can work with literally any other type, subject to requirements that you define.**

A great example of this is creating new data types that can act differently depending on what you need them to do. Swift's own collection types, like the magical Array, do this, so you've used a lot of different generic-powered Swift so far. Now we'll make our own collection type.

Let's make a **queue**: a data type that's first-in first-out, like a queue in the real world. When you add things, they always get added to the back, and when you remove things they always get removed from the front.

Queue requirements

❶ A way to push new items onto the back of the queue

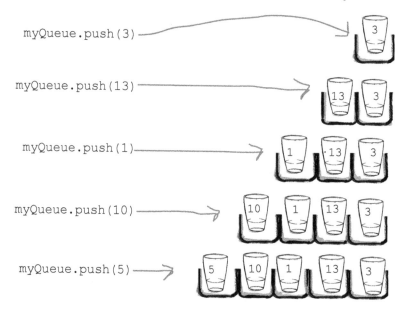

A queue with generics

❷ A way to pop items off the front of the queue, removing them

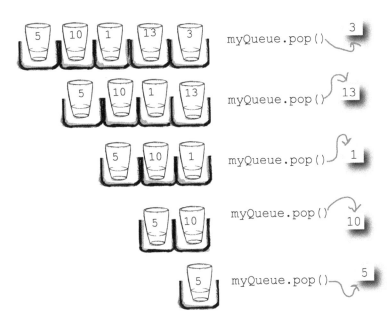

```
myQueue.pop()      3
myQueue.pop()      13
myQueue.pop()      1
myQueue.pop()      10
myQueue.pop()      5
```

❸ A way to get a count of items in the queue

```
myQueue.push(5)
myQueue.push(11)
myQueue.count      2
```

❹ The ability to be created as a queue of any type (Ints, Strings, whatever)
...this is where generics come in!

Here's our new Queue type

This bit is the generic. We put the name of a generic placeholder between < and >.

The T represents the generic type that can then be anything.

All four requirements of the queue are present in our queue.

```
struct Queue<T> {

    private var arrayRepresentation = [T]()

    var count: Int {
        return arrayRepresentation.count
    }

    mutating func push(_ item: T) {
        arrayRepresentation.append(item)
    }

    mutating func pop() -> T? {
        if arrayRepresentation.count > 0 {
            return arrayRepresentation.removeFirst()
        } else {
            return nil
        }
    }

}
```

Inside our Queue, things will actually be represented using an array of whatever type lives in T.

Our Queue's count property will return the count of our internal array.

Our push function allows us to add an item to the queue—an item of type T.

And our pop function returns an item of type T, if there's one to return, from the front of the internal array.

Using your Queue

Create a queue (of Strings in this case).

```
var stringQueue = Queue<String>()
stringQueue.push("Hello")
stringQueue.push("Goodbye")
print(stringQueue.pop()!)
```

Push two Strings onto the queue.

Pop off the front (and print it).

We force unwrap the optional result because, in this case, we're absolutely sure something is inside. But you should do it properly in the real world.

So...again...is that it? Can generics do anything else?

Great question. The classic generics example is functions.

Generic functions are functions that work with any type.

Here's a function that switches two Int values:

```
func switchInts(_ one: inout Int, _ two: inout Int) {
    let temp = one
    one = two
    two = temp
}
```

Now imagine you needed to make a similar function to switch two Doubles, or two Strings, or any other type. You'd need to write a nearly identical function for each case. Enter generics.

Here's our switching function, rewritten as a generic function:

```
func switchValues<T>(_ one: inout T, _ two: inout T) {
    let temp = one
    one = two
    two = temp
}
```

Now you can use `switchValues` to switch any pair of values, regardless of their type:

```
var a = 5
var b = 11
switchValues(&a, &b)
print(a)
print(b)
```

You don't have to refer to your generics as T. You can actually use any name you like. T is just convention. Get creative!

there are no
Dumb Questions

Q: I understand optionals, I think. They let me represent something that's either there and of a certain type, or not there at all?

A: Yes. You can represent the absence, or presence, of something. It's clear and easy to use.

Q: Do I have to unwrap an optional to get access to the actual value?

A: Yes, to get access to the value of an optional you need to unwrap it. To do that, you can use `if let` or `guard let`.

Q: Can I force unwrap optionals too?

A: Yes, to force unwrap an optional you can use the `!` operator. But if you force unwrap something and get nil (i.e., the absence of a value), then your code will definitely crash.

Q: And implicitly unwrapped optionals are kind of like optionals that automatically unwrap themselves?

A: Yes—you can make an optional that's implicitly unwrapped, which makes it behave kind of like it's automatically unwrapped, but basically it just doesn't have the special safety features of optionals.

Q: What about optional chaining? Is it basically doing something to an optional and ignoring the code if the optional turns out to be nil?

A: Got it in one. Optional chaining is a safe way of doing something with an optional that might be tucked in between some other variables that aren't optionals.

Q: And as far as I can tell, nil coalescing is just a way of providing a known safe default value if an optional contains nil?

A: Correct. Nil coalescing is just a fancy way of saying "this provides a default value for a nil value in an optional."

Q: And if I'm making an object that uses optionals, I can make a failable initializer to make sure it's safe?

A: Yeah, the idea with a failable initializer is that you can add the `?` operator to the `init` keyword when defining your initializer, and make sure that the whole object cannot be made if it's created with bad input.

Q: And finally, typecasting... That's just converting one thing to another?

A: Got it in one. Typecasting involves telling Swift you'd like it to provide you something in a different type.

Q: Optionals seem really useful. Why don't other programming languages have those?

A: That's a great question. We have no idea.

Bullet Points

- `nil` represents the absence of a value.
- Using the `!` operator on a type (for example, `Int!`) means that things of that type don't need to be unwrapped before using them—as long as the variable in question doesn't contain `nil`.
- Adding the `?` operator to the `init` keyword allows you to create a failable initializer, which prevents the initializer from completing at all if it would fail with bad data.
- Optionals are a key part of Swift safety. They let you safely work with data that might be missing.

 **Optionalcross**

We've learned a lot about optionals together. Now it's time for some mandatory fun.
See if you can figure out the optional-related terms in this crossword.

Down

1) You must _____ an optional to get to the value inside.

3) Optional ___ is a special version of ___ that supports optionals (same word in both empty spots).

4) The nil _____ operator unwraps an optional and returns a value or a default value.

5) An _____ unwrapped optional does not need to be unwrapped to get at the value inside.

6) You can _____ unwrap to convert an optional to a non-optional type.

8) Optionals are one of the things that helps you write _____ code with Swift.

9) The _____ let syntax lets you unwrap an optional and keep the value usable after.

11) The if ___ syntax lets you unwrap an optional, or do something else if you cannot.

Across

2) An Int that can store an Int or nothing is an _____ Int.

4) Optional _____ is a shortcut to accessing optionals.

7) When you access a type as a (potentially) different type.

10) A _____ initializer is one that might work, but is allowed not to.

12) Name for a missing or no value.

Optionalcross Solution

```
                    ¹U
   ²O  P  ³T  I  O  N  A  L
          R        W
          Y        R
          ⁴C  H  A  I  N  ⁵I  N  G
          O        P     M
          A              P      ⁶F
          L              L      O
   ⁷T  Y  P  E  C  A  ⁸S  T  I  N  ⁹G  R
          S           A     C     U    C
          C           ¹⁰F  A  I  L  A  B  ¹¹L  E
          I           E     T     R     E
          ¹²N  I  L        L     D     T
          G                Y
```

BE the Swift Compiler Solution

A will work. B will not work because force unwrapping the returned value is attempting to unwrap a nil value. C will work. D will not work because force unwrapping the second ship's assignment is attempting to unwrap a nil value.

From page 267.

10 getting started with swiftUI

User Interfaces...Swiftly

It's very important that you know what you're doing once you start drawing...

It's time to use your toolbox full of Swift techniques, features, and components: you're going to start building user interfaces. A Swift UI, if you will. We're going to bring everything together in this chapter to create our first true user interface. We'll build a whole experience using **SwiftUI, the user interface framework for Apple's platforms**. We'll still be using Playgrounds, at least initially, but everything we're doing here will lay the groundwork for an actual iOS application. Get ready: this chapter is full of code and a lot of new concepts. Take a deep breath, and turn the page to dive into *SwiftUI*.

Yes, it's really named that. This isn't another pun...at least, it's Apple's pun, not ours.

What's a UI framework, anyway?

Frank

Judy

Jo

Frank: So, does anyone know what a UI framework is?

Judy: It's a.. framework...for UI?

Jo: It's a set of tools for drawing visual elements on the screen. In this case, it's called SwiftUI, and it's built using the fundamental bits and pieces of Swift we've all been learning.

Frank: So how's it work?

Judy: Is it good?

Jo: You construct you UI programmatically, using structs and properties,and things like that.

Judy: How do you build a UI using structs?

Frank: I assume we'll be using protocols, so that the structs conform to some sort of protocol that SwiftUI supplies?

Jo: Bingo. That's exactly how it works.

Judy: So what sort of UI elements can I use? Buttons? What else?

Jo: There are `Buttons`, of course, `TextFields` for entering text, `Lists`, `Image` views, and all sorts of other useful things.

Frank: So how do you lay things out properly if you have to construct your UI programmatically? I meanwhen I've made UIs in other programming tools, I've been able to lay things out visually. How do I position things properly if it's code?

Jo: You can position and lay things out easily using tools like `NavigationView`, `VStacks` for vertical stacks, `HStacks` for horizontal stacks, and more. By embedding views within other views, you can pretty precisely control the position of things.

Judy: And what platforms can I build UIs for using SwiftUI?

Frank: I think it works on iOS, macOS, tvOS, and watchOS.

Judy: All of Apple's platforms then...

Jo: That's right. It's Apple-only, but it's very good. And it makes making clean, well-designed apps super easy.

Frank: OK, you've convinced me. Where do I start learning SwiftUI?

Judy: Me too. I'm convinced. Let's go.

Jo: Lucky for you, there are some introductory steps on the next page...

I'm sick of everything being text-based. I want to get graphical. I want a user interface. What's it gonna take?

SwiftUI is what it's going to take.

SwiftUI lets you make graphical user interfaces (sometimes called GUIs, or UIs) using straightforward Swift code.

This is a **whole program**, with a (Swift) UI:

```swift
import SwiftUI
import PlaygroundSupport


struct ContentView: View {
    @State var count = 0

    var body: some View {
        VStack {
            Button(action: { self.count += 1 }, label: {
                Text("Press Here")
                .padding()
            })

            if count > 0 {
                Text("The button has been pressed \(count) times.")
            } else {
                Text("The button has not been pressed.")
            }
        }
    }
}
PlaygroundPage.current.setLiveView(ContentView())
```

Test Drive

Create a new Playground, and run the above code. What do you see?

Your first SwiftUI UI

Remember these imports, from the previous page?

```
import SwiftUI
import PlaygroundSupport

struct HuzzahView: View {

    var body: some View {
        Text("Huzzah!")
    }

}
```

We create a view by declaring a type (in this case named HuzzahView) that conforms to the View protocol.

The body variable inside, which is required by the protocol, is a computed property. We use it to provide the content we want drawn.

Inside our body computed property, we combine as many of the primitive views that the SwiftUI framework provides as we like in order to draw what we want.

In this case, we want a Text view, initialized with the text "Huzzah".

```
PlaygroundPage.current.setLiveView(ContentView())
```

We need to ask the Playground to display the view we want to see. In this case, that's HuzzahView.

Run it and see what happens.
Make a new Swift Playground and type the above code into it. Then run the Playground.

▶ Run My Code

This is ugly, and has too much space. But it worked!

Huzzah!

SwiftUI is a declarative, responsive UI framework. It's easy to read the code and mostly figure out what the UI will look like.

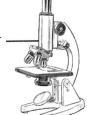

— Anatomy of a View —

❶ The import line

SwiftUI needs to be imported .The import line tells Swift that we want to use the SwiftUI framework.

```
import SwiftUI
import PlaygroundSupport


struct HuzzahView: View {

    var body: some View {
        Text("Huzzah!")
    }

}
```

❷ A struct, named HuzzahView

We create a struct named HuzzahView (a name we choose) that conforms to the View protocol. View is SwiftUI's protocol for things that get drawn on the screen.

❸ A body property

This computed property, body, has the type some View. This means that it'll return (contain) something that conforms to the View protocol, and the some keyword means it always must be the same kind of view being returned.

❹ Something in the view

Here we display some text, using a Text view. This complies with the requirement for body to return some View.

⚠ **Watch it!**

SwiftUI is easy, but it's easy to make mistakes with it. It's very easy to fix them too, though!

SwiftUI is a lot more finicky than Swift itself. It's easy to make a mistake that generates a nonsensical error, and often the error you get as a result will not be related to the actual line where the error was made. Go slowly, and carefully.

> So, what's the deal with this <u>some View</u> syntax? I don't really understand how some View is different from a View.

This is what's called an *opaque return type*.

To explain why this is used, it's better to look at some code. Instead of body's return type being some View, it could actually be a concrete type that *conforms* to View, such as, Text:

```
struct MyView: View {

        var body: Text {

                Text("Hello!")

        }

}
```

But because SwiftUI is designed to let you compose views out of multiple views, a real-world SwiftUI view would have more than just a Text view in it, even if it was just displaying a Text view—it would have a VStack or an HStack or something similar, in order to position it.

This goes back to Swift's **generics**. All of the things you're using that conform to View are generic types. The concrete type of the generic type changes, depending on what's inside.

This can get fiddly and complex fast, as you unpack layers of types. Don't worry about it too much!

For example, if you had a VStack with a Text view and an Image view inside it, then the type of the VStack would be inferred as VStack<TupleView<(Text, Image)>>.

But if you changed the Image view to be a Text view instead, then it would change to VStack<TupleView<(Text, Text)>>.

```
var body: VStack<TupleView<(Text, Text)>> {
        VStack {

                Text("Hello!")
                Text("I'm more text!")
        }
}
```

Because of this, if we used a concrete type for the view that's returned by the body, we'd have to manually change it every time we changed things in the body.

It's much easier to say that the body returns **some** view.

there are no Dumb Questions

Q: Is SwiftUI part of Swift? I don't get it.

A: SwiftUI is a framework for Swift. It's built by Apple, and designed to let you create user interfaces for Apple's platforms: iPadOS, iOS, tvOS, watchOS, and macOS. SwiftUI is a proprietary, closed source framework, and is only available when you're using Swift on an iPad using Playgrounds or on a machine running macOS using Playgrounds or Xcode. That might change in the future, but that's the situation right now.

Q: So SwiftUI is not open source like Swift?

A: That's correct. SwiftUI is closed source.

Q: Does that mean I can't use SwiftUI to make apps for Linux or Windows?

A: As of right now, that is the case. SwiftUI can only be used to make apps for Apple's platforms.

Q: I've heard of this thing called UIKit. What's that got to do with SwiftUI?

A: UIKit is Apple's other UI framework for iOS and iPadOS. It's still around, still being updated, and still awesome, but it's not a native Swift-based framework (although you can use it natively with Swift). It has all the same closed source and platform-specific limitations as SwiftUI, but it's a bit different. We'll be using UIKit views from SwiftUI in this book occasionally, but this book won't teach you UIKit.

Q: So SwiftUI replaced UIKit?

A: No! SwiftUI is built on top of UIKit in places (but not everywhere). Sometimes when you use SwiftUI, you're actually using UIKit underneath. But you don't need to know that. SwiftUI is featureful, fully Swift-native, and powerful. It doesn't matter to you whether SwiftUI is using UIKit to draw a user interface you've created, as you're just using SwiftUI.

Q: SwiftUI having Swift in the name... is that just because it's for Swift, or is it also a fast UI framework?

A: SwiftUI is really fast. Under the hood all the views you create with SwiftUI are optimized to draw as quickly and efficiently as possible, and many use Apple's super-fast Metal framework to draw using the GPU. In short: it's named SwiftUI because it's fast, and because it's for Swift.

Q: Should I learn UIKit at some point, too?

A: If you're interested in getting further into app development for Apple's platforms then it makes sense to graduate to learning UIKit when you're done with this book, yes. But you should really learn SwiftUI first.

Q: I heard that SwiftUI is a declarative framework. What does that mean?

A: SwiftUI is indeed a declarative (as opposed to an imperative) UI framework. We'll explore exactly what this means later in this chapter, but the gist is that you define a set of rules and states and how to move between them, and SwiftUI figures out the rest.

Bullet Points

- Using SwiftUI requires that you import SwiftUI.

- A SwiftUI view is a struct that conforms to the View protocol. The View protocol comes from SwiftUI.

- A user interface is composed of multiple, usually nested, SwiftUI views.

- The code and behavior of your UI are very tightly coupled together, and SwiftUI relies heavily on Swifty concepts like protocols.

- Some SwiftUI views provide common useful UI elements, like `Buttons`, and some provide invisible layout elements, like `VStacks` for vertical alignment and `HStacks` for horizontal alignment.

- It's very quick and straightforward to make a simple UI with minimal code. But things get more complex pretty fast. Move slowly, and carefully.

UI building blocks

Like any good toolkit, SwiftUI has a whole collection of things you can use to assemble a fantastic interface. Here are a few of them:

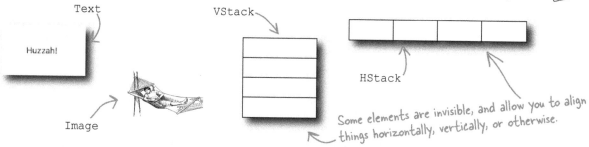

Text	A Text view can display one or more lines of text. The text in a Text view is read-only and cannot be edited by the user.
TextField	A TextField view provides an editable text view. It lets you bind a value to the view that is updated with whatever the user types into the view.
Image	An Image view can display an image. That's it.
Button	A Button view creates and displays a button. It has a label, which is the text on the button, and an action, which is a method or closure to call when the button is tapped or clicked.
Toggle	A Toggle view is a view that can be toggled between an on state and an off state. It can be bound to a Boolean property that reflects the state of the toggle.
Picker	A Picker view lets you display a view that contains a set of mutually exclusive values. One of the values can be picked, and this information can be sent somewhere else.
Slider	A Slider view creates a control for choosing between a bounded range of values. The slider can be bound to a value, which is updated as the user moves it.
Stepper	A Stepper view displays a control that lets the user increment or decrement a value.

Making a list, checking it...quite a few times, to get it perfect

Now that you know a little about how SwiftUI works (you'll learn a lot
more later), we're going to build a slightly more complicated UI.

Here's the UI we want to build:

Here's the steps to make this UI:

① **Create a struct to serve as the view**
The view struct needs to adhere to the View protocol.

② **Implement the protocol requirement: a body property**
The View protocol that we're adhering to requires our view struct to
contain a computed property called body.

③ **Create the list we want**
SwiftUI provides a List container that automatically presents rows of
data, arranged into a single column.

④ **Put some Text views inside our list**
Using SwiftUIs, Text view, we create as many pieces of text as we want
displayed in our list.

Brain Power

Create the List view from the previous page, using SwiftUI. You'll need to use some of the concepts from earlier in the book, and fill in some of the gaps in using SwiftUI by yourself.

Setting up

As usual, we'll be doing our work in a Swift Playground. Create one now, and inside it import both `SwiftUI` and `PlaygroundSupport`.

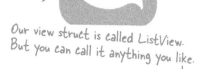

Step 1: Creating our view

Let's make this list. The first thing we need is a struct to serve as our list view. That struct needs to adhere to the `View` protocol.

✳ Create a struct and name it something sensible for a view that will contain a list.

✳ Set the struct so that it adheres to the View protocol.

Step 2: Declare the body

We need a `body` property in order to actually display something. The `body` property is required in order to comply with the View protocol we're adhering to.

✳ Create a variable named `body` that returns `some View`. We'll leave the closure empty for now.

Step 3: Create a list

The main thing we want to put in our view's body is a list. So, for this step, all we need to do is add that list inside the `body` property's closure.

✳ Create a `List` container, leaving its contents empty for now (you'll fill it in the next step).

Step 4: Put some things in the list

The list we want to build has three text entries in it. And that's what we'll put inside the `List` container at this point:

✳ Add a `Text` view that says `"Huzzah!"`

✳ Add a `Text` view that says `"Hooray!"`

✳ Add a `Text` view that says `"Amazing!"`

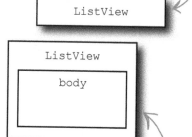

Our view struct is called ListView. But you can call it anything you like.

The body property closure returns "some View" because it needs to return one specific type that conforms to the View protocol, but we don't care what type.

The List container will create a static list containing whatever collection of things that conform to the View protocol get put inside it.

After, don't forget to ask the Playground to display the view we want to see. In this case, that's our ListView.

User interfaces with state

A user interface isn't much use unless it reflects the state of something: some sort of logic, calculation, data from the user, data from a remote server...**some sort of state is vital to a user interface.**

The philosophy of SwiftUI is that *a view is a function of its state.* With SwiftUI, the code that creates a view and the code that understands the state of the view are intertwined. They're often one and the same, as you'll see.

Imagine you're building an app to track your consumption of coffee, tea, and cocktails.

The requirements are as follows:

✳ There are three buttons: one labeled "Coffee", one labeled "Cocktail", and one labeled "Tea."

✳ A number is displayed on each button, as part of the label.

✳ The number reflects the count of each beverage that you've consumed. The number is incremented by tapping the button.

The implementation of our Counter view might look something like this.

This app might look something like this.

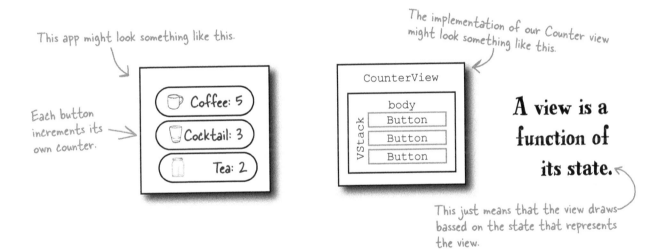

Each button increments its own counter.

A view is a function of its state.

This just means that the view draws bassed on the state that represents the view.

State is only kept while the code is running.

The kind of state we're talking about here is the state of the code while it's running. We're not talking about saving the state of the app when you're no longer running the code in question.

This state is stored in the RAM of the device that the code is running on. It's never written to the disk. If the code is stopped and restarted, the state will be reset to whatever the default is.

Buttons are for pressing

Before you can explore how to make this app, you need to know how `Button` views in SwiftUI work. It's actually very similar to how `Text` views work:

We want a button. →
A button needs an action: something that happens when it's pressed. ←

```
Button(action: {
        print("The button was pressed!")
    }) {
        Text("This is a Button")
    }
```

A closure is provided as the action.

The action, in this case, is calling print to say that the button was pressed.

A closure is also provided as the view. This is the thing that effectively is the button.

This button is going to be some text. Almost any view can be used inside a button, so you could display an image instead, for example.

There's also a shorthand syntax for creating a text-only button, which is likely to be one of the most common kinds of button you create. It looks like this:

A button needs some text to display.

```
Button("I'm also a Button") {
        print("The other button was pressed!")
    }
```

We still want a button.

A closure is provided as the action.

Our action is another call to print to say that the button was pressed.

Sharpen your pencil

Think about how you might write some code to create the app that we've been discussing. Consider how you'd structure it in SwiftUI, based on what you know already, and what SwiftUI views you'd need.

Once you've had a think, turn to actual code and have a go in a Swift Playground. Here are some steps that might be useful:

☐ Create a SwiftUI view struct, named something sensible for a counter app. Add the required `body` computed property so you can implement the view we want inside it.

☐ Inside your view struct, create three variables to keep track of the three counts we want to track. You'll need to make sure they each contain the value 0 to start with.

☐ Create a `VStack` inside the body to position the user interface elements vertically, one on top of the other.

☐ Inside the `VStack`, create three `Button` views. For each button, the title should be composed of an emoji, the name, and the count for its name. The action for each button should be to increment the relevant count by 1.

You can use string interpolation to compose the title.

Once you're done (don't forget to use PlaygroundSupport to display your view), turn the page and we'll have a chat about your solution. Don't worry if you haven't got it working at this point.

Sharpen your pencil
Solution

Your solution might have looked something like the following code. Compare this to what you implemented. Was your code similar? **Why didn't it work?**

```
import SwiftUI                                   Imports are all there, as needed.
import PlaygroundSupport
                                                 A SwiftUI view struct.
struct DrinkCounterView: View {
    var coffeeCount = 0                Some variables inside our view, to track the state for
    var cocktailCount = 0              each of the three counters. Each is initialized to 0.
    var teaCount = 0
                        Our body property.
    var body: some View {                            A VStack, containing three buttons.
        VStack {                                     Lines up things inside it vertically.
            Button(" 🍵 Coffee: \(coffeeCount)") {   Each button's title uses string interpolation
                self.coffeeCount += 1               to display the relevant count...
            }
            Button(" 🍸 Cocktails: \(cocktailCount)") {
                self.cocktailCount += 1   And increments the appropriate counter variable.
            }
            Button(" 🍵 Tea: \(teaCount)") {
                self.teaCount += 1
            }                                  And we ask the Playground to display the
        }                                      counter view that we've created.
    }
}
PlaygroundPage.current.setLiveView(DrinkCounterView())
```

If you run this, you might expect it to work: everything seems to make sense based on what we know about SwiftUI so far. We created a view correctly, and we appropriately used a VStack to place three Button views on top of each other. Each button displayed a count variable, which resided inside the view struct, and incremented the variable appropriately. So, why doesn't this work?

The clue lies in the error you'll receive when you run this.

> Left side of mutating operator isn't mutable: 'self'
> is immutable

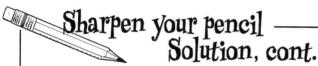

Sharpen your pencil
Solution, cont.

The error tells us that `self` is immutable—`self`, in this case, being the `BirdCounterView` struct that we created.

Because `BirdCounterView` is a struct, it might have been created as a constant. The value of a constant cannot be changed, and this extends to the values of properties of a struct that's been created as a constant.

If our struct had a method inside it that could change the values of its properties, that method would have to have the `mutating` keyword applied (as you learned back in Chapter 6.

However, because this is a SwiftUI view, `body` is a *computed property*. Computed properties cannot have the `mutating` keyword applied.

You need to be able to change the values of variables that are being used as state, though. So how do you fix this?

You fix it by tagging the properties with a special *property wrapper* named `@State`:

```
@State private var coffeeCount = 0
@State private var cocktailCount = 0
@State private var teaCount = 0
```

The `@State` property wrapper attribute ensures that Swift knows to store the value of the tagged property separately, in a manner that allows modification. You should also add the `private` access control tag, since the properties are only intended to be used within that view.

If you modify the code you wrote earlier, adding the `@State` attribute and the `private` access control tag, you should now be able to run it and use the buttons to increment the correct counters.

```
import SwiftUI
import PlaygroundSupport

struct BirdCounterView: View {
    @State var coffeeCount = 0
    @State var cocktailCount = 0
    @State var teaCount = 0

    var body: some View {
        VStack {
            Button("🐦 Coffee: \(coffeeCount)") {
                self.coffeeCount += 1
            }
            Button("🍸 Cocktails: \(cocktailCount)") {
                self.cocktailCount += 1
            }
            Button("🍵 Tea: \(teaCount)") {
                self.teaCount += 1
            }
        }
    }
}
```

< Bird Counter >

🐦 Coffee: 0
🍸 Cocktails: 0
🍵 Tea: 0

Stop

Let's see how far you've come ← *In both inches and centimeters!*

You've got Swift programming down, and you're familiar with the building blocks of SwiftUI. It's time to make something that's actually useful!

Our goal is to make a SwiftUI program that lets us very simply convert from inches to centimeters. It should look a bit like this:

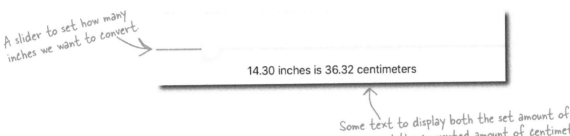

A slider to set how many inches we want to convert.

14.30 inches is 36.32 centimeters

Some text to display both the set amount of inches, and the converted amount of centimeters.

You already know how to use the `@State` property wrapper to work with a value that's involved with the view. The only new concept here is using the SwiftUI `Slider`.

It also needs a closed range, representing the extents of the slider.

You can create a SwiftUI slider view like this:

```
Slider(value: $sliderValue, in: 1...10, step: 1)
```

A slider needs to be bound to a variable. The variable is used to store the slider's current value.

And finally a step, for how much your want the value to change when the slider moves a step.

You can customize and theme your `Slider` the same way you can with most SwiftUI views. For example, if you wanted to change the underlying color of the slider's accent to red, you could do that:

```
Slider(value: $sliderValue, in: 1...10, step: 1)
    .accentColor(Color.red)
```
← *This is called a modifier...*

The $ syntax tells Swift to bind values to things. It's used a lot by SwiftUI.

Or you could put a border around your slider, like this:

```
Slider(value: $sliderValue, in: 1...10, step: 1)
    .border(Color.red, width: 3)
```
— *This is also a modifier.*

Brain Power

You already know how to create a SwiftUI view, so we've made one for you (named `SliderView`). All you need to do is implement the SwiftUI UI we described on the previous page in a Swift Playground.

First, you'll need to add a property tagged with the `@State` property wrapper to the `SliderView`. It will be a double that's used to store the inches represented by the slider.

In the body, inside the `VStack`, create a `Slider`. Set the `value` to the property that you created, the `range` to something sensible (maybe 0 to 100, nothing negative), and the `step` to whatever you'd like the slider to increment the inches by each time it moves (such as 0.1).

Finally, you'll also need some text to describe the conversion. You'll only need to add in the name of the property that stores inches; we've provided the rest for you.

```
import SwiftUI
import PlaygroundSupport


struct SliderView: View {

    ┌─────────────────────────────────────┐
    └─────────────────────────────────────┘

    var body: some View {
        VStack {
            ┌─────────────────────────────────────┐
            └─────────────────────────────────────┘
            Text("\(┌──────┐, specifier: "%.2f") inches is
                    └──────┘
                  \(┌──────┐ * 2.54, specifier: "%.2f")
                    └──────┘
centimeters")
        }
    }
}
```

This specifier is a formatter that tells Swift to display only 2 decimal places of the double, to keep the output neat.

```
PlaygroundPage.current.setLiveView(SliderView())
```

You'll know it's working when you can run the code in the Playground and use the slider to pick an amount of inches, and see the result in centimeters:

38.60 inches is 98.04 centimeters

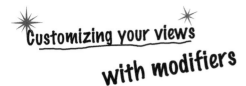

Customizing your views with modifiers

Modifiers in context

❶ The default building block view elements provided by Swift are nice

But most of the time we want to go beyond them, style-wise. We want to make them fit with the design and theme of our programs. We want to customize them. We want to modify them.

❷ View modifiers let you...modify views

A view modifier takes a view that it's applied to, modifies it to some specification, and returns the view looking how you want it to look.

Using view modifiers:

```
Text("Big Red Text")
        .font(.headline)
        .foregroundColor(.red)
        .padding()
```

Big Red Text

Order matters (sometimes):

```
Text("Big Red Text")
    .font(.headline)
    .foregroundColor(.red)
    .background(Color.green)
    .padding()
```

```
Text("Big Red Text")
    .font(.headline)
    .foregroundColor(.red)
    .padding()
    .background(Color.green)
```

The background is applied to a bigger view, because padding came first.

Brain Power

Add another background color (not green) after the padding in the first example with a background color, above. Try to guess where the background will end up, and how it will relate to the other (green) background before you run the code and find out.

Serious Coding

TODO: Put SwiftUI to work

We're going to build our friend a Todo List app. To do this (hah), we'll need to use Xcode, Apple's fancy macOS-based development environment for Swift (and other languages).

Follow along with these steps, and build your own todo app! We'll show you how on the following pages.

- ☐ Create a new SwiftUI Xcode project, for iOS.

- ☐ Create a new type to store a todo item in.

- ☐ Make sure each todo item can be uniquely identified.

- ☐ Create a user interface for the app: a text field to add new todos with, a button to save them, and a list to show all the todos.

- ☐ Implement a way to save the list of todos, so that it persists.

2:27

Todos

Add todo...   +

Get a todo list app

Buy more coffee

Read Practical Artificial Intelligence with Swift book

Re-watch 30 Rock

Go for a swim

Find out if eels hunt in packs

This is the app we'll be building. Looks good, right?

It has a place to add new todo items.

And shows a list of all todos that have been added.

Create a new SwiftUI Xcode project, for iOS

Enough chit-chat. Let's build this todo list. The first thing we need to do is make an Xcode project. (If you haven't got Xcode installed, do that first.)

1 Fire up Xcode.

2 Choose the **Create a new Xcode project** option from the *Welcome to Xcode* screen.

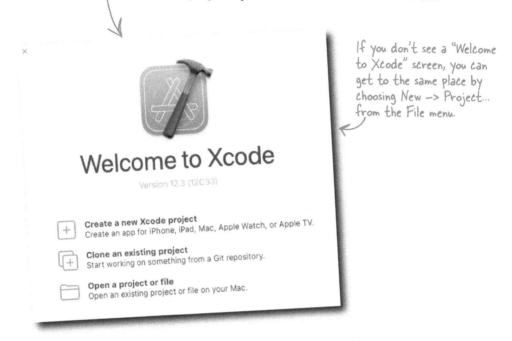

If you don't see a "Welcome to Xcode" screen, you can get to the same place by choosing New –> Project... from the File menu.

Welcome to Xcode

Version 12.3 (12C33)

+ **Create a new Xcode project**
Create an app for iPhone, iPad, Mac, Apple Watch, or Apple TV.

+ **Clone an existing project**
Start working on something from a Git repository.

📁 **Open a project or file**
Open an existing project or file on your Mac.

Bullet Points

- Xcode is a bigger and much more complex, featureful version of Playgrounds.

- Xcode can compile apps that can be run on Apple platforms like iOS, iPadOS, macOS, tvOS, and watchOS, plus other platforms, or the web.

- An Xcode project needs to be saved to a specific location (instead of just magically appearing in the list of things you've made, like in Playgrounds).

- An Xcode project is a folder that contains an *.xcodeproj* file, as well as a collection of specially named internal folders.

- You don't need to work with the Xcode project folder directly. Instead, you work with it via Xcode's UI.

- All of Xcode's functionality is beyond the scope of this book, but as long as you go slowly, and stick to the familiar bits that are consistent between Playgrounds and Xcode, you'll be fine.

❸ In the template chooser, find the App template, select it, and then click the Next button.

You can choose whether you want your app to be Multiplatform, iOS, macOS, or one of Apple's other platforms. This Todo List app will work on most of these, but we recommend leaving Multiplatform selected.

❹ Give your app a product name and an organization identifier, and click the nNext button.

Your organization identifier is usually just your website's domain, backward, with the name of the app at the end. Feel free to make something up for now if you don't have a website.

❺ You'll be asked to pick a location to save the project to, then click Create.

☑ Create a new SwiftUI Xcode project, for iOS.

Your Xcode will look something like this

The code files that make up your project will be here.

You can run your app using the play button here.

You'll see a preview of the current code's UI (if any) here.

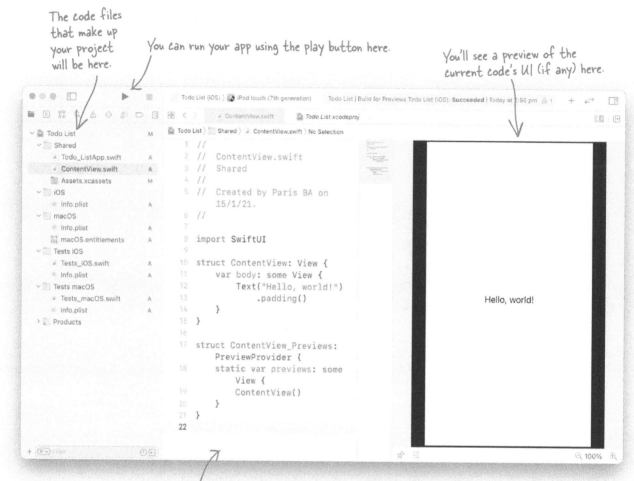

Code for the currently active file will be editable here.

Xcode can be confusing.

But don't worry. It's an important progression from Playgrounds. Most of the features of Playgrounds are still present and use the same interface elements to indicate them. Stick to coding and using the play button, and you'll be fine.

Create a new type to store a todo item in

Our first bit of coding is to create a new type to store each of our todo items in.

1   Create a new Swift file named *Item.swift* to store the code for the new type in.

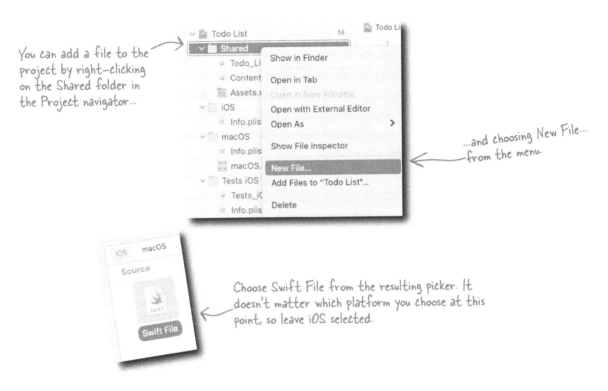

You can add a file to the project by right-clicking on the Shared folder in the Project navigator...

...and choosing New File... from the menu.

Choose Swift File from the resulting picker. It doesn't matter which platform you choose at this point, so leave iOS selected.

2   Inside `Item.swift`, define a new type named Item.

3   Our todo Item will need to store one thing: a String, representing the todo.

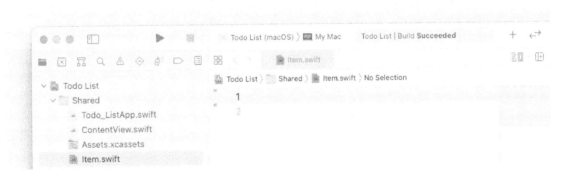

Why are we making our own special type to store todos in? Why not just use a String?

We need to store a little more than just a String.

Each todo will need to store a `String`, which is the todo itself, plus a unique identifier of some sort (eventually).

Creating a type of our own enables us to add features to the todo item that a String doesn't support.

Sharpen your pencil

Your turn. We need to implement the new type. We've given you the basic steps required, so have a go at implementing it in your new project.

You'll probably want to make your new type out of a struct, and it will need to (at the first stage) store a String, representing your todo item.

Once you've created it, you'll add a way to make each todo item uniquely identifiable.

Sharpen your pencil Solution

We need a type to represent a todo item.

The best way to make this is using a struct:

```
struct Item {


}
```

We need to store a String inside this new struct, representing the todo item, so we'll add a property:

```
struct Item {

    var todo: String

}
```

And that's it!

☑ Create a new type to store a todo item in.

Structs

Structs are value types. Every time you create or assign a struct, you're creating a new struct, or a copy of a struct.

This makes a struct the perfect base for our Item type.

We can create items easily, and delete them easily when we're done with them.

```
var todoItem1 = Todo(todo: "Rewatch 30 Rock")
var todoItem2 = Todo(todo: "Learn Spanish")
var todoItem3 = Todo(todo: "Eat a good souvlaki")
```

Make sure each todo item can be uniquely identified

Because we're eventually going to persist the todo list data across app launches, we need to make sure that each todo list item has a stable identity. That is, we need to make sure each instance of our new Item type is uniquely identifiable.

Luckily, Apple makes this easy for us: the Identifiable protocol ships with Swift, and is used to provide unique identities to things.

1 Open your *Item.swift* file, and find the implementation of `Item`:

```
struct Item {
    var todo: String
}
```

This won't be hard, as there should not be anything else in the file.

2 Declare that the `Item` struct will conform to the `Identifiable` protocol:

```
struct Item: Identifiable {
    var todo: String
}
```

2 Implement the necessary property to conform with the `Identifiable` protocol:

```
struct Item: Identifiable {
    let id = UUID()
    var todo: String
}
```

UUID() is part of Apple's Foundation library, and supplies a universally unique value that can be used as the Item's ID.

☑ Make sure each todo item can be uniquely identified.

🔍 Conforming to Identifiable Up Close

Conforming to the Identifiable protocol means that, as a struct, you're required to have an `id` property that will become your identity. If the type is a struct, you'll need to implement this yourself, as we're doing here.

The `UUID` function that we call to supply that identity will generate a big, long unique ID. Nothing magic.

Create a user interface for the app

Now we're going to create the user interface for the app:

1 We need to create some `@State` variables to hold the state of the app. We can figure out what sort of state information we need to hold by thinking about our app's planned UI.

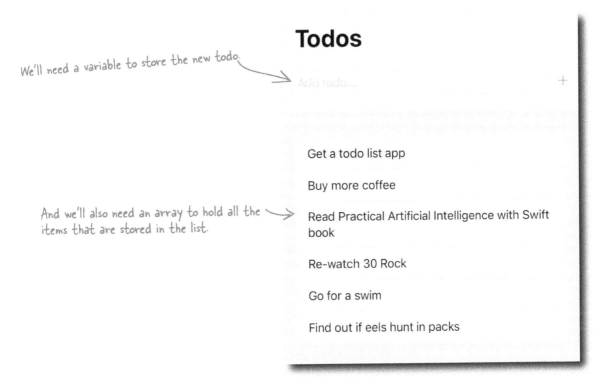

We'll need a variable to store the new todo.

Todos

Add todo...   +

Get a todo list app

Buy more coffee

And we'll also need an array to hold all the items that are stored in the list.

Read Practical Artificial Intelligence with Swift book

Re-watch 30 Rock

Go for a swim

Find out if eels hunt in packs

2 We'll add the two variables to keep track of this state to the `ContentView`, in *ContentView. swift*:

```
struct ContentView: View {
    @State private var currentTodo = ""
    @State private var todos: [Item] = []

    var body: some View {
        Text("Hello, world!")
            .padding()
    }
}
```

This one stores new todos that are currently being created. We'll start it with an empty String.

And this one stores an array of Item instances (which is our custom type for storing a todo), and will be used for the List.

Create a user interface for the app, continued

This is a bit fiddly. Inside the body of ContentView (remove the boilerplate that the project starts with), we will need a NavigationView, with a VStack inside it, with an HStack inside it, with a TextField inside that (a place to type new todos in), with a Button after it to save the new todo. We'll also need to set the NavigationView's navigation bar title to something sensible.

③ Update the body of ContentView to look like the following:

```
var body: some View {
①  NavigationView {
②    VStack {
③      HStack {
④        TextField("New todo..", text: $currentTodo)
              .textFieldStyle(RoundedBorderTextFieldStyle())

⑤        Button(action: {
            guard !self.currentTodo.isEmpty else { return }
            self.todos.append(Item(todo: self.currentTodo))
            self.currentTodo = ""
          }) {
            Image(systemName: "text.badge.plus")
          }
          .padding(.leading, 5)
        }.padding()
      }
      .navigationBarTitle("Todo List")
    }
}
```

Brain Power

Experiment with using different .textFieldStyle parameters to style the TextField. Try SquareBorderTextFieldStyle, DefaultTextFieldStyle, and PlainTextFieldStyle. Which one do you prefer?

What's going on in this user interface?

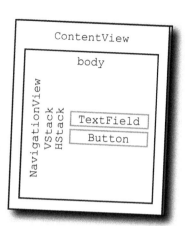

① **NavigationView**
This view allows us to present our user interface as a stack of views. It also gives us an easy way to put a nice name at the top of the screen, by setting `navigationBarTitle` to `"Todo List"`.

② **VStack**
Everything inside our `NavigationView` will live in a `VStack`. This lets us make sure the UI flows top to bottom on the screen, in a sensible way.

③ **HStack**
For now, the only item we'll put in our `VStack` is an `HStack`. We'll use the `HStack` to display things horizontally next to each other. The `HStack` has some padding at the end, too.

④ **TextField**
First, inside the `HStack`, we'll put a `TextField` that allows users to enter some text as a todo. We'll set the label text to "New todo…" and bind it to the `currentTodo` state variable that we created earlier. We also set its `textFieldStyle` parameter to `RoundedBorderTextFieldStyle()`.

⑤ **Button**
After this, we need a `Button` to add the current todo. The `Button` has a closure as its action that guards on the `newTodo` variable being empty (which would mean no text has been entered), and otherwise appends the contents of `newTodo` as an item in the `todos` array we created earlier. Finally, we display an `Image` as the button's label. The `Button` has some leading padding added, too.

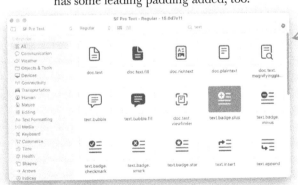

Visit https://developer.apple.com/sf-symbols to download the app to browse symbols!

Useful Icons
The text badge plus icon that we summon using the Image(systemName: "text.badge.plus") call in our Button summons an image that comes from a useful library of images that Apple ships called SF Symbols. SF Symbols has hundreds of different icons available freely for use in your apps on Apple platforms.

Todo List

At this point, your app—if you run it—looks something like this. We really need to add the actual list....

Todo List (iOS) ⟩ iPod touch (7th generation)

New todo..

You can run your app in an iOS simulator by clicking on the play button up in the top-lefthand corner of Xcode.

Make sure you have an iOS device type selected here, for your simulator.

How's my todo list app going? I can't wait forever, you know. I'm just getting more behind.

Create a user interface for the app, continued, continued

Our app looks a bit empty without its primary feature: a List. So we're going to add that now. The List will go inside the VStack we created, but outside and after the HStack.

 Update the body of ContentView to look like the following, adding a **List**:

```swift
var body: some View {
    NavigationView {
        VStack {
            HStack {
                TextField("New todo..", text: $currentTodo)
                    .textFieldStyle(RoundedBorderTextFieldStyle())

                Button(action: {
                    guard !self.currentTodo.isEmpty else { return }
                    self.todos.append(Item(todo: self.currentTodo))
                    self.currentTodo = ""
                }) {
                    Image(systemName: "text.badge.plus")
                }
                .padding(.leading, 5)
            }.padding()

            List {
                Text("This is something in my list!")
                Text("This is also in my list!")
                Text("And another thing!")
            }
        }
        .navigationBarTitle("Todo List")
    }
}
```

← The List is a view of its own.

← Everything inside the List is displayed, in a List.

Making the List actually list todos

5 To make the `List` actually list todos, we need to use a `ForEach` block, iterating through the items in the `todos` array and displaying each one as a `Text` view inside the `List`. First, we'll add the `ForEach`:

```
List {
    ForEach(todos) { todoEntry in
        Text("This is something in my list!")
        Text("This is also in my list!")
        Text("And another thing!")
    }
}
```

It's the same three lines of text, repeated each time the ForEach encounters an item in the todos array. Looks busier, but it's not very useful yet, is it?

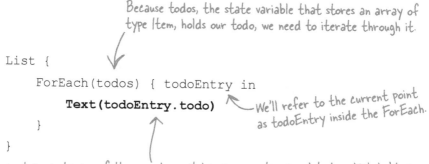

Todo List

This is something in my list!

This is also in my list!

And another thing!

This is something in my list!

This is also in my list!

And another thing!

This is something in my list!

This is also in my list!

6 If you ran the app at this point, you'd see the three lines of text repeated again and again for each item you add to the todo list using the `TextField` and the `Button`. Go ahead, give it a try; it won't bite. What you won't see is the contents of each todo item, unfortunately. Let's fix that. Remove the three `Text` views from inside the `ForEach`, and add:

Because todos, the state variable that stores an array of type Item, holds our todo, we need to iterate through it.

```
List {
    ForEach(todos) { todoEntry in
        Text(todoEntry.todo)
    }
}
```

We'll refer to the current point as todoEntry inside the ForEach.

And because todos contains instances of Item, we know it has a property named todo, which holds a String representing the todo item. So we display that as a Text view inside the List.

☑ Create a user interface for the app: a text field to add new todos with, a button to save them, and a list to show all the todos.

 Test Drive

Todo List (iOS) ⟩ iPod touch (7th generation)

Run the app and see what happens...

You can add entries by typing in here...

...and then hit this button.

Carrier 🗢   5:39 PM

Todo List

New todo...

Eat a burrito

Have a good long nap

Your entries will appear in the list!

Rewatch Frasier

Drink 8 cups of water

Practice insulting people in French

Implement a way to save the list of todos

1 Now we must return to *Item.swift*, and update our Item type so that it can be encoded and decoded. This is a fancy way of saying *saved and loaded*. The only thing we need to do to make Item codable is add a conformance to the Codable protocol:

```
struct Item: Identifiable, Codable {
    let id = UUID()
    var todo: String
}
```

Behind the Scenes

Codable is a `typealias` for Decodable & Encodable, making it easy to allow your type to convert itself to and from an external representation. In other words, it asks Swift to make it so that our type can be encoded into and decoded from a serialized format, like JSON, usually so we can store it on disk.

Making data codable is useful for saving it to disk, sending it across a network, or passing it to an API.

Under the hood, Swift will attempt to create the code required to encode and decode an instance of a type that conforms to `Codable`.

For a type to be able to conform to `Codable`, its stored properties also need to be `Codable`. Thankfully, Swift's standard types—`String`, `Int`, `Double`, `Array`, and so on—are already codable.

If your properties are `Codable`, then your type will automatically conform to `Codable` when you declare that conformance.

This:

```
struct Item: Identifiable, Codable {
    let id = UUID()
    var todo: String
}
```

Is exactly the same as this:

```
struct Item: Identifiable, Encodable, Decodable {
    let id = UUID()
    var todo: String
}
```

But you could pick and choose just `Encodable` or `Decodable`, if you only needed one for some reason.

Next, we're going to go back to *ContentView.swift* and create three methods in the `ContentView` struct:

> **save()**
> We need a method that can encode all the `Items` in the todos array
> and save it.

```
private func save() {
  UserDefaults.standard.set(
    try? PropertyListEncoder().encode(self.todos), forKey: "myTodosKey"
  )
}
```

`UserDefaults` lets you store a small amount of data as part of the user's profile in the device. It makes it easy to store simple things quickly. The syntax is:

```
UserDefaults.standard.set("Data to be stored", forKey: "keyName")
```

So, our `save` method is using a `try` to attempt to get the encoded form of the `todos` Array and save it with the key `myTodosKey`.

> **load()**
> We'll also need a counterpart method that can load all the Items from
> the save back into the `todos` array.

```
private func load() {
  if let todosData = UserDefaults.standard.value(forKey: "myTodosKey") as? Data {
    if let todosList
        = try? PropertyListDecoder().decode(Array<Item>.self, from: todosData) {
      self.todos = todosList
    }
  }
}
```

Our `load` method reads from `UserDefaults` using the same key, `myTodosKey`, and asks for it as `Data`. Once it's got some `Data`, it attempts to use a `PropertyListDecoder` to decode the data that's stored in `UserDefaults` and place it back into the `todos` array.

↑
Swift's Data type allows you to store raw bytes. It's useful when
you need to save or load data, or transmit it across a network.

delete(at offset: IndexSet)
Finally, we'll need a method that can be used to delete an individual todo entry from both the list and the saved copy.

```
private func delete(at offset: IndexSet) {
  self.todos.remove(atOffsets: offset)
  save()
}
```

The `delete` method takes an `offset` parameter, of type `IndexSet`. An `IndexSet` stores a collection of unique integer values that represent the indexes of elements in another collection. Basically, it stores a sorted collected of integers that represent positions in a collection type.

In this case, we take an `IndexSet` parameter, `offset`, and use that to remove one or more entries from the `todos` array.

Then we call our `save` method. That's it!

 ## Sharpen your pencil

It's your turn again. See if you can figure out the appropriate place to call all the methods we've just made.

We need to call `save()` when a new todo is added.

We need to call `load()` when the `NavigationView` appears.

And we need to call `delete()` when a `List` item is deleted.

To assist you, consider the following:

- `List` has a method named `onDelete`, which has a parameter named `perform`, which can take a method as its argument. This will implicitly be passed an `IndexSet` when it's called, which represents the item that was selected for deletion.

- Similarly, the `NavigationView` view (and all other views) has a method called `onAppear`, which has a parameter named `perform`, which takes a method as its argument.

⟶ Answers on page 318.

 Implement a way to save the list of todos, so that it persists.

And that's it. You're ready to test your fabulous new todo app.

Run the app to test it!

You can add todos, and delete todos by swiping on them and tapping delete—and closing and relaunching the app will still show you your todo list, without losing data! Amazing.

Hey, this is pretty good, eh? I wonder what else you could make for me. I have lots of friends who also need apps.

Sharpen your pencil
Solution

From page 316.

```
var body: some View {
    NavigationView {
        VStack {
            HStack {
                TextField("New todo..", text: $currentTodo)
                    .textFieldStyle(RoundedBorderTextFieldStyle())

            Button(action: {
                guard !self.currentTodo.isEmpty else { return }
                self.todos.append(Item(todo: self.currentTodo))
                self.currentTodo = ""
                self.save()
            }) {
                Image(systemName: "text.badge.plus")
            }
            .padding(.leading, 5)
        }.padding()

        List {
          ForEach(todos) { todoEntry in
            Text(todoEntry.todo)
          }.onDelete(perform: delete)
        }
      }
      .navigationBarTitle("Todo List")
    }.onAppear(perform: load)
  }
```

So, that's a UI framework?

Frank: So, that's a UI framework?

Judy: I'm not that impressed.

Jo: I'm impressed. I mean, I already was impressed, but now I'm even more impressed. It's really good.

Judy: So, what should we do with it next?

Frank: Yeah, where to next? It's a bit overwhelming. I feel like I know enough to be dangerous, but not enough to build anything particularly large.

Jo: Never fear. We'll build something even bigger than the todo app next time. Maybe even something that connects to the internet! You'll see how SwiftUI scales and gets more complex, while still being very Swifty.

Judy: I'd like to learn about connecting to the internet, that sounds useful. Downloading things and whatnot...

Frank: Me too!

Jo: Great. Keep learning!

Bullet Points

- SwiftUI is a declarative UI framework, designed around the strengths and features of Swift.
- You can use SwiftUI to make UI-driven apps for Apple's platforms.
- You need to import SwiftUI to use it.
- A SwiftUI view is created by declaring a struct (by convention named `<SomethingView>`) that conforms to the View protocol.
- The View protocol is a core part of SwiftUI, and must be adopted by everything you make in SwiftUI that will be drawn onscreen.
- Inside your view struct, you declare a computed property named body that has the type `some View`.
- `some View` means that it will return something that conforms to the View protocol, but it must always return the same kind of View (it can't sometimes be one type that conforms to View, and sometimes be another type that conforms to View).
- SwiftUI elements are coded inside the `body` computed property. For example, `Text("Hello")` displays a `Text` view that says "Hello."
- Some SwiftUI view elements are invisibile, like `VStack` and `HStack`; they are used solely to lay things out.
- SwiftUI is powerful, but it can start to feel pretty fragile if you don't get your views in the right order. Take extra care to check that everything is in place.

 SwiftUIcross

We've strategically hidden everything you've learned about SwiftUI in this chapter in this crossword. Use it as a palate cleanser before continuing.

Across
2) The _____ property stores the content for our views.
4) This protocol is used for things that need a stable identity.
6) An _____ arranges thing horizontally.
7) Properties that are tagged with _____ indicate variables that relate to the UI.
8) A SwiftUI view conforms to the _____ protocol.
9) A _____ arranges things vertically.
10) A _____ view creates an interface element that lets the user pick between a bounded range of values.
11) This IDE is the primary environment for writing Swift for Apple's platforms.

Down
1) This protocol is used to allow things to be saved to and loaded from disk.
3) A _____ is a SwiftUI view that provides an editable area for text.
5) SwiftUI is a _____ framework (as opposed to imperative).
7) _____ is a library of useful icons and symbols.

Answers on page 324.

Pool Puzzle

Note: each thing from the pool can only be used once! Or not at all.

Your **job** is to take lines of code from the pool and place them into the blank lines in a Playground. You may **not** use the same line more than once, and you won't need to use all the lines. Your **goal** is to make the code that will generate the output shown.

78.30 F is 25.72 C

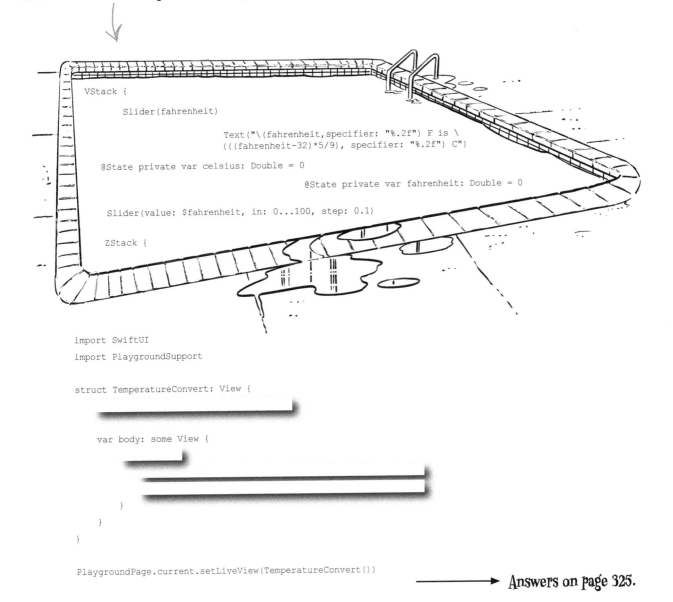

```
VStack {

        Slider(fahrenheit)

                        Text("\(fahrenheit,specifier: "%.2f") F is \
                        (((fahrenheit-32)*5/9), specifier: "%.2f") C")

    @State private var celsius: Double = 0

                            @State private var fahrenheit: Double = 0

    Slider(value: $fahrenheit, in: 0...100, step: 0.1)

    ZStack {
```

```
import SwiftUI
import PlaygroundSupport

struct TemperatureConvert: View {


    var body: some View {




        }
    }
}

PlaygroundPage.current.setLiveView(TemperatureConvert())
```

Answers on page 325.

BE the Swift Compiler

Each of the Swift code snippets on this and the following page represents a SwiftUI view. Your job is to play Swift compiler, and determine whether each of these will run or not. If they will not compile, what's wrong with them?

Assume each snippet was run in a Playground, importing SwiftUI appropriately, and using this command.

```
PlaygroundPage.current.setLiveView(MyView())
```

A

```swift
struct MyView: View {
    var dogs = ["Greyhound", "Whippet", "Italian Greyhound"]
    @State private var selectedDog = 0

    var body: some View {
        VStack {
            Text("Please select your favorite dog breed:")
            Picker(selection: $selectedDog, label: Text("Dog")) {
                ForEach(0..<dogs.count) {
                    Text(self.dogs[$0])
                }
            }
            Text("\(dogs[selectedDog]) is your favorite breed.")
        }
    }
}
```

C

```
struct MyView: View {
    var body: View {
        VStack {
            Text("Hello")
            Text("SwiftUI!")
        }
    }
}
```

B

```
struct MyView: View {
    var body: some View {
        Image(systemName: "star.fill")
            .imageScale(.large)
            .foregroundColor(.yellow)
    }
}
```

E

```
struct MyView: View {
    @State private var lovelyDayStatus = true

    var body: some View {
        Toggle( isOn: $lovelyDayStatus) {
            Text("Is it a lovely day?")
        }

        if(lovelyDayStatus) {
            Text("It's a lovely day!")
        } else {
            Text("It's not a lovely day.")
        }
    }
}
```

D

```
struct MyView: View {
    var body: some View {
        List {
            Text("This is a list!")
            Text("Hello")
            Text("I'm a list!")
        }
    }
}
```

F

```
struct MyView: View {
    @State private var coffeesConsumed = 0

    var body: some View {
        Stepper(value: coffeesConsumed) {
            Text("Cups of coffee consumed: \(coffeesConsumed)")
        }
    }
}
```

⟶ Answers on page 325.

SwiftUIcross
Solution

From page 320.

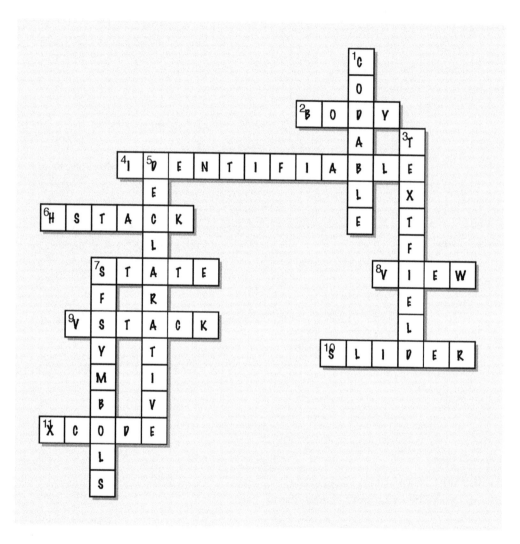

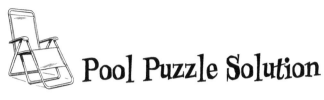

Pool Puzzle Solution

From page 321.

```
import SwiftUI
import PlaygroundSupport

struct TemperatureConvert: View {
    @State private var fahrenheit: Double = 0

    var body: some View {
        VStack {
            Slider(value: $fahrenheit, in: 0...100, step: 0.1)
            Text("\(fahrenheit,specifier: "%.2f") F is \
              (((fahrenheit-32)*5/9), specifier: "%.2f") C")
        }
    }
}

PlaygroundPage.current.setLiveView(TemperatureConvert())
```

BE the Swift Compiler Solution

From page 322.

A, B, D, and E all work fine.

C is missing the keyword some in the body.

F is missing the $ from the binding of coffeesConsumed in the Stepper.

11 putting swiftUI into practice

Circles, Timers, Buttons—Oh My!

All the UI elements of the rainbow.

> There are a lot of elements in SwiftUI, and when your UI gets advanced, it can feel like you're trying to juggle them all.

SwiftUI lets you do more than work with Buttons and Lists.

You can also use shapes, animations, and more! In this chapter, we're going to look at some of the **more advanced ways you can construct a SwiftUI UI,** and connect it to a data source that isn't just user-generated content like todo items. SwiftUI lets you **build responsive UIs** that handle **events** coming from all sorts of places. We'll be working with Xcode, Apple's IDE, and we'll be focusing on iOS apps, but everything you'll learn is applicable to SwiftUI on iPadOS, macOS, watchOS, and tvOS as well. It's time to explore the depths of SwiftUI!

What fancy things can be done with a UI framework?

Frank: So, we've learned what a UI framework is...

Judy: We even built a pretty good todo List app...

Jo: But what else can we do?

Frank: I imagine we could build another app!

Judy: Well yeah, we could. And we should. But what features haven't we learned yet? There's more to it than we've learned so far, isn't there?

Jo: Well yes, there are some more advanced SwiftUI concepts we haven't looked at yet.

Judy: Shall we build something with one or two of them, then?

Jo: I'd also like to see how we can make a website with Swift. I heard that it's pretty easy to do that.

Frank: Yeah, websites! I mean, can we use SwiftUI for a website?

Judy: No, we can't, but there's a framework called Vapor that lets us make a website in Swift. I think we'll get to it soon.

I like to relax a lot. Can you help me build me an app that allows me keep track of how long is left in a meeting, so I can efficiently get back to my hammock?

SwiftUI can help us build a timer for meetings.

SwiftUI has all sorts of useful building blocks that let us build a timer.

A useful representation of a timer is a circle, so we might make our timer look like a circle that steadily shrinks.

Serious Coding
Making a timer ⟵

We're on the clock here...(we're
not really...take your time).

We're going to build an Executive Timer app for the CEO. Once again, we'll be using Xcode, Apple's IDE for Swift and SwiftUI development. We'll need to complete the following steps to create the Executive Timer:

☐ Create a new SwiftUI Xcode project, for iOS.

☐ Create the basic elements of the Executive Timer app.

☐ Do some setup so that the UI can function.

☐ Create all the pieces of the UI.

☐ Combine all the elements!

☐ Make the timer update the UI, so it all works.

⟵ Follow along with these
steps yourself, and build
your own Executive Timer.

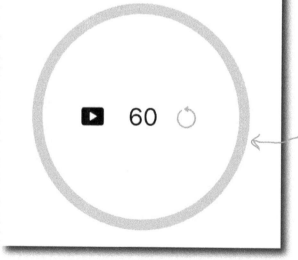

The Executive Timer app is
going to look like this.

This circle represents the time we're...
timing. It shrinks as the time reduces.

Let's get building...

Create a new SwiftUI Xcode project, for iOS

Once again, we need to start by creating an Xcode project. This is pretty similar to in the previous chaptrer (in fact, it's exactly the same).

1 Fire up Xcode.

2 Choose the **Create a new Xcode project** option from the *Welcome to Xcode* screen.

If you don't see a "Welcome to Xcode" screen, you can get to the same place by choosing New –> Project... from the File menu.

3 In the template chooser, find the App template, select it, and then click the Next button.

You can choose whether you want your app to be Multiplatform, iOS, macOS, or one of Apple's other platforms. This Todo List app will work on most of these, but we recommend leaving Multiplatform selected.

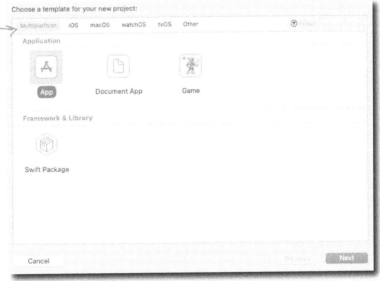

Create a new SwiftUI Xcode project, for iOS, continued...

4 Give your app a product name and an organization identifier, and click the Next button.

5 You'll be asked to pick a location to save the project to, then click Create.

☑ Create a new SwiftUI Xcode project, for iOS.

Bullet Points

- Selecting the SwiftUI project settings in Xcode does not do anything special. Every project type in Xcode provides a sensible set of defaults appropriate to what you're trying to make. Because we want to make an iOS app written with SwiftUI, we select those settings for the project.

- We could also make this timer app for macOS, or even watchOS, using exactly the same code (SwiftUI makes that very easy), but because this book tries to keep things straightforward for teaching, we've stuck with iOS. In your own time, it's a good learning exercise to figure out how to make your timer app cross-platform!

- Our timer app is going to make use of some basic shapes in order to represent parts of its user interface. This is because we want our timer to be a circle, and SwiftUI doesn't come with any building blocks that naturally represent a circular timer: we need to make one. And we will.

The Executive Timer UI and features

This is what our Executive Timer UI will look like, and do:

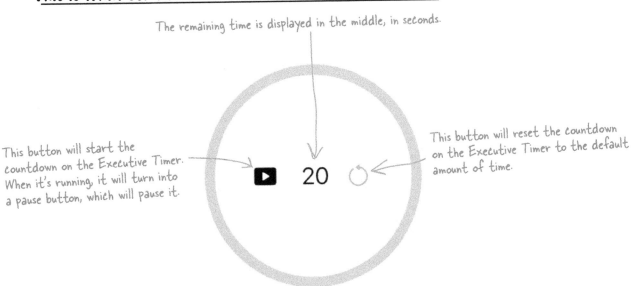

The remaining time is displayed in the middle, in seconds.

This button will start the countdown on the Executive Timer. When it's running, it will turn into a pause button, which will pause it.

This button will reset the countdown on the Executive Timer to the default amount of time.

And this is what the UI will look like in the various different states:

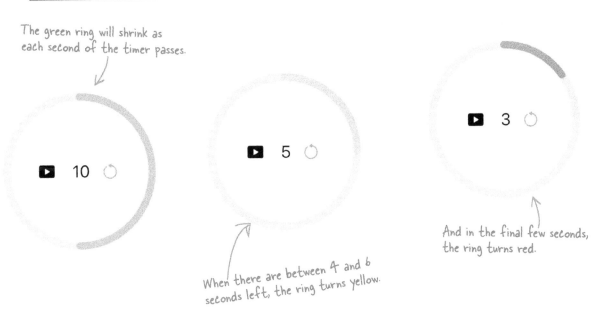

The green ring will shrink as each second of the timer passes.

When there are between 4 and 6 seconds left, the ring turns yellow.

And in the final few seconds, the ring turns red.

Creating the basic elements of the app

We need to do a tiny bit of setup to make our Executive Timer app. We'll start by creating some places to store state, and then the timer itself. Then we'll do some UI setup to actually draw the timer on the screen.

① Set up a place to store the default time—in other words, the time the Executive Timer will count down from. We'll use a `CGFloat` for this, which is just a `Float`, but for graphics-related things (like a user interface):

```
let defaultTime: CGFloat = 20
```

This is the time in seconds.

② Create some properties using the `@State` keyword to store UI-related state elements:

```
@State private var timerRunning = false
@State private var countdownTime: CGFloat = defaultTime
```

This Boolean will reflect whether the timer is active.

This CGFloat will store the time remaining to count down.

We'll make it the defaultTime to start with: the time remaining starts with however long the timer is for.

③ Make a `Timer` so that, you know, the Executive Timer can actually count down:

```
let timer = Timer.publish(every: 1, on: .main, in: .common).autoconnect()
```

Behind the Scenes

The `Timer` is created using the `publish` method, specifying a time interval (1 second in this case) and running on the main loop. Because we used the `publish` method to create the `Timer`, it will publish (or emit) its data over time (every 1 second, in fact).

A Swift publisher's data can be received in a variety of ways, including by SwiftUI views, which can act on the updates each time they are received.

Publishers are part of a library Apple supplies called **Combine**. YWe're not covering everything about Combine, but it supplies a lot of useful things for receiving data from other places in your apps.

 Create the basic elements of the Executive Timer app.

Pieces of the UI

The gray circle
First you'll need a gray circle. This will go underneath everything, to be revealed as the primary circle shrinks as the Executive Timer counts down.

1

The primary circle
2 Then you'll need a primary circle, which will be trimmed to the right size based on how much time is left.

The time and buttons
And finally, you'll need the play/pause button and the reset button, as well as the time remaining in seconds.

3 20

 20

We'll code these in a moment...

Brain Power

Create a Playground and draw some shapes with SwiftUI.

We recommend starting with a Triangle:

```
Triangle()
    .stroke(Color.green, style:
      StrokeStyle(lineWidth: 5, lineCap: .round, lineJoin: .round))
    .frame(width: 300, height: 300)
```

Setting up the UI of the Executive Timer

Now we're going to do the UI setup to draw the timer.

1   Create a **closure** that returns the correct color, depending on the state of
`countdownTime`:

```
let countdownColor: Color = {
    switch (countdownTime) {
        case 6...: return Color.green
        case 3...: return Color.yellow
        default: return Color.red
    }
}()
```

2   Define a `strokeStyle`, so it's easy to experiment with new looks for the timer later:

```
let strokeStyle = StrokeStyle(lineWidth: 15, lineCap: .round)
```

3   Define a `buttonIcon`, so that the timer start and pause button switches between the
correct icons at the appropriate time, based on the state of `timerRunning`:

```
let buttonIcon = timerRunning ? "pause.rectangle.fill" : "play.rectangle.fill"
```

This is the ternary operator.

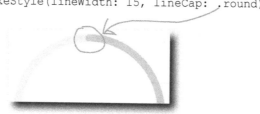

☑   Do some setup so that the UI can function.

Coding the pieces of the UI

❶ Coding the gray circle

To draw the gray circle, we need to draw...a gray circle! Since this is going to be the static UI element beneath everything else, it doesn't actually need to do aything; it just needs to exist.

SwiftUI has a lot of useful UI view building blocks, like `Text`, `Image`, `VStack`, and `HStack`, but it also has a lot of primitive shapes for you to use, like `Rectangle`, `Ellipse`, `Capsule`, `RoundedRectangle`, and `Circle`.

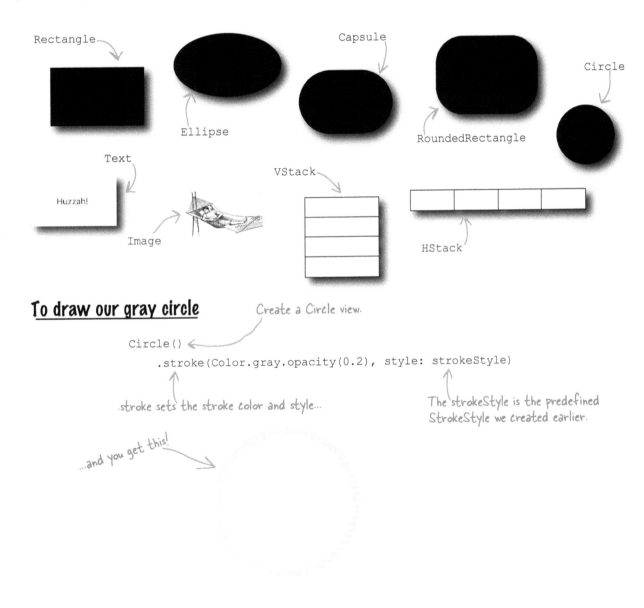

To draw our gray circle

Create a Circle view.

```
Circle()
    .stroke(Color.gray.opacity(0.2), style: strokeStyle)
```

.stroke sets the stroke color and style...

The strokeStyle is the predefined StrokeStyle we created earlier.

...and you get this!

❷ Coding the primary circle

The primary circle is a little more complex than the gray circle. The primary circle needs to shrink its ring based on how much time is left, and needs to animate nicely as it shrinks.

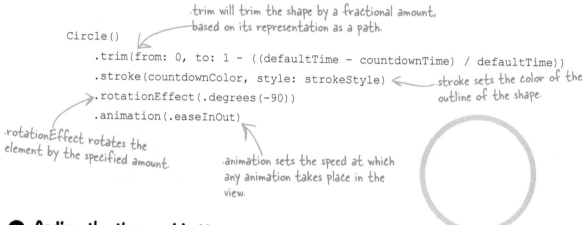

.trim will trim the shape by a fractional amount, based on its representation as a path.

```
Circle()
    .trim(from: 0, to: 1 - ((defaultTime - countdownTime) / defaultTime))
    .stroke(countdownColor, style: strokeStyle)
    .rotationEffect(.degrees(-90))
    .animation(.easeInOut)
```

.stroke sets the color of the outline of the shape.

.rotationEffect rotates the element by the specified amount.

.animation sets the speed at which any animation takes place in the view.

❸ Coding the time and buttons

The time and buttons are not displayed using shapes, like the two circles you've drawn so far, but with elements you've used previously, to make the Todo List.

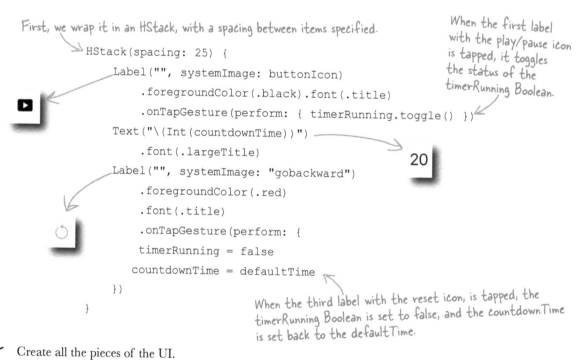

First, we wrap it in an HStack, with a spacing between items specified.

```
HStack(spacing: 25) {
    Label("", systemImage: buttonIcon)
        .foregroundColor(.black).font(.title)
        .onTapGesture(perform: { timerRunning.toggle() })
    Text("\(Int(countdownTime))")
        .font(.largeTitle)
    Label("", systemImage: "gobackward")
        .foregroundColor(.red)
        .font(.title)
        .onTapGesture(perform: {
            timerRunning = false
            countdownTime = defaultTime
        })
}
```

When the first label with the play/pause icon is tapped, it toggles the status of the timerRunning Boolean.

20

When the third label with the reset icon, is tapped, the timerRunning Boolean is set to false, and the countdownTime is set back to the defaultTime.

☑ Create all the pieces of the UI.

Sharpen your pencil

Take a look at the follow snippets of SwiftUI code. For each of them, draw what you think they'll output, or if they're not going to draw anything, and try to describe what's wrong and try to fix it.

Assume that SwiftUI and PlaygroundSupport are imported, and they're running in a Playground that's drawing the view using:

```
PlaygroundPage.current.setLiveView(ShapeView())
```

☐
```
struct ShapeView: View {
    var body: some View {
        VStack {
            Rectangle().padding()
            Ellipse().padding()
            Capsule().padding()
            RoundedRectangle(cornerRadius: 25).padding()
        }
    }
}
```

☐
```
struct ShapeView: View {
    var body: some View {
        VStack {
            Circle()
            Circle()
        }
    }
}
```

☐
```
struct ShapeView: View {
    var body: some View {
        VStack {
            RoundedRectangle(cornerRadius: 100).padding()
        }
    }
}
```

→ Answers on page 343.

Combining the three elements

Have a think about what a ZStack might do. We'll discuss it in a moment.

To create the view we need, we need to combine all three elements in order, inside a ZStack:

```
ZStack {
    Circle()
❶      .stroke(Color.gray.opacity(0.2), style: strokeStyle)
    Circle()
        .trim(from: 0, to: 1 - ((defaultTime - countdownTime) / defaultTime))
❷      .stroke(countdownColor, style: strokeStyle)
        .rotationEffect(.degrees(-90))
        .animation(.easeInOut)
    HStack(spacing: 25) {
        Label("", systemImage: buttonIcon)
            .foregroundColor(.black).font(.title)
            .onTapGesture(perform: { timerRunning.toggle() })
        Text("\(Int(countdownTime))")
❸          .font(.largeTitle)
        Label("", systemImage: "gobackward")
            .foregroundColor(.red)
            .font(.title)
            .onTapGesture(perform: {
            timerRunning = false
            countdownTime = defaultTime
        })
    }
}.frame(width: 300, height: 300)
```

We've framed the ZStack to a nice 300x300 square, so the circle for the countdown isn't to big.

☑ Combine all the elements!

Wait, what's a ZStack? I've used HStack, for horizontal layouts, and VStacks for vertical layouts, but I don't know what a ZStack does!

A ZStack is like an HStack or a VStack, but instead of being on the h- or v-axis, it's on the z-axis. Also known as: depth.

In the case of our Executive Timer app, we need to use a VStack because we want to place the gray circle underneath everything, with the primary circle on top of it (so that the gray circle is revealed when the primary circle shrinks), and the time and buttons on top of everything else.

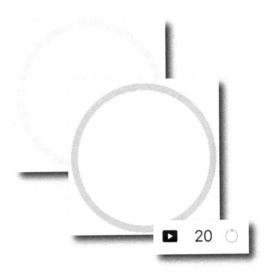

Brain Power

Create a new Swift Playground, add some Text views, maybe in an HStack or a VStack or two, and an image if you want to get fancy. Then, experiment with wrapping it all in a ZStack, and see what happens. Experiment with ZStack's embedded inside each other, each with some Text views inside.

You'll quickly get a feel for how ZStack's work!

The finishing touches

The last piece of the puzzle is adding an `onReceive` event action to the view. This will allow the view to respond to the timer we created earlier, and do things with that information:

The three visual bits of the UI you created go here. They've been snipped out to fit this code on the page.

```
ZStack {
    ❶ ❷ ❸
}.frame(width: 150 * 2, height: 150 * 2)
.onReceive(timer, perform: { _ in
    guard timerRunning else { return }
        if countdownTime > 0 {
            countdownTime -= 1
        } else {
            timerRunning = false
            countdownTime = defaultTime
        }
    })
```

The perform parameter specifies the method to be run when the specified publisher (in this case, timer) emits something.

.onReceive is an instance method available on views that lets you specify a publisher to respond to, and a method to run when that publisher emits data.

The method we run is a closure that guards on timerRunning (i.e., it only continues if the timer is running). It subtracks 1 from the countdownTimer if the timer is above 0, or turns the timer off and resets the time to the default if it isn't.

☑ Make the timer update the UI, so it all works.

And now you're ready to test your Executive Timer!

Working with Publishers

Our `timer` is effectively a mutable piece of state that dictates what the Executive Timer UI is going to do: the UI needs to display the number of seconds remaining on the timer, as well as update the ring to reflect the time left.

The `onReceive` method tells SwiftUI that we want to receive emissions from the thing specified (`timer`, in this case) and **perform** a function when an emission is received.

The things we **perform** update the value of `countdownTime`, which the UI uses to draw its state.

Test Drive

Executive Timer ⟩ 📱 iPhone 12 Pro Max

Run the app and see what happens...

You should see something pretty similar to this!

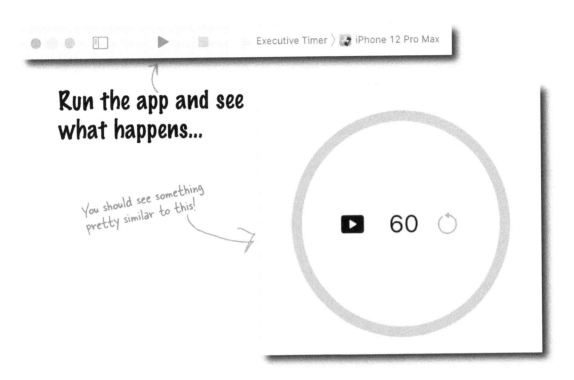

▶ 60 ↻

Sharpen your pencil
Solution

From page 339.

Tabbed views for a clean UI

> Hey, so, most of my favourite iOS apps have a nice tabbed view. How do I do that in SwiftUI? I just can't get my head around how that would work. Help!?

SwiftUI has a number of useful container views, and makes it easy to put any view you might want on a separate tab.

`TabView` is one such useful **container view**. Unsurprisingly, it allows you to put different views on different tabs in your app.

To use a `TabView`, you need to do three things:

❶ Create however many different views you need

Each tab needs something to display, so you'll need to make sure you have some views available to put in the tabs.

❷ Build a TabView containing your views

You'll use SwiftUI's `TabView` container view to hold your tabs and display the tab UI.

❶ Create however many different views you need (to live in tabs)

Use the File menu to add a new file to your project.

Then select SwiftUI View from the template chooser.

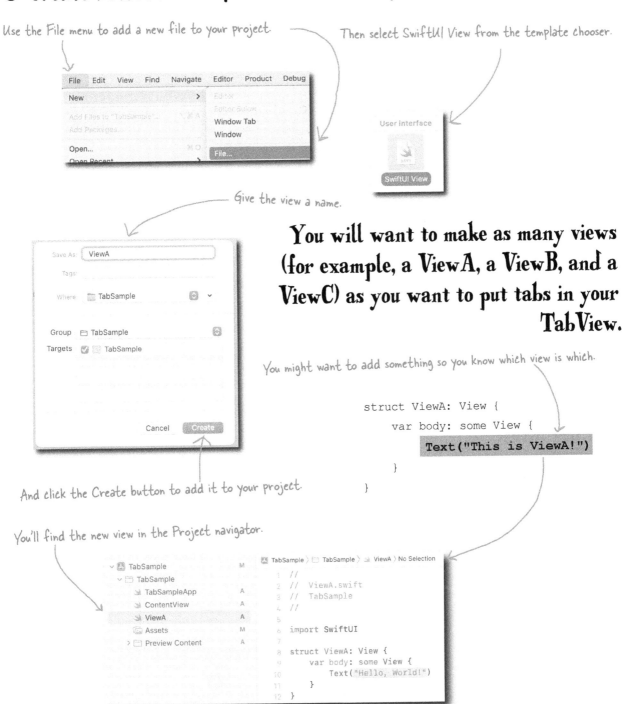

Give the view a name.

And click the Create button to add it to your project.

You'll find the new view in the Project navigator.

You will want to make as many views (for example, a ViewA, a ViewB, and a ViewC) as you want to put tabs in your TabView.

You might want to add something so you know which view is which.

```
struct ViewA: View {
    var body: some View {
        Text("This is ViewA!")
    }
}
```

❷ Build a TabView containing your views

With your views ready to go...

⤷ ViewA
⤷ ViewB
⤷ ViewC

Wrap everything in a TabView.

In whatever view you want to display the tabs:

```
struct ContentView: View {
    var body: some View {
        TabView {
            ViewA()
                .padding()
                .tabItem {
                    Image(systemName: "a.square")
                    Text("View A")
                }
                .tag(1)
            ViewB()
                .padding()
                .tabItem {
                    Image(systemName: "b.square")
                    Text("View B")
                }
                .tag(2)
            ViewC()
                .padding()
                .tabItem {
                    Image(systemName: "c.square")
                    Text("View C")
                }
                .tag(3)
        }
    }
}
```

❶

And call each view (in this case ViewA).

With some appropriate padding.

And the details you want shown on a tab: in this case, an image from SF Symbols, and some text.

❷

Plus a numbered tag, for order of the tabs.

❸

Whatever views you put inside a TabView will be displayed, tab-by-tab. The tabItem modifier allows you to add details that are display on a tab.

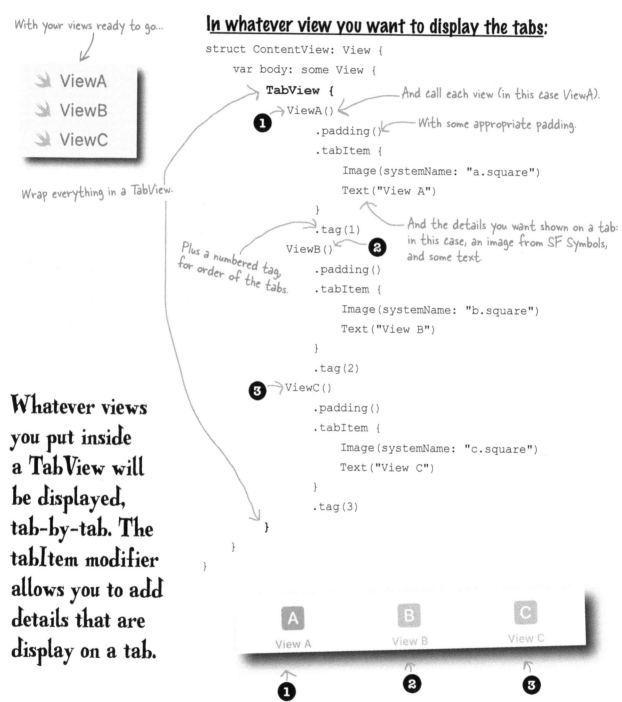

A — View A   ❶
B — View B   ❷
C — View C   ❸

The resulting tabs

If you created three views, and a TabView containing them, you might end up here:

Introducing Labels

Instead of combining an `Image` and a `Text` view, we could instead use a `Label`. A `Label` combines an image and some text.

So, one of our tabs could look like this:

```
Label("View B", systemImage: "b.square")
```

Instead of:

```
Image(systemName: "b.square")
Text("View B")
```

Test Drive

Update the code for the three tabs to use `Label` views, instead of an `Image` view and a `Text` view together.

Hmm...Can you put some settings for my nice Executive Timer...great work by the way...on a separate tab? That sounds great...all my favorite iOS app have tabs. OK, back to my snooze now.

This is easy! Just wrap the view with the timer, and a new Settings view in a TabView.

You already know how to do everything you need to do, assuming the Settings view is empty (we'll get to that in a moment).

Exercise

Update your Executive Timer to have two tabs, one for the Timer and one for a Settings view. You'll need to undertake the following steps to do this:

☐ Rename the ContentView that displays the timer to TimerView. You'll need to rename both the ContentView struct (to TimerView) and the file (using the Xcode sidebar).

☐ Create a new SwiftUI View file in the project, and name it ContentView.

☐ Inside the new ContentView, add a TabView and a tab displaying the TimerView.

☐ Create a new SwiftUI View file in the project, and name it TimerSettingsView.

☐ Add TimerSettingsView as a second tab in the TabView in the ContentView.

Exercise Solution

Rename the existing Executive Timer ContentView <u>file</u>:

Select the ContentView in the Project navigator on the lefthand side of the Xcode window.

And change the name from ContentView.swift to TimerView.swift on the righthand side of the Xcode window, in the File Inspector.

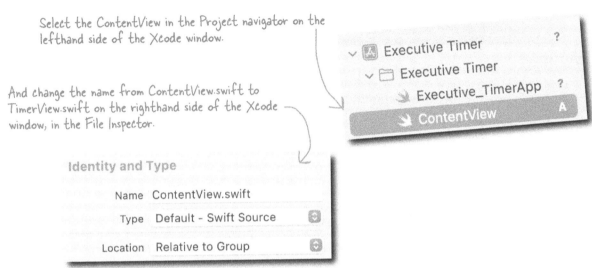

Identity and Type

Name ContentView.swift

Type Default - Swift Source

Location Relative to Group

Rename the existing Executive Timer ContentView <u>struct</u>:

In the code in the newly renamed TimerView.swift, rename the view struct from ContentView to TimerView.

```swift
struct ContentView: View {
```

```swift
struct TimerView: View {
```

<u>Your newly renamed TimerView should look like this:</u>

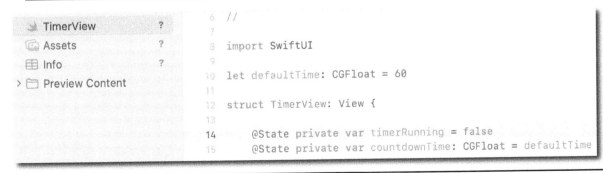

```swift
6  //
7
8  import SwiftUI
9
10 let defaultTime: CGFloat = 60
11
12 struct TimerView: View {
13
14     @State private var timerRunning = false
15     @State private var countdownTime: CGFloat = defaultTime
```

Creating a new tabbed ContentView

To display the tabs, we need a new view containing a `TabView`. This new view will be called `ContentView`, taking over from the previous `ContentView` (which we just renamed to `TimerView`).

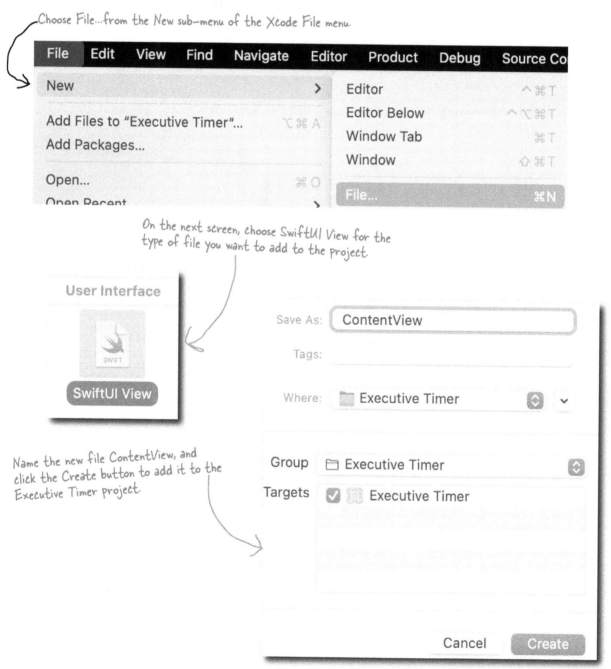

Choose File...from the New sub-menu of the Xcode File menu.

On the next screen, choose SwiftUI View for the type of file you want to add to the project.

Name the new file ContentView, and click the Create button to add it to the Executive Timer project.

Creating the tabs and the TabView

In our brand new ContentView we need to create a TabView. Add a TabView as follows:

```swift
import SwiftUI

struct ContentView: View {
    var body: some View {
        TabView {

        }
    }
}
```

Inside the TabView, add a Tab to display our timer:

```swift
TimerView()
    .padding()
    .tabItem {
        Image(systemName: "timer")
        Text("Timer")
    }
    .tag(1)
```

This creates an instance of our TimerView.

❶ Create an empty TimerSettingsView view

Save As: TimerSettingsView

Tags:

Where: 📁 Executive Timer

Group: 📁 Executive Timer
Targets: ☑ 📱 Executive Timer

Cancel   Create

You don't need to modify the code that's provided, unless you want it to display something different. We'll create some actual timer settings next.

```swift
import SwiftUI

struct TimerSettingsView: View {
    var body: some View {
        Text("Hello, World!")
    }
}
```

```
∨ 📱 Executive Timer
  ∨ 📁 Executive Timer          ?
      Executive_TimerApp    ?
      ContentView           A
      TimerSettingsView     A
      TimerView             ?
      Assets                ?
      Info                  ?
  > 📁 Preview Content       ?
```

❷ Add the second tab to the TabView in the ContentView

Our `ContentView` currently looks like this, and only has one tab (the `TimerView`). We're going to add the (currently empty) `TimerSettingsView`:

```
struct ContentView: View {
    var body: some View {
        TabView {
            TimerView()
                .padding()
                .tabItem {
                    Image(systemName: "timer")
                    Text("Timer")
                }
                .tag("Timer")
        }
    }
}
```

Add the TimerSettingsView here as a tab, with some padding, and a tag (it's tab 2), and a similar set of .tabItem modifiers to the first tab.

```
TimerSettingsView()
    .padding()
    .tabItem {
        Image(systemName: "gear")
        Text("Settings")
    }
    .tag("Settings")
```

You might have noticed we've updated the .tag modifier on the first tab to be a String (and used a String for the second tab). This makes it easier to refer to tabs in our code elsewhere, by this tag name.

We're basically done! The Executive Timer now has tabs:

☑ Rename the `ContentView` that displays the timer to `TimerView`. You'll need to rename both the ContentView struct (to TimerView) and the file (using the Xcode sidebar)..

☑ Create a new SwiftUI View file in the project, and name it `ContentView`.

☑ Inside the new ContentView, add a `TabView`, and a tab displaying the `TimerView`.

☑ Create a new SwiftUI View file in the project, and name it `TimerSettingsView`.

☑ Add `TimerSettingsView` as a second tab in the `TabView` in the `ContentView`.

Running your new tabbed Executive Timer

Run the Executive Timer, and witness the power of your fully operational tabs!

The first tab will display the TimerView.

The second tab will display the unfinished TimerSettingsView.

So, that's everything I need to know about SwiftUI? I'm good to go now?

Well, yes and no.

It would take a whole additional Head First book to cover SwiftUI in all its glory.

This taste of SwiftUI was intended to give you a little bit of everything: to familiarize you with the fundamentals so that when you tackle other parts of SwiftUI you'll already know what you're doing.

Clever, right?

SwiftUIcross

We've strategically hidden everything you've learned about SwiftUI in this chapter, as well as a few related concepts, in this crossword. Use it as a palate cleanser before heading to the last chapter.

Across
3) Apple's library of icons and symbols.
6) A library that works with Swift to process events asynchronously.
7) A float, but one that's used for graphics.
8) A class that does something at a certain rate.

Down
1) A controlled transition from one thing to another using SwiftUI.
2) A UI element to help position overlapping things on top of each other.
4) This method lets a view respond to something a publisher emits.
5) Something that can emit its value at regular points.

SwiftUIcross Solution

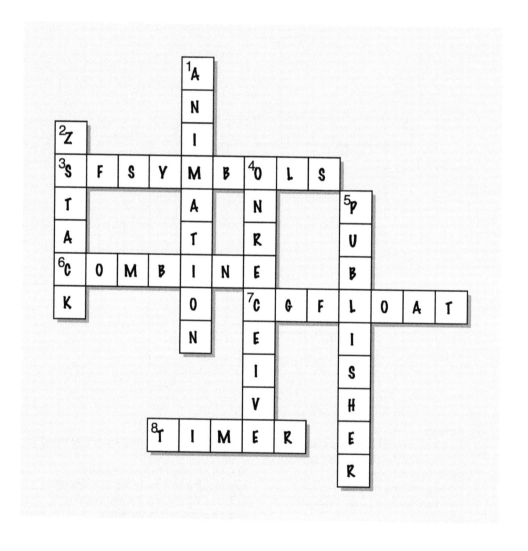

12 apps, web, and beyond
↓
Putting It All Together

↑
Let's spend one more chapter together...

I've got so many new toys...
it's hard to decide which
ones to play with first!

You've done lots of Swift. You've used Playgrounds and Xcode.

We knew you'd have to **say goodbye** eventually, but the time has finally arrived. It's hard to part, but we know you've got what it takes. In this chapter, our final chapter together (at least in this book), we're going to do a **final pass through many of the concepts** you've learned, and build a handful of things together. We'll make sure your Swift is shipshape, and give you some **pointers on what to do next**. Some homework, if you will. It'll be fun, and we'll part on a high note.

This is the chapter equivalent of the scene in the detective novel where the great detective summons everyone to the drawing room and summarizes the case.

A journey must end...

You've learned a lot of Swift, but there's still time to spend one more chapter together...

Variables

Constants

Types

Operators

Strings

Collections

Conditionals

Loops

Switches

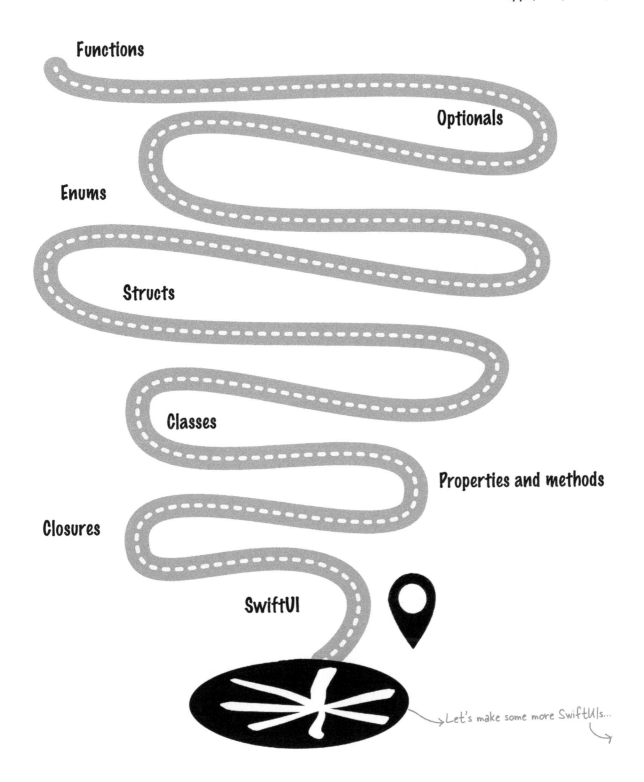

Functions

Optionals

Enums

Structs

Classes

Properties and methods

Closures

SwiftUI

Let's make some more SwiftUIs...

Something like this?

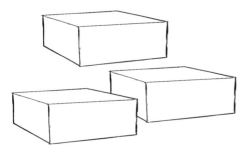

SwiftUI makes it easy to construct a nice welcome screen out of pieces.

Let's walk through how you can use the building blocks of SwiftUI to make a welcome screen.

The welcome screen is made of the same basic building blocks you've already used in SwiftUI, quite a few times.

There's nothing mysterious here, just some `Text`, some `Spacers`, some `HStacks`, `VStacks`, some `Images`, and a `Button`.

Sharpen your pencil

What do you think the primary elements of the welcome screen that we want to build might be?

We've drawn a sketch of the welcome screen. Have a go at identifying what sorts of SwiftUI building blocks you might compose it from.

We've started you off with a few hints....

The big welcome message is composed of some Text views in a VStack, so they're on top of each other. We'll color one of them blue.

What does the rest of the welcome screen need? Don't forget VStacks, HStacks, and Spacers!

Sharpen your pencil
Solution

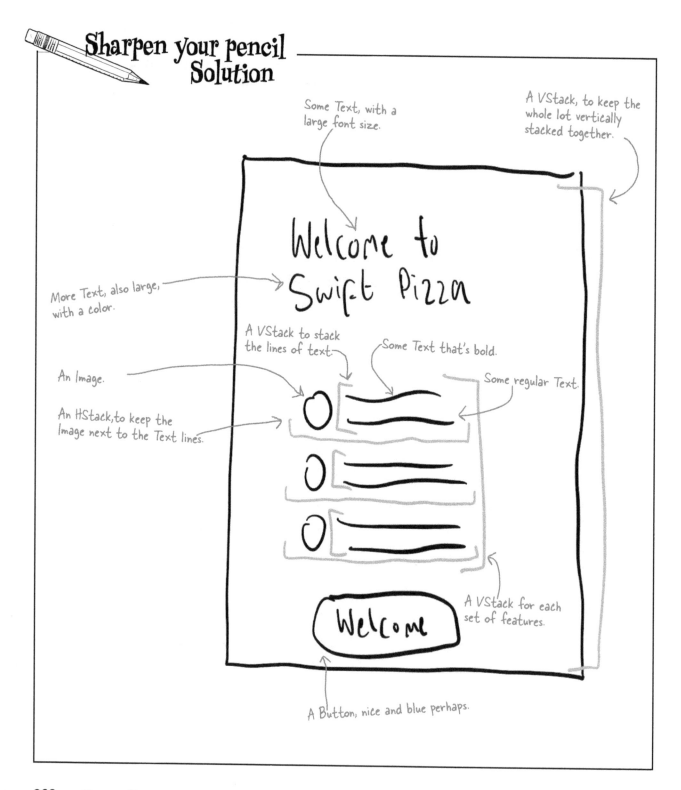

Some Text, with a large font size.

A VStack, to keep the whole lot vertically stacked together.

Welcome to Swift Pizza

More Text, also large, with a color.

A VStack to stack the lines of text.

Some Text that's bold.

Some regular Text.

An Image.

An HStack, to keep the Image next to the Text lines.

A VStack for each set of features.

Welcome

A Button, nice and blue perhaps.

> So, how do we build this thing with SwiftUI? It's got concepts I'm familiar with, but I need help!

A recipe for a welcome screen

1 Make sure your `ContentView` struct is ready to go. We'll leave the name as `ContentView`, which is SwiftUI's default name for the first view in an Xcode project.

2 Likewise, make sure your `body` is ready to go. Nothing mysterious here.

3 Create a `VStack` for everything to sit inside, and give it some padding.

4 Add the two `Text` views to display the "Welcome to Swift Pizza" message, and style it appropriately.

5 Add a `Spacer` view.

6 Add the views for the three featured items: a `VStack` to keep them all together, and then three identical `HStacks`, each with an `Image`, and then another `VStack` in each containing two `Text` views.

7 Add another `Spacer` view.

8 And finally, add a `Button`, appropriately styled.

Step by step assembly of the welcome screen

① The ContentView

```
struct ContentView: View {


}
```

ContentView can be named <u>whatever</u> you like, but the template for a SwiftUI app looks for a view named ContentView by default.
(You <u>can't change</u> the name of the body, though.)

② The body

```
var body: some View {


}
```

③ The all-encompassing VStack

```
VStack (alignment: .leading) {


}.padding(.all, 40)
```

Setting everything to .leading alignment means that it'll be aligned to the left-side in left-to-right locales, and the right side in right-to-left locales.

This adds 40 units of padding to everything inside the VStack.

Welcome to
Swift Pizza

④ The welcome text

```
Text("Welcome to")
        .font(.system(size: 50)).fontWeight(.heavy)
        .foregroundColor(.primary)
Text("Swift Pizza")
        .font(.system(size: 50)).fontWeight(.heavy)
        .foregroundColor(Color(UIColor.systemBlue).opacity(0.8))
```

⑤ A Spacer

```
Spacer()
```

A Spacer will take as much space as is available, in whatever axis it can expand in. Because this Spacer is inside the all-encompassing VStack, it will expand vertically until it cannot anymore. This gives us some nice space in the welcome screen.

❻ The highlighted features

All three featured items are stacked vertically.

Each featured item is in an HStack, which allows us to horizontally place the image to the left of the text.

```
VStack (alignment: .leading, spacing: 24) {
    HStack (alignment: .top, spacing: 20) {
            Image(systemName: "bag").resizable()
                    .frame(width: 40, height: 40)
                    .foregroundColor(Color(UIColor.systemBlue).opacity(0.8))

            VStack (alignment: .leading, spacing: 4) {
                Text("Order Everything").font(.headline).bold()
                Text("Our whole menu is available in the app.")
                    .font(.subheadline)
            }
    }
```

Order Everything
Our whole menu is available in the app.

This structure is replicated for all three of the featured items.

```
    HStack (alignment: .top, spacing: 20) {
            Image(systemName: "giftcard").resizable()
                    .frame(width: 40, height: 40)
                    .foregroundColor(Color(UIColor.systemBlue).opacity(0.8))

            VStack (alignment: .leading, spacing: 4) {
                Text("Buy Gift Cards").font(.headline).bold()
                Text("Buy a gift card, check card balance, and more.")
                    .font(.subheadline)
            }
    }
```

Buy Gift Cards
Buy a gift card, check card balance and more.

The images used come straight from Apple's SF Symbols.

```
    HStack (alignment: .top, spacing: 20) {
            Image(systemName: "fork.knife").resizable()
                    .frame(width: 40, height: 40)
                    .foregroundColor(Color(UIColor.systemBlue).opacity(0.8))

            VStack (alignment: .leading, spacing: 4) {
                Text("Customize Pizzas").font(.headline).bold()
                Text("Easily View Stock Options, Quotes, Charts etc.")
                    .font(.subheadline)
            }
    }
}
```

Customize Pizzas
Pick and choose ingredients to make your dream pizza.

Another Spacer

7 `Spacer()`

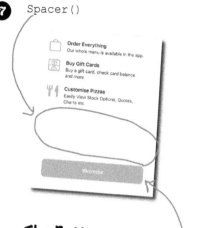

The Button

8

```
Button(action: {}) {
    Text("Welcome").foregroundColor(.white).bold()
}.frame(width: 350, height: 60)
    .background(Color(UIColor.systemBlue)
    .opacity(0.8)).cornerRadius(12)
```

Spacers vs. Padding

You might be wondering what the difference between using a `Spacer` and adding padding to SwiftUI views is. The answer is simple. `Spacers` expand to fill all the space available between SwiftUI views (in whatever direction they can, based on whether they're inside, for example, a `VStack` or an `HStack`).

Padding lets you have much more exact control over the spacing of things: you can ask for a specific amount of padding on a specific side of a view. If you ask for padding on a view without specifying an amount, the system will do its best to work out what you need.

Serious Coding

Now that you've seen each of the elements, fire up Xcode and see if you can reconstruct the Swift Pizza welcomne screen using these techniques.

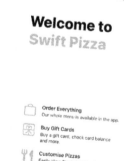

Feel free to come up with new features to highlight, use different icons, or spice up the colors you use a bit!

You'll want to create a new Xcode project, with an empty iOS project.

SwiftUI actually automatically supports Dark Mode! In many cases you won't need to do anything at all.

But the automatic support only goes so far, so sometimes you need to step in and override things.

For example, if we had the following code in our app, displaying a map centered on Times Square in New York City:

What about Dark Mode? How do I make sure my apps work with Dark Mode?

```
import SwiftUI
import MapKit
```
← Because we're using a map, we need to import MapKit.

```
struct ContentView: View {
    @State private var region: MKCoordinateRegion =
        MKCoordinateRegion(center:
            CLLocationCoordinate2D(latitude: 40.75773, longitude: -73.985708),
            span: MKCoordinateSpan(latitudeDelta: 0.05, longitudeDelta: 0.05))
```

We'll use a state variable to define the map region we want to look at.

This points to Times Square, in New York City, New York.

```
    var body: some View {
        Map(coordinateRegion: $region)
            .edgesIgnoringSafeArea(.all)
    }
}
```

This displays a map, using the region we defined above. The extra parameter tells iOS to push the map all the way to edges of the display.

If you try this in the simulator, you'll see something like this.

If you use the simulator's Toggle Appearance function, you'll switch it to Dark Mode.

And then you'll see something like this. Magic!

Brain Power

Try making your own simple SwiftUI UI to test the automatic implementation of Dark Mode. It's so simple it barely deserves an exercise, but try it out anyway because it's awesome!

DIY Dark Mode

☐   Create a brand new iOS application, using Xcode.

☐   In the empty `ContentView` that's supplied for you, create a `VStack`.

☐   In the `VStack`, add some `Text`, some `Images` from SF Symbols, some `Buttons`, and whatever else you can think of.

☐   Add a `Map`, if you're feeling spicy.

☐   Fire up your app in the iOS Simulator, and see what it looks like.

☐   Use the Toggle Appearance menu item to switch to Dark Mode. How's it look?

Features   Debug   Window   Help
Face ID
Simulate Fall
Authorize Apple Pay
Toggle Appearance
Toggle In-call Status Bar
Increase Preferred Text Size
Decrease Preferred Text Size
Toggle Increased Contrast
Trigger iCloud Sync
Location

What looks wrong?
What doesn't look wrong?

I'm getting to grips with SwiftUI...but I still don't really understand state and what that means?

SwiftUI views are functions of their state.

What this means in practice is that when we want a view to change we change the data—the state — that's used to derive the view, and the view automatically updates to reflect it.

The SwiftUI Stepper view.

In more concrete terms, SwiftUI provides a handful of ways to store that state.

You've already worked one with of these quite a bit: the **@State** property wrapper. Here it is in action:

```
struct ContentView: View {

    @State private var number: Int = 0

    var body: some View {

        Stepper(value: $number, in: 0...10, label: {Text("Number is \(number)")})

    }

}
```

— We create a property to hold a number, tagged with @State.

—And here's a Stepper view, bound to the number.

A Stepper view is a control that lets you increment or decrement something.

The use of **@State** in front of the property declaration (which is otherwise just a regular int) tells Swift we want it to manage this property and keep it persistent in memory while the view it belongs to sticks around. Because the property is tagged with @State, SwiftUI will automatically redraw the view when the property changes.

←This is relevant because SwiftUI views are structs, and as you know from working with structs earlier, a struct can't be changed.

Using @State allows us to effectively work with any property that belongs to a single, specific view and isn't important, relevant, or used outside of that view. That's one of the reasons it's also marked as **private**.

The state never leaves the view it belongs to. Hence it is private.

~~Smash~~ Share the state

@State

@State is the simplest of the bunch. You've used it already. It's a simple source of truth for a view in your apps. It contains simple values, like Int, String, Bool. It's not intended to be used for fancy reference types or types that you might've made yourself using classes and structs.

@State causes the body variable of the view it's attached to be recomputed any time the property it's attached to updates.

@StateObject

@StateObject is a little more complex than @State. It tells SwiftUI that we would like our body variable recomputed if any properties that have the @Published property wrapper change within the object that is marked with the @StateObject property wrapper.

Any object marked with @StateObject must conform to the type ObservableObject (which is a protocol).

@ObservedObject

@ObservedObject allows us to keep track of @StateObjects that have already been created.

When you need to pass a @StateObject between views, any view that isn't the one that created it tags the property as an @ObservedObject. The @ObservedObject tells Swift that the object has already been created, and that you just want the (child) view that's accessing it to get access to the same data, without re-creating the object.

@EnvironmentObject

An @EnvironmentObject accesses a @StateObject that was created somewhere in your views and attached to a specific view. When you need to use it in a child view a long way from the view that owns it, you use @EnvironmentObject to access it. It looks for something of the same type, which means you cannot have more than one @EnvironmentObject in the same view tree that has the same type.

It's time for our old friend...
contrived example → @StateObject and @ObservedObject

Here's a type that represents the score of a game:

```
class GameScore: ObservableObject {
    @Published var numericalScore = 0
    @Published var piecesCaptured = 0
}
```

GameScore conforms to ObservableObject. This allows instances of GameScore to be used inside a view, and makes the view reload when GameScore changes.

The @Published property wrapper tells SwiftUI to specifically trigger view updates when one of these properties changes its value.

Here's some views that use our class:

```
struct ContentView: View {
    @StateObject var score = GameScore()

    var body: some View {
        VStack {
            Text("Score is \(score.numericalScore),
                \(score.piecesCaptured) pieces captured.")
            ScoreView(score: score)
        }
    }
}
```

The object being made here must conform to ObservableObject. Luckily, it does.

Our score property, an instance of the GameScore type we made, uses the @StateObject property wrapper. @StateObject means the view is ready to reload whenever any properties marked as @Published within the ObservableObject change.

Here we create the second (ScoreView) view, passing in the score property.

```
struct ScoreView: View {
    @ObservedObject var score: GameScore

    var body: some View {
        Button("Bigger score!") {
            score.numericalScore += 1
        }
        Button("More pieces!") {
            score.piecesCaptured += 1
        }
    }
}
```

Our score property in this view, which is going to be used inside the ContentView, does not need to create a new instance of score; it just needs to keep track of an already instantiated property (that uses the @StateObject property wrapper). Because of this, score here is an @ObservedObject.

Updating properties of score updates the original @StateObject.

Building an app with multiple views that share state

↳ @StateObject and @EnvironmentObject

Here's the first view of our hypothetical app:

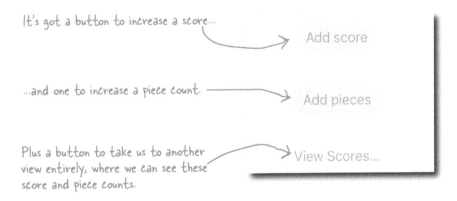

It's got a button to increase a score...   Add score

...and one to increase a piece count. ──────→ Add pieces

Plus a button to take us to another   View Scores...
view entirely, where we can see these
score and piece counts.

Here's the second view of our hypothetical app:

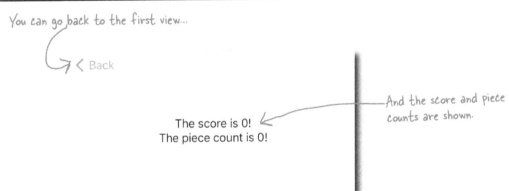

You can go back to the first view...

‹ Back

And the score and piece
counts are shown.

The score is 0!
The piece count is 0!

Brain Power

See if you can build some, or all, of this app. Start with an empty SwiftUI iOS app in Xcode, and stick to a single source file (*ContentView.swift* by default). You'll need to create a class that represents a GameScore, holding a score and a pieces property (and conforming to ObservableObject). Use your knowledge of state to create the rest. If you can't figure out how to split the app into two views that can be moved between, put it all on one screen.

Building a two-view score tracker

Exercise

Here's what we'll need to do:

☐ Implement a GameScore class to store the score and the piece count, conforming to ObservableObject.

☐ Assemble the ContentView (the first view), holding a GameScore type @StateObject and all the needed components.

☐ Create a ScoreView (the second view), using an @EnvironmentObject to gain access to the GameScore type @StateObject from the first view and all the needed components.

☐ Make sure we can navigate from one to the other, and back again.

The ObservableObject

1 We need a new type to store two things: a score and a piece count. Both are integers.

```
class GameScore {
    var score = 0
    var pieces = 0
}
```

This class allows us to store two integers, and update the view of any SwiftUI views that use an object of this type as a property when one of its two integer properties changes.

2 We need to conform the type to ObservableObject, which allows us to publish some of its properties using the @Published property wrapper.

```
class GameScore: ObservableObject {
    @Published var score = 0
    @Published var pieces = 0
}
```

Suspiciously easy or what...

 Implement a GameScore class to store the score and the piece count, conforming to ObservableObject.

The first view

Our ContentView is a pretty straightforward thing, initially: a @StateObject (storing a GameScore), and two Buttons and a Text view in a VStack. Easy.

```
struct ContentView: View {
    @StateObject var gameScore = GameScore()

    var body: some View {
        VStack {
         ❶ Button("Add score") {
                gameScore.score += 1
            }
            .buttonStyle(.bordered)
            .padding()

         ❷ Button("Add pieces") {
                gameScore.pieces += 1
            }
            .buttonStyle(.bordered)
            .padding()

         ❸   Text("View Scores...")
            .padding()
        }
    }
}
```

Our instance of GameScore is created with the @StateObject property wrapper, as we're going to share it between multiple views.

We increment the score property and the pieces property, respectively, that live in our GameScore instance when the appropriate Buttons are pressed.

This will ultimately be our link to the second view, but for now it's nothing special. Just a Text view.

The Button to increase the score...

Add score ❶

The Button to increase the piece count Add pieces ❷

View Scores... ❸

And some text, which will eventually take us to the second view.

☑ Assemble the ContentView (the first view), holding a GameScore type @StateObject and all the needed components.

The second view

Our ScoreView is also pretty straightforward. We use an @EnvironmentObject to refer to the GameScore, and the rest is just a VStack with a couple of Text views showing the score, the pieces count, and a Spacer.

```
struct ScoreView: View {

    @EnvironmentObject var gameScore: GameScore

    var body: some View {
        VStack {
            Text("The score is \(gameScore.score)!")
            Text("The piece count is \(gameScore.pieces)!")
            Spacer()
        }
    }
}
```

@EnvironmentObject allows us to access a @StateObject-tagged instance of GameScore that was created in another view and attached to that view.

1

2

We display the score and pieces properties of the gameScore in some Text views.

You might notice that we haven't implemented the Back button anywhere...it's coming.

⟵ Back

1
The score is 0!
The piece count is 0!
2

And the score and piece counts are shown.

☑ Create a ScoreView (the second view), using an @EnvironmentObject to gain access to the GameScore type @StateObject from the first view and all the needed components.

Relax

This is a lot to take in one go, but it's using concepts you've already used multiple times. It's just combining them together in new ways.

All the other state-sharing systems work fundamentally the same way as @State does; they just offer more flexibility. And navigating between views is no trickier than wrapping something in a VStack or an HStack.

The first view, again

1 We need to update our ContentView so that we can move from it into the second view (ScoreView). To do this we need to add a NavigationView and a NavigationLink.

```
struct ContentView: View {
    @StateObject var gameScore = GameScore()

    var body: some View {
        NavigationView {
            VStack {
                Button("Add score") {
                    gameScore.score += 1
                }
                .buttonStyle(.bordered)
                .padding()

                Button("Add pieces") {
                    gameScore.pieces += 1
                }
                .buttonStyle(.bordered)
                .padding()

                NavigationLink(destination: ScoreView()) {
                    Text("View Scores...")
                        .padding()
                }
            }
        }
    }
}
```

NavigationView is a special container view that allows you to manage other views.

To move from one view to another inside a NavigationView, you use a NavigationLink. A NavigationLink is a special kind of Button that triggers another view to appear on top of the current view, and automatically handles adding a Back button to the new view.

We specify that we want our destination to be a ScoreView, and leave the same Text view we had before inside. The Text will be tappable now.

Think of NavigationView as a counterpart to other container views, like VStack and HStack. Instead of stacking things on the screen, it stacks a collection of views that can be traversed. On small screens, like iPhones, the views replace each other. But on bigger screens, like iPads and Macs, the first view might appear in a left column, and the second view in a right column.

The First View, again, continued

2 Next, in order to make the data stored in our GameScore property available to the second view, we need to add an .environmentObject() modifier to the ContentView. This makes the data available to any views inside (in this case, our ScoreView).

```
struct ContentView: View {
    @StateObject var gameScore = GameScore()

    var body: some View {
        NavigationView {
            VStack {
                Button("Add score") {
                    gameScore.score += 1
                }
                .buttonStyle(.bordered)
                .padding()

                Button("Add pieces") {
                    gameScore.pieces += 1
                }
                .buttonStyle(.bordered)
                .padding()

                NavigationLink(destination: ScoreView()) {
                    Text("View Scores...")
                        .padding()
                }
            }
        }.environmentObject(gameScore)
    }
}
```

We add the .environmentObject() modifier to the NavigationView, as we need the gameScore to be available to any views inside it (which will be our ScoreView, when we navigate to it via the NavigationLink).

☑ Make sure we can navigate from one to the other, and back again.

3 At this point, if you've been following along in Xcode, you can run your app and it should work! You should be able to increment both the score and the pieces count, and then move to the second view to see the counts.

Bullet Points

- You can use the `@State` property wrapper for sharing simple pieces of data, like Int, String, and Bool between views. It's useful for sharing very straightforward pieces of state, like numbers, or whether a toggle is on or off.

- `@StateObject` is for sharing types that are more complex. Any data shared using `@StateObject` must conform to `ObservableObject`, and any properties within that type that should cause a view to update must have the `@Published` property wrapper.

- The `ObservableObject` protocol lets an object notify other objects when the value of any of its properties that are marked with the `@Published` property wrapper change.

- The `@StateObject` property wrapper is necessary when something is being instantiated for the first time.

- `@ObservedObject` is used to access an already-instantiated piece of data that conforms to `ObservableObject` and was created by the parent of the current view using the `@StateObject` property wrapper.

- `@EnvironmentObject` can access a `@StateObject` piece of data that conforms to `@ObservableObject` from anywhere in a view hierarchy if the `@StateObject` was attached to the view it was created in using the `.environmentObject()` modifier.

- `NavigationView` is a special kind of container view that allows you to traverse between multiple views.

- `NavigationLink` is a special kind of `Button` that allows you to trigger a move between views inside a `NavigationView`.

- iOS (and the other supported SwiftUI operating systems) automatically handles adding back buttons, and similar cues, to move back and forward between views.

Hmm.. how do I use Images in my SwiftUI apps if they're not coming out of the SF Symbols collection?

Working with local images is easy with SwiftUI.

But you probably already guessed that. Most apps are likely to need to display local images at some point. Local images don't come from the internet, and aren't downloaded while the user is running the app. They ship with the app.

Swift does indeed make this easy, but you need a little help from Xcode.

Adding Local Images Up Close

To add a local image to your app, you need to add it to app's asset catalog in your app in Xcode. You can then refer to it by name from your Swift code.

❶ In an Xcode project

Look for the Assets entry in the Project navigator in the left sidebar.

❷ Drag images in from the Finder

Drag whatever images you want from the Finder into the asset catalog in Xcode.

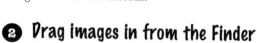

❸ Verify your images are there

Xcode will copy them into your project, and add them to the assets. You can rename them here, if you want.

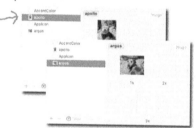

❹ Use the images in your code

Use the images in your Swift code by referring to them by name in an Image view.

```
struct ContentView: View {
    var body: some View {
        VStack {
            Image("argos")
                .resizable()
                .aspectRatio(contentMode: .fit)
            Spacer()
            Image("apollo")
                .resizable()
                .aspectRatio(contentMode: .fit)
        }
    }
}
```

This modifier tells Swift to automatically size the image, so that it fills all available space.

And this modifier tells Swift to maintain the image's aspect ratio. You can also use .fill, if you want it to ignore the image's aspect ratio, and push it to all the edges of the space it's in.

Bullet Points

- The SwiftUI Image view lets you display an image by name.

- The images you can display by name come from the project's asset catalog. To add images to the assets, you can drag them in from Finder.

- By default, images will display at their full size, which makes they might be too big for the view you're using them in.

- To make an Image fill the entire available screen area more sensible, you can add the `.resizable()` modifier to it.

- To keep an image at its original aspect ratio (so it does not become distorted or skewed), you can apply the `.aspectRatio(contentMode: .fit)` modifier.

- You can also position the image in a custom frame by using the `.frame(width: 100, height:100)` modifier, with appropriate values.

- You can specify `.top`, `.bottom`, `.right`, `.left`, or `.center` alignment to push the image in a certain direction: `.frame(width: 100, height: 100, alignment: .top)`.

- And you can clip an image to a certain shape by adding the `.clipShape()` modifier, with a specific shape inside, like `.clipShape(Circle())`.

- As with any SwiftUI view, you can add a border with the `.border` modifier and appropriate values like `.border(Color.red, width: 2)`.

Sharpen your pencil

Have a go at replicating this view using your SwiftUI skills.

You can subtitute your own pictures for these incredibly handsome dogs, if you must.

⟶ Answer on page 385.

The _order_ in which you apply modifiers to a SwiftUI can impact how the view ends up looking.

It might sound like a silly question, but how do I load an image from the web?

SwiftUI makes it easy to load an image from the web.

It's not a silly question at all. So many apps pull images from online via a URL that it's almost an essential feature of SwiftUI!

Meet `AsyncImage`, another useful building block provided by SwiftUI.

AsyncImage works kind of like Image.

```
AsyncImage(url: URL(string: "https://cataas.com/cat?type=square"))
    .frame(width: 300, height: 300)
```

But it can take a URL.

I know what a URL is...but what's a URL in Swift? A type?

URL is a type provided by Swift.

A URL can be created from a String. Many parts of Swift can use a URL to load things, and a URL can refer to a remote or local file.

It's just a type like any other.   And it takes a string parameter.

```
let myLink = URL(string: "https://secretlab.games/")
```

But it can also be created relative to another URL.

```
let mySecondLink = URL(string: "headfirstswift/", relativeTo: myLink)
```

And you can get an (Optional) String out if it. if you need one.

```
let firstLinkString = myLink?.absoluteString
let secondLinkString = mySecondLink?.absoluteString
```

`The first link is: https://secretlab.games/`

```
print("The first link is: \(firstLinkString!)")
print("The second link is: \(secondLinkString!)")
```

`The second link is: https://secretlab.games/headfirstswift/`

A fancy AsyncImage

Sometimes you want to be a bit fancy when you're loading images from the internet, and add a nice little progress spinner that shows when the image is downloading, then ultimately replace that with the image.

Like this:

Where, while the image is loading, we get a nice spinning view... That gets replaced by the image, when it's downloaded.

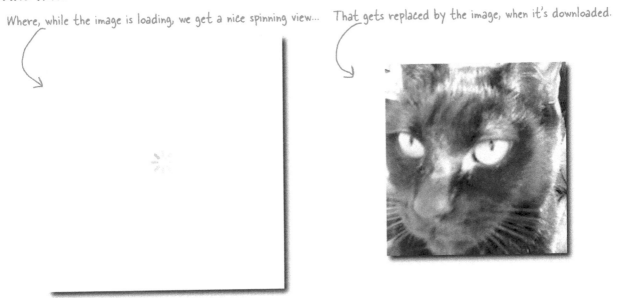

We do this:

```
struct ContentView: View {

    var body: some View {
        VStack {
            AsyncImage(url: URL(string: "https://cataas.com/cat?type=square")) { image in
                image.resizable()
            } placeholder: {
                ProgressView()
            }
            .frame(width: 300, height: 300)
        }
    }
}
```

When AsyncImage actually manages to get an image, it puts it into image. image is a SwiftUI Image, which you already know how to use.

We can just apply the .resizable() modifier to it, because it's just an image at this point.

ProgressView is a useful little SwiftUI view that displays a spinner that will animate forever. It will never go away unless you make it go away. It just spins eternally.

We could replace ProgressView() with something else, like Text("Image loading!"), if we wanted. Anything in the placeholder closure will be displayed until AsyncImage has managed to get hold of an image.

Exercise

Take a look at the code below. It's an even fancier version of what you've already learned to build. We've left some bits empty, and would like you to fill them in.

```
struct ContentView: View {

    var imageURL = URL(string: "https://cataas.com//cat?type=square")

    var body: some View {
        VStack {
            AsyncImage(url: imageURL) { phase in
                switch phase {
                case .empty:



                case .success(let image):




                case .failure:




                default:
                    EmptyView()
                }
            }
        }
    }
}
```

AsyncImage can work with a closure that receives an AsyncImagePhase that indicates the state of the image load.

So we switch on that phase...

If it's empty, it's still loading.

If it's success, we grab the image.

If it fails, we hit failure.

And if something weird happens, we get an EmptyView.

You'll need to put a ProgressView here, to display while the image is loading. You can put text inside a ProgressView("Like this...")

This syntax binds the associated value (associated with the enum where .success is coming from) with a constant we name image. This lets us get the image.

Use image here, and display it with the .resizable() modifier, fit to its view, in a 300x300 frame.

Display an image from SF Symbols here. We recommend shippingbox, but feel free to get creative.

EmptyView is a SwiftUI view that doesn't contain anything at all. It's useful when you need an actually empty view.

Loading cat...

.empty

.success

.failure

→ Answers on page 386.

Sharpen your pencil
Solution

From page 381.

```swift
struct ContentView: View {
    var body: some View {
        VStack {
            Image("argos")
                .resizable()
                .frame(width: 300, height: 300)
                .aspectRatio(contentMode: .fill)
                .border(Color.green, width: 3.0)
            Spacer()
            Image("apollo")
                .resizable()
                .aspectRatio(contentMode: .fit)
                .clipShape(Capsule())
        }
    }
}
```

> We were told we could make websites with Swift. How do we do that? I feel pretty confident with Swift, but I don't know how to make a website...

It's time to (very briefly) meet Vapor.

Vapor is an expressive, event-driven, protocol-oriented web development framework written in, and for Swift. It gives you everything you need to build amazing modern web services and websites using Swift.

Vapor is not an Apple project; it's part of the vibrant Swift open source community.

Exercise
Solution

From page 384.

```
struct ContentView: View {

    var imageURL = URL(string: "https://cataas.com//cat?type=square")

    var body: some View {
        VStack {
            AsyncImage(url: imageURL) { phase in
                switch phase {
                    case .empty:
                        ProgressView("Loading cat...")
                    case .success(let image):
                        image.resizable()
                            .aspectRatio(contentMode: .fit)
                            .frame(maxWidth: 300, maxHeight: 300)
                    case .failure:
                        Image(systemName: "shippingbox")
                    default:
                        EmptyView()
                }
            }
        }
    }
}
```

Loading cat...

.empty →

.success

.failure →

Meet Vapor, the Swift web framework

With Vapor installed, there's a **3-step process** to get an **Xcode project** you can work with.

We're not going to cover installing Vapor, since it's fiddly, but head over to https://vapor.codes in your web browser to get started.

❶ You can make a <u>new Vapor project</u> with the following command:

```
vapor new mysite -n
```

You'll see something like this when it's done.

❷ Change into the Vapor <u>project's directory</u> with this command:

```
cd mysite
```

> ⚠️ **Watch it!**
>
> **You can't do this bit on an iPad.**
>
> *While everything else we've been doing is equally doable on an iPadOS or macOS device, Vapor is only useful for developing on a macOS device.*
>
> *So, sorry: you'll need to fire up your Mac for Vapor!*

❸ Then run this to <u>open</u> the new Vapor project <u>in Xcode</u>:

```
open Package.swift
```

✳ Fetching swift-nio (22%)...

When the project opens in Xcode, the Swift
Package Manager will download a bunch of things.

Swift Package Dependencies
- 📦 async-http-client
- 📦 async-kit
- 📦 console-kit
- 📦 multipart-kit (fetching...)
- 📦 routing-kit
- 📦 swift-backtrace
- 📦 swift-crypto
- 📦 swift-log
- 📦 swift-metrics
- 📦 swift-nio (fetching...)
- 📦 swift-nio-extras
- 📦 swift-nio-http2
- 📦 swift-nio-ssl
- 📦 vapor
- 📦 websocket-kit

You'll be able to see the packages as they are
downloaded and added to the project in the sidebar.

Test Drive

Click the run button in Xcode, and wait for
the project to build. Once it's built, look in the
Xcode log area for a URL. Try visiting the URL,
and see what you find. Then take a look at the
routes.swift file and see if you can figure out
what's going on.

```
[ NOTICE ] Server starting on
           http://127.0.0.1:8080
```

- ∨ 📦 mysite
  - 📄 Package.swift
  - ∨ 📁 Sources
    - ∨ 📁 App
      - > 📁 Controllers
      - 📄 configure.swift
      - 📄 routes.swift
    - > 📁 Run

> I can see how the routes maybe map to what I see. But what if I want to make it do something more complex than say hello?

Routes get you places.

Vapor lets you create routes to define what happens in different circumstances. We're not going to go into a full example here, but if you open the *routes.swift* file in the Xcode project you're using and add a new route, like this:

```
app.get("swift", "awesome") { req ->
String in
    return "Swift is awesome!"
}
```

You will have created a new route.

This route handles a GET request. It's a closure, and each parameter is a path parameter for the URL you want the route to be for (in this case */swift/awesome*).

So now, when you visit the URL of your local machine */swift/awesome*, the text you specified for this route will be returned.

Useful, right?

Sending data over the web with Vapor

You can also collect data from URLs using GET requests, and use that to display a specific greeting to someone, based on the name they put in the URL.

❶ Create a new closure, with a dynamic parameter:

```
app.get("hello", ":name") { req -> String in




}
```

This is technically still just a String. But Vapor knows to look for the : at the beginning, which means it's treated as a dynamic parameter. This is a Vapor convention, not a Swift convention.

❷ Add a guard let to unwrap the optional parameter:

```
app.get("hello", ":name") { req -> String in
    guard let name = req.parameters.get("name") else {
        throw Abort(.internalServerError)
    }

}
```

Here we use guard let to unwrap the optional, and throw a big error if we couldn't. We haven't really covered errors in the book, but this code throws an error from an enum of errors provided by Vapor.

❸ Return what you need to return

```
app.get("hello", ":name") { req -> String in
    guard let name = req.parameters.get("name") else {
        throw Abort(.internalServerError)
    }
    return "Hello, \(name)!"
}
```

And finally, we return a String, which includes the name variable!

4 Visit your new URL

Hello, paris!

The page will display the name that's passed in as the second component of the URL!

Bullet Points

- Vapor lets you create modern web apps and websites using Swift.

- After installing Vapor, you can use Xcode to define routes, and what different pages do, and create other features for your web app.

- Vapor can return text, or JSON, and work with packages from the Swift Package Manager to do all sorts of amazing web things.

- There are packages that let you use Vapor with everything from MySQL to JQuery, Redis, Apple's Push Notification Service, and beyond.

Brain Power

Add some routes to your web app that /add and /multiply numbers based on what's passed in to the URL (for example, /add/2/10 would add 2 and 10, and display 12). See if you can figure out the best place to put the code for adding, and how to break the code into pieces that make sense.

So, we know Swift is open source. But what does that mean, exactly> Does it mean I can help work on Swift itself? It seems like a worthy project to help out on...

The Swift Evolution process is the best way to get started contributing to Swift.

The Swift Evolution process is designed and facilitate bringing new people, insights, ideas, and experience into the Swift community.

Swift is a big, complex project, so even though it's open source — it's not feasible to just accept literally every idea that's proposed.

That's what Swift Evolution is for. In this forum, anyone is welcome and invited to propose, discuss, and review new ideas for Swift.

The format for posting new ideas is designed to be consistent and easy to understand.

The Swift project keeps track of where ideas are in the process, so you can always check on their progress.

To get started, head over to the Swift website.

```
let swiftWebsite =
    URL(string: "https://swift.org")
```

The Swift Evolution process lets everyone have a direct impact on the project, if they want.

Grab the code from this book, as well as some bonus exercises, at secretlab.com.au/books/head-first-swift

Frank: Is that it? We're done?

Judy: We're done with this book, I think.

Jo: What do we do now?

Sam: Well, I think we know all the Swift?

Frank: I don't think so. I think we've just learned all the building blocks we need, and all the skills we need to learn everything else Swift.

Jo: There's MORE Swift to learn? This book was already so long!

Judy: Well yeah, I think the point was to introduce the different bits and pieces of Swift, and now we're on our own.

Sam: We can deal with that! Onward!

SwiftUIcross

We've strategically hidden everything you've learned about SwiftUI from this chapter in this crossword. Have a go, before you leave the safety of the book...

 SwiftUIcross

Down

1) A view that fills all the space available between other views.

3) A SwiftUI view is a function of its _____.

5) _____ is used to keep track of a @StateObject from another view.

6) A special container view that's used to wrap multiple different views and transition between them.

8) This modifier is used to make sure images automatically size to the available space.

9) A _____ view is used to enable users to navigate between views.

12) An _____ catalog stores images in an Xcode project.

Across

2) This property wrapper is used to mark which properties are used to trigger automatic updates of a view they're used in.

4) The Swift _____ process is used to manage community requests and ideas for the Swift language.

7) _____ mode is automatically supported by MapKit.

10) A @State property wrapper operates on properties that are _____ to the view they're used in.

11) An exact amount of space you add to specific sides of a view.

13) A @StateObject that's been attached to another view is accessed using _____ in another view.

14) _____ is like @State, but for when you want to share state over multiple views.

15) This modifier can be used to clip an image in SwiftUI inside a Circle or a Capsule.

16) This view lets you download an image from the web, if it's available, and display it.

SwiftUIcross Solution

Index

Symbols

E

F

G

O'REILLY®

There's much more where this came from.

Experience books, videos, live online training courses, and more from O'Reilly and our 200+ partners—all in one place.

Learn more at oreilly.com/online-learning

©2019 O'Reilly Media, Inc. O'Reilly is a registered trademark of O'Reilly Media, Inc. | 175

Lightning Source UK Ltd.
Milton Keynes UK
UKHW031822231121
394411UK00005B/18

9 781491 922859